ADDRESSES

UPON

THE AMERICAN ROAD

1945–1948

ADDRESSES

UPON

THE AMERICAN ROAD

BY

Herbert Hoover

1945-1948

1949

D. VAN NOSTRAND COMPANY, Inc.

TORONTO   NEW YORK   LONDON

NEW YORK

D. Van Nostrand Company, Inc., 250 Fourth Avenue, New York 3

TORONTO

D. Van Nostrand Company (Canada), Ltd., 228 Bloor Street, Toronto

LONDON

Macmillan & Company, Ltd., St. Martin's Street, London, W.C. 2

PRINTED IN THE UNITED STATES OF AMERICA

Contents

PART I: FOREIGN POLICIES

POSTWAR FOREIGN LOANS   3
  [*Executives' Club, Chicago, Illinois, September 17,
  1945*]

ON VIEWS ON NATIONAL POLICIES AS TO THE
  ATOMIC BOMB   14
  [*North American Newspaper Alliance, New York
  City, September 27, 1945*]

ON THE PALESTINE QUESTION   16
  [*New York World-Telegram, November 19, 1945*]

ON CONSTRUCTION OF THE ST. LAWRENCE
  WATERWAY   18
  [*Letter to Senator Carl A. Hatch, February 12,
  1946*]

ON APPRAISAL OF THE WORLD SITUATION
  AND OUR POLICIES IN RELATION TO IT   20
  [*Press Statement, Salt Lake City, Utah, August 12,
  1946*]

ON YUGOSLAVIAN INCIDENT   22
  [*Press Statement, August 26, 1946*]

ON FINLAND   24
  [*Press Statement, New York City, October 14,
  1946*]

25981

PART II: DOMESTIC AFFAIRS AND ECONOMICS

ECONOMIC RECOVERY FROM THE WAR   29
[Fiftieth Anniversary of Clarkson College of Technology, Potsdam, New York, October 8, 1945]

MORAL AND SPIRITUAL RECOVERY FROM WAR   36
[Seventy-fifth Anniversary of Wilson College, Chambersburg, Pennsylvania, October 13, 1945]

AN EXTEMPORANEOUS ADDRESS CLOSING THE YAMA CONFERENCE OF 1945   44
[Absecon, New Jersey, November 10, 1945]

THE OBLIGATION OF THE REPUBLICAN PARTY   49
[Lincoln Day Dinner, National Republican Club, New York City, February 12, 1946]

ON CONGRESSIONAL ELECTION   54
[Press Statement, New York City, November 5, 1946]

THE RIGHT TO STRIKE   55
[This Week Magazine, December 29, 1946]

ADDRESS BEFORE THE HOLLAND SOCIETY OF NEW YORK   58
[Waldorf Astoria Hotel, New York City, November 20, 1947]

ADDRESS BEFORE THE SONS OF THE REVOLUTION   61
[Washington's Birthday Banquet, Waldorf Astoria Hotel, New York City, February 23, 1948]

THIS CRISIS IN AMERICAN LIFE   67
[Address before the Republican National Convention at Philadelphia, June 22, 1948]

THE MEANING OF AMERICA   74

[*Homecoming Address at the Reception Tendered by West Branch, Iowa, on the speaker's 74th Birthday, August 10, 1948*]

PART III: REPARATIONS AND ECONOMIC SUPPORT TO THE WORLD

ON THE NECESSARY STEPS FOR PROMOTION OF GERMAN EXPORTS, SO AS TO RELIEVE AMERICAN TAXPAYERS OF THE BURDENS OF RELIEF AND FOR ECONOMIC RECOVERY OF EUROPE   83

[*Report to the President, March 18, 1947*]

ON JAPANESE REPARATIONS   98

[*Letter to the Honorable Robert Patterson, Secretary of War, May 7, 1947*]

WE MUST SPEED PEACE   103

[*On Food and Relief Requirements for Germany, Japan and Korea; Letter to Congressman John Taber, May 26, 1947*]

THE LIMITS OF AMERICAN AID TO FOREIGN COUNTRIES   109

[*Letter to Senator Styles Bridges, June 13, 1947*]

DESTRUCTION AT OUR EXPENSE   119

[*Foreword Written for Common Cause, Inc. Magazine, December 27, 1947*]

THE MARSHALL PLAN   120

[*Statement to Senator Arthur H. Vandenberg, Committee on Foreign Relations, United States Senate, January 18, 1948*]

THE MARSHALL PLAN BILL   131
    [*Statement to Speaker Joseph W. Martin, House of Representatives, March 24, 1948*]

PART IV: EDUCATIONAL, SOCIAL
AND SCIENTIFIC

ON THE TWENTY-FIFTH ANNIVERSARY OF RADIO   141
    [*Broadcast—Columbia Broadcasting System, November 10, 1945*]

ON THE EXCHANGE OF STUDENTS WITH FOREIGN COUNTRIES   146
    [*Letter to Senator J. W. Fulbright, February 8, 1946*]

ON SUPPORT OF NATIONAL BOYS' CLUB WEEK   149
    [*Article for Boys' Clubs of America, International News Services, April 16, 1947*]

GRIDIRON DINNER   152
    [*Address, Washington, D. C., May 10, 1947*]

IN CELEBRATION OF THE BICENTENNIAL ANNIVERSARY OF PRINCETON UNIVERSITY   156
    [*Address, Princeton, N. J., June 16, 1947*]

PART V: WORLD FAMINE, 1946-1947

ON PRESIDENT TRUMAN'S APPEAL TO SAVE FOOD   163
    [*Press Statement, New York City, February 8, 1946*]

ON WORLD FAMINE   165
    [*Statement before the Famine Emergency Committee Meeting, Washington, D. C., March 11, 1946*]

ON WORLD FAMINE 167
[*Broadcast over the National Broadcasting Company, March 14, 1946*]

ON WORLD FAMINE 169
[*Broadcast over the American Broadcasting Company, March 16, 1946*]

ON WORLD FAMINE CRISIS 172
[*Reply to the French Minister of Foreign Affairs at
Luncheon in Paris, March 21, 1946*]

ON THE FOOD STORY OF ITALY 174
[*Rome, March 25, 1946*]

ON THE FOOD SITUATION IN FRANCE 176
[*Broadcast over Blue Network Radio from Paris,
March 27, 1946*]

ON FOOD CONDITIONS IN CZECHOSLOVAKIA 179
[*Prague, March 28, 1946*]

REMARKS AT DINNER OF PRESIDENT BIERUT 181
[*Warsaw, Poland, March 29, 1946*]

ON THE FOOD SITUATION IN POLAND 183
[*Warsaw, March 30, 1946*]

ON FOOD ADMINISTRATION IN FINLAND 185
[*Helsinki, April 1, 1946*]

EMERGENCY CONFERENCE ON EUROPEAN
CEREAL SUPPLIES 187
[*Address, London, England, April 5, 1946*]

ON THE WORLD FOOD CRISIS 193
[*Broadcast over Mutual Broadcasting Company
from Cairo, Egypt, April 19, 1946*]

ON THE WORLD FOOD SITUATION 199
[*Broadcast from Bombay, India, April 24, 1946*]

ON FOOD DIFFICULTIES IN INDIA 203
[*Bangalore, April 26, 1946*]

ON THE FOOD PROBLEM IN THE PHILIPPINES 206
[*Manila, April 29, 1946*]

ON THE FOOD NEEDS OF CHINA 207
[*Shanghai, May 3, 1946*]

ON THE JAPANESE FOOD SUPPLY 208
[*Tokyo, May 6, 1946*]

ON THE EFFECTS OF THE RAILROAD STRIKE
ON WORLD FAMINE 209
[*San Francisco, May 10, 1946*]

WORLD FAMINE 210
[*Report to The President, May 13, 1946*]

WORLD FAMINE SITUATION 221
[*Address under auspices Famine Emergency Committee, Sherman Hotel, Chicago, May 17, 1946*]

A NEW WORLD FOOD ORGANIZATION NEEDED 229
[*Address before the Food and Agricultural Organi-
zation of the United Nations, Washington, D. C.,
May 20, 1946*]

ON EFFECT OF RAILROAD STRIKE ON RELIEF
TO FAMINE AREAS 232
[*Press Statement, Washington, D. C., May 25,
1946*]

THE MISSION TO DETERMINE NEEDS OF THE
FAMINE AREAS 233
[*Mexico, D. F., May 28, 1946*]

ON WORLD FAMINE 235
[*Bogota, Colombia, May 31, 1946*]

ON THE FOOD MISSION 237
[*Quito, Ecuador, June 1, 1946*]

ON THE WORLD FAMINE CRISIS 238
[*Address at Luncheon given by the President of Peru at Lima, June 2, 1946*]

ON THE WORLD FOOD CRISIS 245
[*Address at Luncheon given by American Ambassador to Chile at Santiago, June 5, 1946*]

ON THE WORLD FOOD CRISIS 252
[*Buenos Aires, Argentina, June 10, 1946*]

ON COMMUNIST PRESS PRACTICES 254
[*Rio De Janeiro, Brazil, June 15, 1946*]

ON THE LATIN-AMERICAN FOOD SITUATION 256
[*Press Statement, Washington, D. C., June 19, 1946*]

REPORT ON THE WORLD FAMINE 259
[*Address broadcast over the Canadian Broadcasting Company from Ottawa, June 28, 1946*]

ADDRESS AT A BANQUET IN HONOR OF HIS EXCELLENCY, THE PRIME MINISTER OF GREECE 267
[*New York City, December 16, 1946*]

GERMAN AGRICULTURE AND FOOD REQUIREMENTS 269
[*Report to The President, February 26, 1947*]

ON RELIEF ASSISTANCE TO COUNTRIES DEV-
ASTATED BY WAR   286
    [*Statement before the Committee on Foreign Af-
    fairs, House of Representatives, February 28, 1947*]

ON AUSTRIAN AGRICULTURE AND FOOD RE-
QUIREMENTS — ECONOMIC REORGANIZA-
TION   294
    [*Report to The President, March 11, 1947*]

ON GREEK INDEPENDENCE DAY   303
    [*Remarks before Greek War Relief Dinner, New
    York City, March 25, 1947*]

ON THE GERMAN FOOD CRISIS   305
    [*Press Statement, New York City, May 15, 1947*]

THE WORLD FOOD SITUATION   306
    [*Address at Madison Square Garden, New York
    City, September 21, 1947*]

INDEX   311

PART I

FOREIGN POLICIES

Postwar Foreign Loans

Executives' Club, Chicago, Illinois
[September 17, 1945]

Members of the Executives' Club:

I AM deeply grateful for your generous reception; and I am especially touched that General Dawes should have consented to come here to introduce me today, for General Dawes has been my friend and my colleague ever since I entered public life.

I shall respond to the invitation of your members that I should discuss the proposals for large postwar loans or financial aid from our government for relief and reconstruction of our former allies. I refer to direct aid from our government over and above our indirect commitments already made through Bretton Woods, the Export-Import Bank, and UNRRA.

Let me say at the outset that I favor such financial assistance under safeguards and defined fiscal policies.

Never in human history has there been such an imperative need for wisdom and imagination in facing the common problems of mankind. They call for concepts of great generosity and tolerance that faith may be restored on this earth.

We in America can let no child, woman, or man starve—whether friend or enemy—as long as we have an ounce of surplus. When it comes to financial assistance for postwar reconstruction, however, if we act without wisdom and without regard to experience, far from curing the ills of the world, we will make them worse.

It is therefore the defined policies and the safeguards around such operations with which I am concerned at this occasion. They are very serious, and if properly imposed, will require great frankness, courage, and boldness in leadership.

On this problem I speak as the sole surviving American official from World War I who combined the functions of authority over a portion of the loans made during and after the first world war; who was also a member of the Debt Commission that renegotiated these loans, and who subsequently had to deal with the earlier efforts at their repudiation by the debtors. Knowing the conclusions of my many eminent colleagues of those times who can no longer speak, imposes an even more specific duty upon me.

The world had little experience in lending huge sums by governments before World War I. There were mistakes made at that time, but whatever the mistakes, they were the mistakes of pioneers in unknown lands. There will be greater mistakes and losses in handling the problem from World War II unless heed is taken to lessons of World War I.

To follow experience in these matters is the hard way. But if we would promote the ultimate recovery of America and a demoralized world, and if we would promote the long-view good feeling among nations, we shall require very much more realism than the easy road of starry-eyed sentimentalism. The problem of the American people today is to act from their idealism and at the same time keep their feet on the ground.

Now, in order to make the subject perhaps more clear, I will first relate some history, and then I will appraise some economic matters, both of which comprise the ground on which we must stand. Finally, I will offer some policies to be pursued.

SOME HISTORY

During World War I, our government loaned about seven billions to foreign governments for war purposes prior to the armistice and about three and a half billions after the armistice for relief and reconstruction. This did not include private loans, which I am not here discussing. These government loans were made to nineteen different countries. To make these loans the United States Government sold bonds to our own people, and it was agreed by the foreign governments that they would pay principal and interest in such a fashion as to equal the principal and interest which would fall upon the American taxpayer for the bonds that had been issued.

After the war, it became evident that the borrowers could not raise and pay the annual amounts that would be required. The world was in a better condition to pay then than it is now.

The World War Debt Commission was created by Congress to renegotiate the loans. The Commission was set up on the thesis that the settlements should be based upon the annual capacity of each individual nation to pay. While the principal sum of the debt was never theoretically diminished, yet deferments, interest rates, and the period of repayment were so manipulated that the loans to the different countries were reduced all the way from 30 per cent to 75 per cent to adjust them to capacity to pay. The aggregate annual payments of the combined debtors on all loans were reduced about 70 per cent and never exceeded 250 million dollars per annum up until their repudiation in 1933. This amount did not represent any insuperable economic difficulty either in paying or receiving under normal conditions.

However, when the hurricane of the great depression started in Europe in 1931, the annual payments on intergovernmental debts between other nations, added to the payments to us, became a stifling burden on the stability of exchanges and in the currencies of the whole world. You may recollect that at that time I secured an 18-month moratorium on intergovernmental debts all over the world. I further urged upon the Congress in 1932 that the Debt Commission be authorized to again renegotiate the debts so as to determine if the payments to us for the future seemed more than the capacity of any debtor to meet and at the same time make his own internal recovery.

In any event, every nation except Finland repudiated or, more euphoniously, ceased payment on their debts in 1933.

How much Congress contributed to this by refusing my request for renegotiation nobody can tell. I was always of the opinion that had Mr. Roosevelt secured that authority from Congress, he might have saved something. And this was more possible as by devaluation of the dollar he had, in effect, reduced the payments by about a further 50 per cent.

Up to the cease-payment signal, the actual sum paid upon the original principal of ten and a half billion was less than four and a half per cent. The interest payments amounted to only about twenty per cent of what our taxpayers had paid out on the American bonds issued to make these loans.

At this point, I wish to call your attention to the fact that this repudiation covered not only war loans, that is the equivalent of our lend-lease during the present war, but it included also the three and a half billion of relief and reconstruction loans made after the war was over. If you will conceive that all payments on principal made by the European debtors were applicable to the reconstruction advances alone, then only about thirteen per cent of that segment was repaid with interest. No nation except Britain paid more than ten per cent of the postwar loans. If all payments of that country be applied to postwar loans alone, then Britain paid an amount equal to the principal and interest of the postwar loans of about 600 million and a small amount of interest on the war loans of about three billion eight hundred million. So much for history.

SOME LESSONS

Here enter two great lessons from experience. The first is the moral and emotional coloring matter which infiltrates into these war and postwar financial transactions between governments; and second, there are certain economic phenomena which lie inherently in them.

Right or wrong, the color of the majority American view after the first world war was that we had no part in its origins; that we were in no danger of invasion; that we entered to save the Western democracies from defeat by Germany after Russia had deserted them. When it came to the peace, we waived any part of the indemnities to which we might have been entitled or any part of the territory two-thirds as large as the United States which the Allies acquired. Americans felt that we had made a great sacrifice to save the Allies and that we had continued these sacrifices in the debt settlements.

Right or wrong again, the coloring matter of the European view was that they had saved us from destruction by Kaiser Wilhelm; that they had held the line alone for two years defending us; that our sacrifice of blood and treasure was much less than theirs; and that, therefore, we still owed them something.

Anyway, statesmen and demagogues in every debtor country at once appealed for votes on the platforms of repudiation of our claims with this sort of justification. Foreign taxpayers naturally took to this idea of getting rid of taxes. Thereby, in the European view, our national visage changed from a great idealistic nation, crusading for the right, to that of Uncle Shylock; and a host of domestic fellow travelers echoed these cries.

I make this point because we must avoid such a situation again; and I make it because this interminable question of who saved who enters into these postwar financial transactions with great force. Nor is this history confined to the aftermath of the last war. As late as three weeks ago, the former prime minister of Great Britain, protesting against our stoppage of lend-lease, accused us of a rough and a harsh manner to a faithful ally who held the fort alone for us for over two years. Propaganda has again begun that we are delinquent in our contribution to this war, although we have spent more per capita than any other country.

But aside from these emotional questions, there is an economic question of first importance involved in lending and repayment of these great sums between governments. Outside of some proportionately small movement of gold and services, these sums must in the end be translated into movement of commodities. Whatever we may loan in the future will in reality be goods. Whatever we get back will be goods, and here comes in a vast difference between our situation and that of the European borrowers. Our economy is so self-contained that we normally import under seven, perhaps under six, per cent of the goods we consume; and we normally export about the same percentage of what we produce. Any great imports beyond certain limits tend to create unemployment in the United States by displacing our workmen on one hand, or on the other hand, too great exports might drain our own resources for recovery. The borrowing nations, however, normally depend all the way from twenty to sixty per cent upon imports with corresponding exports. Thus, they can take far larger amounts of goods on loan without damaging their employment than we can take on repayment. Aside from the economic difficulties involved, they naturally consider any opposition by us to receiving unlimited goods from them in repayment as justification for ceasing payments.

I am fully aware that some of our economists disagree with this. Some of them contend that if we would take down our tariffs, we can ultimately secure full payment in goods for any financial aid we may give. I might suggest, however, that there is a very serious danger to our national defense if we were to abandon our self-sufficiency in many of our products. This war has been a day-by-day illustration of that fact.

I am not, however, going to discuss the merits of free trade or protection. I might suggest a little experience. Indeed, Old Man Statistics enters at this point with certain sardonic humor. For, if we compare the four years from 1926 to 1930 prior to the depression with the four years from 1936 to 1940 after Mr. Hull's systematic lowering of American tariffs, we find that both our imports and our exports decreased instead of increased. Apparently, it didn't work in practice. In the four years from 1926 to 1930 prior to the depression, the goods we imported annually averaged $33.60 per capita with our exports a bit larger at $39.10 per capita. In the four years from 1936 to 1940, after Mr. Hull's systematic lowering of American tariffs, our annual imports averaged only $18.79 per capita and our exports dropped to $24.40 per capita. Put on a quantity basis, the showing is even worse. On an index number of 1913 equaling 100, our per capita imports before taking the lowered tariffs stood at 142, whereas after taking, they stood at 127. The indexes for exports were respectively 115 and 92.

Whatever the answer to that question may be, we are here, however, considering a different phenomenon.

The economic reality is that these huge loans of peace-time goods are mostly consumed by the borrowers to fill a vacuum without creating a corresponding surplus on their side, which they could use for export. There is also a great disparity in the variety and volume of goods that they can give or that we can take. Nor can these disparities be overcome through triangular trade. In sum, we simply cannot be repaid in full for such advances, tariffs or no tariffs.

I might also emphasize that these advances of money or credit by our government did not seem to stimulate international good will. Our greatest failure was Italy, where our government made over a billion of war loans and 800 million of postwar loans for reconstruction. She repaid less than four per cent of even the reconstruction loans, and ultimately declared war on us.

Now all this experience with emotional and moral coloring and economics certainly should be of a little guidance because human nature is still about the same.

First: When our government makes postwar loans in excess of a few tens of millions, they are only going to be partly repaid at best.

Second: Loaning money is a poor road to international friendship. Despite all this, there is the one over-riding necessity. We want to aid our allies to recover, and we want within all of our capacities to help them.

THE PRESENT ECONOMIC SITUATION

In the present situation Europe is very much more impoverished by this war than the last one, but Europe should not ignore the fact that we also are more greatly impoverished by this war than the last one.

America's recovery and financial stability is the first need of the world. Unless we recover, no one will recover.

There is a limit to the aid that thirty million American families can give to the 300 million families abroad who are hoping for postwar help. While we must provide some postwar credits, yet sooner or later most of these credits will come from our taxpayers. The burdens upon them are already gigantic. Even after the transition period, our federal expenses for many years will require from twenty to twenty-five billions annually. Such a federal tax alone spread over thirty million families comes to $600 or $800 annually per family. It is nonsense to claim that taxes are paid by the rich. A tax of 100 per cent on all personal incomes over the level of the United States Senator would yield only about one-fifth of our future annual budget. It is also foolish to believe that corporation taxes are not in the end passed on to the consumer. Thus it is those who toil and those who produce who will pay these taxes.

We have already pledged billions of postwar aid to foreign countries through the International Bank, the Stabilization Fund, and the Export-Import Bank. We have rightly assumed great burdens to feed the hungry all over the world through UNRRA.

Even if all these already made postwar commitments or any future ones are assumed to be repayable, yet our government will have to increase our national debt by borrowing from the American people by just that much. That limits our own capital for conversion and puts that much more strain on our governmental financial structure.

SOME POLICIES TO BE PURSUED

Taking all of these complexities together, I would like to make a suggestion for navigating through these difficult channels.

First: I should like to make a suggestion to dispose of lend-lease and all the other World War debts out of this war. Although I do not believe that we shall be repaid very much, if anything from our forty billions of lend-lease, yet I believe we should not cancel it now. We should, instead, propose a worldwide moratorium on all intergovernmental war debts for five years. Five years hence when the shape of the world is more clear, we should join with our Allies in settling the disposition of all these debts. This should include the debt relations of mother countries with dominions, including our own relations with the Philippines. In the meantime, we ought to demand that all weapons that we have sent on lend-lease should be destroyed.

Second: As to future postwar advances, loans, or financial aid from our government, we should remember that peace is not yet a month old. We do not know how our own reconversion will go. We cannot for a year hence appraise either our domestic situation or the effect of the great foreign commitments we have already made. Moreover, these new demands will come not from one foreign government, but from many. We must, in the interest of our recovery, take time to consider how much further burdens we can assume to aid others and still remain solvent.

Third: Both we and our allies need time to find out the actual needs of borrowing countries. Some of the Western European countries still have very considerable balances and assets in the United States. There is also a considerable amount of refugee assets in the United States. These things should be made known in order to enable us to appraise the situation.

Fourth: We cannot afford to just make general loans or give unrestricted financial aid as our government did in large part after the last war. We cannot today afford having our resources used to keep up armies, to engage in non-productive enterprises, to pay debts to other countries, or to pay for propaganda to upset our way of life.

Fifth: The redeeming part of this situation is that there exist today certain commodities in all nations which are on surplus. They are needed by other nations. We have a surplus of wheat, cotton, machinery, some metals, etc. The British Empire has rubber, tin, etc. The Russians have manganese and pulp, and the Dutch have more rubber and tin. The exchange of these surpluses at once is in obvious mutual interest.

Sixth: All loans or credits should be reduced to terms of commodities. We should open a credit to each particular nation who needs aid, and that credit should be available to purchase commodities in the United States such as we can approve. That will assure the employment of our own people in producing those commodities.

The borrowing nations will be exporting goods to the United States in the ordinary course, and that will secure some needed supplies for them without credits. A wise policy would seem to be, for the present, that we fill in by credits their deficient needs for commodities. In other words, until we can see more clearly, it is the part of wisdom to limit our credits to sums that would pay for temporary programs of actual goods. Certainly we should lower the sights as to size of our financial aid a long way from the current newspaper discussion of billions. Four hundred million dollars' worth of peace-time commodities in any one year to any individual nation in addition to the natural result of their trade is an awful lot of commodities. It is more than any one country took from us before the war in any one year, once or twice over.

Seventh: When the Allied governments receive cotton or other commodities from us, they sell those commodities for cash in their own currencies to their own people. It would seem only fair that these sums should be credited to our account, and while that cash possibly cannot be turned at once into dollars, it will purchase in their countries certain commodities which can be shipped to us without disturbing their economy.

Eighth: The whole world food and fuel program for the next winter cries for organization that would abolish its horrid inefficiency and power politics and that would prevent starvation.

Ninth: As we are going to get back only a part of any advances for relief and reconstruction, there are some indirect benefits which we might receive. We should insist that there be no quotas against us, no discriminatory tariffs against us, no dumping of goods upon us, no cartel operations against us. Quotas and discriminatory tariffs are not equal opportunity. Dumping is selling below cost to the injury of our workmen and farmers. Cartels are monopolies for the purpose of fixing prices and driving free enterprise from business. Therefore, we must have some socialized foreign trade. Such trade contains both the essence of dumping and cartelization. There should also be agreement of no trade discriminations in spheres of influence against us in favor of the dominant power.

Tenth: There should be agreement that no propaganda against the American system of life will be carried on. Such agitation creates uncertainty in a free enterprise system that undermines domestic confidence in our own stability and lessens our ability to help.

Eleventh: If we would avoid the ill will which will arise among our respective peoples from the emotional and moral coloring of these transactions, it should be agreed on both sides that at the end of ten years we will reconsider the situation of these postwar credits by governments which may have been opened on all sides. That should prevent propaganda of hate against us for cancellation.

Twelfth: While I am not here discussing private loans from our bankers and others to foreigners, yet they must be regarded so as to prevent their being applied to any other than directly reproductive enterprise. Otherwise, American investors will not get their money back.

CONCLUSION

In conclusion, again I repeat. We must help! We should keep our feet on the ground. We should limit our help to what our taxpayers can afford. We should consider our own employment. We should organize our aid so as to minimize any ill will that might arise over these transactions. We should do it with the knowledge that we must make sacrifices to aid humanity to recover from the greatest disaster of all history.

On Views on National Policies as to the Atomic Bomb

North American Newspaper Alliance, New York City
[September 27, 1945]

AS THE secret of the atomic bomb is only the "know-how" of manufacture, the scientists of other nations could make it if they had uranium ore, a billion or so of money, and some 2,000 contributing industries at their disposal. All this would take several years and would be even longer if we keep the practical methods of manufacture a secret.

In the meantime it gives the United States and Britain the power to dictate political policies to the whole world if we want to use it. No matter how desirable these policies might be we are not going to use it for this purpose. Therefore we should consider how we can prevent anyone else doing it.

This is the most terrible and barbaric weapon that has ever come to the hand of man. Despite any sophistries its major use is not to kill fighting men, but to kill women, children, and civilian men of whole cities as a pressure on governments. If it comes into general use, we may see all civilization destroyed.

The whole subject needs an entirely different approach. Aside from trying to prevent war, what we ought to be doing is to devise methods to prevent nations from using the bomb in any event. In the meantime we ought to keep the secret if for no other reason than to give time to devise methods for its control. Also possessing the secret gives power in negotiating on the subject.

If we consider methods of control, we have one precedent of some interest. We made international agreements among practically all nations not to use poison gas in war. Those agreements were generally adhered to during this last war. It was about the only agreement that was not seriously violated. The reason was not the sacred honor of our enemies, not perhaps of ourselves. It was the fear of reprisals upon the first to break the agreement. Such an agreement and such a fear would be no complete guaranty that the atomic bomb would not be used in case of war, but at least it would cause hesitation.

Another approach might be through control of uranium ores by the Security Council of the United Nations. That idea would be for all nations to agree that any uranium ores in their territory should be placed under the jurisdiction of joint representatives of other nations with resident inspectors in each country possessing such ores. This, if faithfully carried out, would limit their use to the peaceful arts. In consideration of such an agreement and its faithful adherence, the United States and Great Britain could agree not to use the bomb nor to disclose the method of manufacture.

Certainly the idea that the making of this hideous instrument should be encouraged by giving any other nation, or the world, the method of its making is the negation of trying to keep it under control in the interest of civilization as a whole.

On the Palestine Question

New York World-Telegram
[November 19, 1945]

THERE is a possible plan of settling the Palestine question and providing ample Jewish refuge. It at least is
worth serious investigation for it offers a constructive
humanitarian solution.

In ancient times the irrigation of the Tigris and Euphrates
Valleys supported probably ten million people in the Kingdoms
of Babylon and Nineveh. The deterioration and destruction of
their irrigation works by the Mongol invasion centuries ago and
their neglect for ages are responsible for the shrinkage of the
population to about 3,500,000 people in modern Iraq. Some
30 years ago, Sir William Willcocks, an eminent British engi-
neer, completed a study of the restoration of the old irrigation
system. He estimated that about 2,800,000 acres of the most
fertile land in the world could be recovered at a cost of under
$150,000,000. Some progress has been made under the Iraq
Government, but their lack of financial resources and the delays
of the war have retarded the work greatly. Some years ago it
was proposed that this area should be developed for settlement
by Jewish refugees. This did not, however, satisfy the Jewish
desire for a homeland.

My own suggestion is that Iraq might be financed to complete this great land development on the consideration that it
be made the scene of resettlement of the Arabs from Palestine.
This would clear the Palestine completely for a large Jewish
emigration and colonization. A suggestion of transfer of the

Arab people of Palestine was made by the British Labor Party in December, 1944, but no adequate plan was proposed as to where or how they were to go.

There is room for many more Arabs in such a development in Iraq than the total of Arabs in Palestine. The soil is more fertile. They would be among their own race which is Arab speaking and Mohammedan. The Arab population of Palestine would be the gainers from better lands in exchange for their present holdings. Iraq would be the gainer for it badly needs agricultural population.

Today millions of peoples are being moved from one land to another. If the lands were organized and homes provided, this particular movement could be made the model migration of history. It would be a solution by engineering instead of by conflict.

I realize that the plan offers a challenge both to the statesmanship of the Great Powers as well as to the good-will of all parties concerned. However, I submit it and it does offer a method of settlement with both honor and wisdom.

On Construction of the St. Lawrence Waterway

Letter to Senator Carl A. Hatch

[February 12, 1946]

New York, N. Y.

Honorable Carl A. Hatch
United States Senate
Washington, D. C.

My dear Senator:

I have your request for my views upon the construction of the St. Lawrence Waterway.

At my instance, as Secretary of Commerce, President Coolidge in 1924 created the first St. Lawrence Waterway Commission. I served as Chairman of that body until 1928. A parallel body was created by the Government of Canada and under the two commissions exhaustive economic and engineering investigations were completed. The economic studies demonstrated great public usefulness of the undertaking and the engineering studies greatly advanced the engineering problems.

In 1929, as President, I initiated negotiations for a treaty with Canada providing for the construction of the waterway and settling various interrelations in respect to it. This treaty was signed on July 18, 1932 and was sent by me to the Senate with an urgent recommendation for its ratification.

During this period of nearly eight years of close association with the problem, I made something like thirty statements, addresses and reports, and appeared a number of times before

Congressional Committees, all advocating the undertaking. In those statements I canvassed the reasons for and against the construction, and except for minor changes which time implies, those statements are applicable today.

No doubt these statements and reports can be had from the files of the Department of Commerce if they are wanted and it is unnecessary for me to repeat the gist of them now.

I did not at the time of my association with the problem believe—and I do not now believe—that the Federal Government should undertake to operate and distribute the electric power which will be a by-product of the enterprise. The sale of the power on a long-term contract to public bodies and private power companies under regulations which protect the consumer, as in the case of the Colorado River dam, will be in much greater public interest.

I do not consider the construction of the waterway will injure the existing American transportation system or our ports. The natural increase in goods movements which should take place during the long period of construction should more than compensate any diversion.

Nor should we begrudge any added prosperity to Canada that may come from this enterprise, for her prosperity is as much our prosperity as that of any group of our own states.

It was obvious in 1924 that aside from its great peace time importance the waterway would have been of immense value in prosecuting World War I. Had the treaty of 1932 been ratified at that time, and construction followed, the waterway would have directly or indirectly paid for itself several times over in World War II. There can be no doubt as to its value as a defense measure.

From an economic point of view, it could be said as an axiom that every improvement of transportation brings not only visible economic benefits but a host of invisible ones—for cheapening of transport benefits both the producer and the consumer in lessening costs. I have no hesitation in my belief as to the economic value of the project.

On Appraisal of the World Situation and Our Policies in Relation to It

Press Statement, Salt Lake City, Utah
[*August 12, 1946*]

M Y BLUNT answer to the request for an appraisal of the world situation and our policies in relation to it are as follows:

1. There were several conclusions besides the food situation which I arrived at in recent conversations with top officials and other citizens in thirty-eight nations.

2. The dominant note in the world a year after World War I was hope and confidence; today it is fear and frustration. One year after the first World War we had signed peace; today there is no peace.

3. Today there is universal desire in all nations except Russia to make and preserve peace. My own impression is that Russia is obstructing to gain time for the elimination of all non-Communist elements behind the Iron Curtain and Manchuria, and thus the consolidation and practical absorption of those areas. Her invigorated fifth columns in every country add to the confusion. The rest of the world is rapidly concentrating its fears, and consequently its animosities, toward her.

4. Far from freedom having expanded from this war it has shrunk to far fewer nations than a quarter of a century ago. In addition there are at least 15,000,000 people in concentration or

forced-labor camps who are slaves in every sense of the word. Several scores of millions more are practically serfs.

5. The dismemberment of the German state and the attempt to reduce the German people to a level of perpetual poverty will some day break into another world explosion.

6. The destruction and deterioration of the world's productive equipment are unmeasurable. Our own country has suffered great depletion of reserves and equipment. We are burdened with fabulous debt and are slow in recovery of production.

7. In all this unhappy situation, necessity requires that the United States should observe three major policies:

A. In the economic field we must now conserve our resources, improve our equipment and reduce our spending. We must end our role of Santa Claus. Now that world famine No. 2 is about over we should announce that our economic relation with other nations is a two-way street—and balanced traffic at that.

B. In national defense we should hold the atomic bomb until there is real cooperation for lasting peace which must include general disarmament in the world—allies as well as enemy countries. Our military are today spending large sums to improve the bomb so as to keep ahead of other nations. It is nonsense to think we can keep ahead and at the same time give away the blueprints.

We should be willing to agree that it will never be used except in defense of free men. That trust we should keep, but until the world returns to keeping agreements and peaceful action —keep our powder dry.

C. We should devote ourselves to cooperation in the United Nations to maintain peace and to do so, appeasement must cease. To hold up the moral banners of the world we should at all times assert the principles of the Atlantic Charter for which we fought the war and to which all other nations pledged themselves to us.

On Yugoslavian Incident

Press Statement, Pasadena, California
[August 26, 1946]

ALTHOUGH Yugoslavia's attacks on American planes "seem like a pretty poor return" for all the assistance given to her by the United Nations Relief and Rehabilitation Administration, the Yugoslav people cannot properly be blamed for lack of appreciation, because they are kept in ignorance by their Communist regime, Herbert Hoover said today.

In an interview at the home of his son, Herbert Hoover Jr., the former President said that the United States had furnished 75 to 80 per cent of UNRRA's food and funds, of which Yugoslavia received more than any other country.

"One thing that can be said for the Yugoslav people: The fact that we contributed anything to UNRRA or to them is unknown to anyone in Yugoslavia," Mr. Hoover said. "It is a Communist state, with a completely controlled press.

SIZE OF ARMY IS CITED

"Tito has an army of 750,000 men out of a population of 14,000,000. These men should have been home farming and rehabilitating the nation. Instead, directly or indirectly, UNRRA was supporting Tito's army. Altogether it is a very sad chapter.

"We contributed to the liberation of Yugoslavia at a cost of American blood. Tito's Government is not carrying out the Yalta Agreement. There has been no general election. It is an imposed regime of true Communist order."

[Mr. Hoover declared that the United States should stop relief shipments to Yugoslavia until free elections were held there, The Associated Press reported.]

Generalizing on his observations during his recent world tour as famine investigator for President Truman, Mr. Hoover asserted that the Russians were "obstructing all peace measures and all progress toward peace."

"The Russians want time," he said, "completely to consolidate Communist control of people in those States east of the Iron Curtain and in Manchuria.

DEPORTATIONS CHARGED

"They are eliminating all dissident elements. They are setting up concentration camps in each of those countries and deporting many to Siberia."

In free elections in the Russian-dominated European countries, the Communists would have only small minorities, he said.

In Latin America, Mr. Hoover added, Communist newspapers have quintupled in number in the last sixteen months.

The former President reported that famine conditions had ended everywhere in the world except China and India, where rice harvests should bring relief in November. He credited the United States, Canada, Australia and Argentina with helping 300,000,000 persons who once had less food than Buchenwald prisoners and 500,000,000 more less seriously undernourished.

Mr. Hoover came here for a trustees' meeting at the Huntington Library. As chairman of the Carnegie Institution's Astronomical Committee, he plans also to confer with California Institute of Technology and Mount Wilson Observatory officials before going on to his home in Palo Alto on Thursday.

On Finland

Press Statement, New York City
[October 14, 1946]

SOMEONE should speak up for the Finns. The next few days in Paris will be their last chance.

This little nation of 3,400,000 people is peaceloving and absolutely democratic. For over 400 years they have struggled for independence. They gained it in 1919 at the insistence of the United States and our Allies.

In 1939 Russia made an aggressive war upon them. It was so denounced by the League of Nations, by Mr. Churchill and Mr. Roosevelt. After fearful losses they were overwhelmed and sacrificed one-fifth of their farmlands and suffered the expulsion of 400,000 of their people to get peace.

In 1941, with the hopes of righting this wrong, they made the mistake of joining the Germans in war on Russia. They were never Nazis. They wanted to regain their homes. In 1944, the Finns—on demand of the United States among others—sued the Russians for peace. The price of peace was not only that they give up the farmlands they had again recovered but that they surrender an additional one-fifth of their country, including their mines and their fisheries. They were also required to wage war to expel the German Army. The Germans turned upon the Finns and destroyed the homes and schools of 400,000 more of them. Today there are 800,000 destitute refugees dependent upon the other 2,600,000.

America never declared war upon Finland. We are the only possible friend they have left. They are now, in addition to all the Russian annexations of their lands, confronted with an indemnity of 300 million dollars to Moscow. Much of it has to be paid in kind at 1939 prices which makes it still worse. In proportion to their national wealth this amount would be equal in size to an indemnity of 200 billion dollars upon the United States. Italy, with ten times the population, is required to pay little more than Finland. In proportion to their population, the terms are very much more hard than those imposed on Bulgaria and Roumania.

The Finns have shown their desire for friendly relations with Russia by taking Communists into their Ministry although only a small percentage of their people or their legislative body are Communists.

They cannot pay this indemnity and buy the food and clothes they must import to live. If they default they, too, will disappear behind the Iron Curtain.

Mr. Churchill one time said:

"Only Finland superb—nay sublime—in the jaws of peril shows what free man can do. The service rendered by Finland to mankind is magnificent. . . . If the light of freedom which still burns so lightly in the frozen north should be quenched . . . every vestige of human progress during two thousand years might be engulfed."

Mr. Roosevelt also said:

"It is tragic . . . to realize that wanton disregard of law. . . . The people and government of Finland have a long honorable wholly peaceful record."

Why has America raised no effective voice in this settlement at Paris? Is the Atlantic Charter signed by all the United Nations wholly dead?

PART II

DOMESTIC AFFAIRS AND ECONOMICS

Economic Recovery from the War

Fiftieth Anniversary of Clarkson College of Technology

Potsdam, New York

[October 8, 1945]

IT IS a great pleasure to attend the 50th Anniversary of Clarkson College of Technology. This institution holds a high place among all engineers. It has during this half century sent an unending stream of constructive men into American life. And they are indeed needed now.

This year 1945 marks the end of a hideous era. Now we must take up the responsibilities of the new era which confronts us. It can be a glorious era, if we have the skills and the vision.

The first job is reconstruction from the most devastating war in history. And that reconstruction must be moral and spiritual as well as economic.

Time limits me to discussion of but one sector of the economic side. It is a sector which concerns engineers. In this sector there lies our major hope of the economic future. And in it we can find courage, inspiration and faith in our future.

We have gigantic losses from the war. We have lost thousands of bright minds, who would have given leadership to our people, and other thousands are cripples for life. We have lost five years' output of men and women trained in technical skills. Our peacetime industrial plant is greatly run down, and our working capital greatly impaired. Some of our natural resources have been greatly exhausted. Our people are burdened with fabulous debt and taxes.

However, the recuperative powers and in fact the economic

wealth of a nation is its ability to produce. The war has proved we have the skills and ability to produce such as history has never witnessed. From the tasks of war thousands of men have been developed in qualities of initiative and leadership. In the last five years we have accumulated new and great assets from the discoveries in science and advances in invention. From these possibilities of increasing efficiency in production and distribution we can, if we have wisdom, overcome our losses. And we can add more than ever before to the security and comfort of our people.

THE ROAD TO RECOVERY AFTER PREVIOUS WARS

It is exactly from great increases in national efficiency and consequently in production that the world has in the past received its major aid in recuperation from devastating wars.

After the Napoleonic wars the plight of Britain seemed hopeless. But the application of the steam engine so increased the productivity of her people that in time the burden of huge debt became easy, the standard of living increased and employment expanded.

After our Civil War the expansion of railway transportation stimulated the productivity of the fertile Mid-West. It opened the mines of the Far West. With these aids, in a few years the United States overcame the economic losses of that war and was again on the march of progress.

After World War I there blossomed a great advance in scientific knowledge and technical skills. It brought expansion in electric power, radio, telephone, motor transportation and the application of a thousand labor-saving devices and improved methods. Again we increased our productivity until the losses of that war were soon overcome. A great advance in the standards of living and comfort were again on the march.

I do not assume these stimulants to productivity were the sole forces of recovery but without them it would have been slow if not impossible.

Now do not get the idea into your heads that these surges

of efficiency were the product of war. They have occurred in peace. No doubt their suspension during war cumulates their force when peace comes.

THE EXPERIENCE AFTER WORLD WAR I

I should like to dwell upon that period of ten years after the first World War a little more for it contains a lesson and at the same time re-enforces our confidence today.

In the early twenties a committee of engineers over which I presided announced an economic doctrine that, while not wholly new, was only discovered by many economists some time later. Amplified a little for clarity, we said the way to increase national efficiency and productivity was:

1. Through scientific research with its discoveries and invention of labor-saving devices and better methods;
2. Through the elimination of waste in industry and better utilization of our natural resources;
3. Through improved technical training.

Thereby the costs of articles and services could be reduced, prices could be decreased, the standard of living increased, people could buy more and thus more jobs could be created. The tax income of the Government would grow and the debts decrease.

From the social profit could come shorter work hours, increasing comfort, more music, more movies, and more chance to go fishing.

Toward the end of that decade of the twenties I appointed an able committee of business men and economists with representatives of agriculture and labor to examine among other things what had happened to our national efficiency during the ten years after World War I. The report showed that during the ten years we had increased the production of commodities and services on a per capita basis by over 35 per cent above pre-war. Real wages increased over 30 per cent, and working hours decreased by 15 per cent. We built more homes and great city buildings, more public improvements than in the previous three decades. There was never such an advance in so short a time in all our history.

This study showed that these results in the twenties were not the product of any single revolutionary invention. We had developed inventions and improved methods in a thousand directions. We had systematically eliminated wastes. We had greatly increased the number of our laboratories and of our skilled scientists, engineers and executives, and had given them better training in our colleges and universities.

The economic doctrine stated by the engineers prevailed during the ten years except in one spot. The weakness was that industrial labor and management skimmed off the cream of these gains and mostly left the farmers and white collar classes out of the benefits. Wages had taken about 70% of the increased gains, profits about 15%. Prices and the cost of living decreased only slightly during the decade. Thus the farmers and white collar classes who did not participate in increased incomes could not buy their share of increased commodities and services. Then we began to overproduce and the increase in profits led to unrestrainable speculation. An inevitable slump resulted in 1929. Just as we were convalescing from our economic sins the hurricane of European financial panic struck us down into the great depression of 1931.

Yet the engineers' doctrine was right and I am going to assume the next generation will have the wisdom not to make the mistake. The lesson from that one economic sin, however, is not the main theme. Today we can well examine the prospect we have for another postwar increase of efficiency.

THE ROAD TO ECONOMIC RECOVERY AFTER WORLD WAR II

From scientific discovery and invention we have today a host of potential new expansions—many of them suspended by war, others stimulated by the war. None of them are immediately revolutionary, but of great cumulative effect. Indeed the whole gamut of science and its application has opened a new frontier to the expansion of American life.

1. We shall see a great expansion in air transport as a result of improvements we now know.

2. There will be great expansion in the application of diesel and turbine gas engines. Among other services, they will expedite and cheapen railway and highway transport.

3. We shall see a great expansion in the new art which we now call electronics with its multitude of new gadgets. The radar and electronic microscope are new to industry and research.

4. There will be great improvements in synthetic or chemical materials, such as plastics, specialized rubber, glass and chemicalized wood. There will be a great expansion in synthetic textiles.

5. There will be much wider use of light metals.

6. We have developed better seeds, many improvements in farm machinery and larger industrial uses of farm products.

7. We will save great wastes by the improvements in weather forecasting.

8. We have seen the development of a host of labor-saving machine tools, big and little, during the past ten years. There is a great improvement in "know how" in the use of these tools and methods.

9. There are a host of new openings for reduction of waste by standardization and simplification of industrial methods and products through cooperation in industry and distribution.

10. We have seen startling discoveries in medicine, the sulfa drugs, penicillin, blood plasma, vitamins, D.D.T. and a host of others which will reduce the waste of sickness and prolong skilled lives.

11. We have made great advances in manipulation of the molecular structure of hydro-carbons, among them improved gasoline and a new host of hydro-carbon products.

ATOMIC POWER

12. The most dramatic of all advances is the manipulation of the structure of the atom. The atomic bomb has awakened high

hopes of application of such power to industrial purposes. There is danger of too high hopes. Up to now there is no reason to believe the explosive qualities of these elements can be tamed down so that they run an engine directly with the amiability of the explosion of gasoline. There will be improvements in the applications of radiation in healing and some industrial uses. There are intermediate and controllable steps in the transformation of Uranium 235, or 238, where a great volume of heat is generated. We are likely to see this indirect application to some power purposes within the next ten years. That, however, would produce no great industrial revolution. The fuel element in the cost of modern services and manufactured articles is a very small percentage. If all of these per cents were saved, it would not be a revolution. And certainly even the preliminary priming of Uranium for action is an expensive business.

But when we look at the last dozen years' march of scientific thought on the atom we can expect more from such great minds as Lawrence, Oppenheimer, Bush, Millikan, Compton and their host of young colleagues, perhaps much more than even they now know.

13. We have had a great expansion of our scientific and industrial laboratories which will daily add to these forces of greater productivity.

14. And to give impulse to all these forces we have a vast vacuum of goods to fill.

The sum of all these possibilities is not only recovery but a renewed march in progress.

THE RESERVATIONS

But now I come to some reservations. Whether we realize these great possibilities and all their train of social good depends upon the moral, social and political climate with which these beneficent forces are surrounded.

They can be crippled by a host of destructive actions:

1. Monopolies that restrict production in order to force up prices or restrain competition from reducing them;

2. Labor union rules that limit the output of men during their agreed hours of work; the gigantic wastes of strikes and lockouts; misguided labor that seeks to secure the benefits of increased productivity before it is accomplished;

3. Foolish industrial labor and management policies that again seek to skim off the cream of increased productivity and leave too little by reduced prices to the consumer who is the farmer and the white collar group as well as labor;

4. Government policies which jeopardize stability of the currency and credit;

5. Taxes which destroy the incentives of men by taking away the reward of their efforts;

6. Bureaucracy which stymies productive forces by stupid meddling;

7. Starry-eyed Utopias which deny men reward for their efforts and thus frighten them from new adventure.

In a word, these forces of science and technology can save this nation from being crushed by the burdens of war. But, to do it, men must be free in mind, spirit and creative power so long as they do no injury to their neighbors. They must be confident of the future.

Clarkson College and all our technical institutions have a great part to play in this recovery. From them must come our trained men. And in their laboratories must develop much of our research. We are confident of the contributions to these ends from Clarkson College.

Moral and Spiritual Recovery
from War

Seventy-fifth Anniversary of Wilson College,
Chambersburg, Pennsylvania
[October 13, 1945]

W E HAVE ended a bloody and horrible era of history.
It has been a war in which the enslavement, the starvation and killing of women, children and civilian
men have returned to the levels which we thought had gone by
a thousand years ago.

America has emerged as the most powerful of nations if we
wish to use that power. In any event, we now have the opportunity to give leadership in a new era for humanity. What the
distant future of this new era will be depends much upon our
institutions of higher learning. They must mould the leadership of the nation.

But beyond this the war has imposed upon you who are en-
joying the privileges of this institution, and all the men and
women of our colleges, an immediate responsibility to the
American people such as you have never hitherto known.

We hear much about the reconversion of economic life from
war to peace. We hear little about reconversion of our intellectual, moral and spiritual life from the shock of war to a life
of peace. Yet that is the first necessity if civilization itself is to
recover.

Surely if the new era upon which we enter is to be an era of
progress it must rest upon the rebirth of truth and justice and

tolerance. It must rest upon intellectual and spiritual freedom and upon a live public sensitiveness to wrong and a resentment of brutality. The redemption of mankind will depend upon those who can give intellectual, moral and spiritual leadership in these immediate years.

To indicate how much reconversion we need in this field we should frankly examine some examples of the degeneration of our ideals during this war. Such an appraisal will not be popular with those whose war emotions still drown their reason, although I shall speak with restraint. Yet facing these facts is the first step to redemption. And now is the time to face them.

THE DEGRADATION OF TRUTH

Let us examine what has happened to truth. It is the first fatality of any war. And total war results in the mass slaughter of truth. Propaganda is one of the weapons of war. And propaganda is at best but half truth. It tells only one side. Its justification is that strategy requires that the enemy be misled. Morale at home in war also requires a boost of spirit by suppression of some things and emphasis on others. War controls are used to cover up blunders and failures. Another taint of untruth still hangs heavy in the air. One of Lenin's principles of propaganda was to confuse vocabularies. At one time America had simple and well-understood expressions, such as self-government, independence of nations, democracy, personal freedom and liberalism. The war leaves us with these phrases stuffed with perversions of truth.

Exploitation of emotion, regimentation of the press and confusion are not operations in pure intellectual honesty. And these practices leave an imprint of the usefulness of lies. The consequence is that the habit of the war-perfected skills of government propaganda are carried over into peace. There is no national permanence in falsehood. There will be no lasting integrity in citizens unless there be intellectual honesty in government.

THE DEGENERATION OF JUSTICE

The war has temporarily injured something in our ideals of justice. Our righteous indignations at the crimes which brought this war and the brutalties of the enemy have clouded our vision of justice.

Justice demands that the men responsible for this must be punished. It requires that the military castes and their weapons be destroyed and be kept destroyed.

But justice also requires that we do not visit on the children of millions of Germans and Japanese the sins of their fathers. Nor can we justly indict and punish two hundred million people. Vengeance and revenge are not justice. Measures which reduce the economic life of coming generations to the low levels of an agricultural state are neither justice nor good policy. That will create gigantic cesspools of hate, poverty and conspiracy against the world. There is no such thing as a "hard peace" or a "soft peace." It must be a just peace if we are to restore justice in the world. And without justice there is no peace.

THE GROWTH OF BRUTALITY

We have lost something in our sensitiveness to brutality. For instance, before the war we protested in deep indignation the bombing of children, women and civilian men by the Japanese at Nanking, the Russians at Helsinki, the Germans at Warsaw and London. We said war must be confined to clashes of armed men, not the killing of civilians. Yet did we not wind up the war by killing tens of thousands of women and children at Hiroshima and Nagasaki? Even if we grant that it was necessary, it is not a matter to exult over.

Thousands of people are still being committed to concentration camps in Eastern Europe without a semblance of justice or compassion. Under the name of reparations men are being seized, and prisoners are being worked under conditions reminiscent of Roman slavery. Yet we have become so habituated to brutality that we are tolerating it with little protest.

THE DEGENERATION OF FREEDOM

We have lost something of our ideals of freedom. We went into the war under the persuasion of such ideas as the Four Freedoms and the Atlantic Charter. This was to be our second and last crusade to free the world from domination, from despotism, from imperialism, from brutality, from fear. Our banners have always proclaimed the freedom and the rights of nations and of men.

Now we find hundreds of millions of human beings breathe less independence, less liberty, less freedom from fear than before we started on this crusade. Their successful rescue at that time was the justification of our first crusade. Can we honestly say that we have not surrendered these peoples on the altar of appeasement?

THE LOSS OF TRAINED MINDS AND SKILLS

The war has brought us a loss in our intellectual life from another direction. In our lists of dead are a multitude who would have given intellectual leadership to our people. Of those who survived, the draft and diversion to war have cost us the equivalent of six annual crops of young men trained in the professions and the arts. I regret to say that, after the interruptions of war, too small a part of them are returning to colleges for training. Worst of all, by continuing the draft of boys between 18 and 21 since the war has ended, we are destroying still another crop. There will sometime be a shortage in scientists, teachers, doctors, engineers, lawyers and our leaders in the humanities. It is not even intelligent of our military forces to continue depriving our future defense of these skills.

OTHER DEGENERATIONS

I will not dwell on more examples of our moral, spiritual and intellectual losses. I could rail against the rise of nationalistic and group selfishness. I could bewail the decrease of compassion which distinguishes Christianity. I could deplore the growth of intolerance. I could expand upon the impairment of the whole cultural structure of the world. I could emphasize the loss of faith in our American system of life.

However, these degenerations in ideals and standards, this insensitiveness to wrong are common to all wars. We have recovered from them before and we can recover from them again, if we have wisdom and courage.

The immediate danger to the world is a sense of frustration in America at the failure of our crusade for freedom and our continued moral and spiritual losses from the war. For from frustration can come bitter isolationism.

THE WAR IS NOT ALL LOSS

And do not get the idea that I am saying the consequences of the war are all bad. The war involved questions of national defense. We made important scientific discoveries, especially in the manipulation of the atom. The heroic deeds of America's sons and daughters have added to the glory of the nation. They have enriched our traditions of valor. The war resulted in the extirpation of three of the festering sores of military aggression in the world. We have a start at world cooperation at least to maintain military peace.

But I am not here discussing our world situation. I am concerned with the recovery of our own American intellectual and moral and spiritual standards from their war degeneration.

THE PART OF OUR EDUCATIONAL INSTITUTIONS

Some one may say that for regeneration of moral and spiritual ideals we should again return to the Sermon on the Mount. That is right, but the responsibility for the idealism of America does not rest alone on the Church. It rests also upon our institutions of higher learning, for such institutions have loyalty to standards as vital as to patriotism itself. They also have the responsibility to proclaim truth and tolerance, to insist upon justice, to awaken a sensitiveness to wrong, to selfishness, to brutality.

Indeed, without these values, there can be no successful re-conversion of even the economic world from war to peace. Adam Smith taught that all material wealth comes from the earth with its increment of value from labor and skill. But he mostly overlooked the most important asset of nations without which no amount of soil or mines or labor can produce lasting wealth. That indispensable asset is moral and spiritual; it is integrity, justice and a willingness to unselfish cooperation of its citizens.

LEADERSHIP

It is a commonplace to say that in this complex modern civ-ilization no nation can survive without leadership. And by leadership I do not speak of public life alone. We must have leadership in every branch of life from the shop foreman to the President. We must have leadership among the neighbors and in the home.

One of the riches of American life is the vast reservoir of leadership in the people. But leaders are not found like queen bees. Neither does heredity produce them and certainly bu-reaucracy does not do so. It is our educational system rooted in the whole people upon which we must depend to develop leaders. That is, the mechanism of free men through which youngsters with qualities of mind and character are promoted from the whole people and trained for leadership. From here must come the constant stream of young men and women who will refresh our ideals.

No doubt there are men and women who rise to leadership without the full help of our colleges. But our national supply would be poor indeed if we had to depend upon this method.

But an intangible corruption has come into our concepts of leadership during the past few years. It is dinned into us that this is the century of the common man; that he is going to do this and demand that—the idea seems to be that common man has come into his own at last. Certainly he is a good vote-getting attachment.

Thus we have developed a cult of the common man. I have not been able to find any definition of who this common man is. Most American men and especially women will fight if called common. Likewise in humility we refer to ourselves as made from common clay but we get mad when anyone says our feet are made of clay.

However, whoever this political common man is, I want him to have all the unique benefits of the American way of life including full opportunity to rise to leadership. But if we are to have leadership in government, in science, in education, in the professions and in the home, we must find and train some uncommon men and women.

The only seriously objectionable part of this deification of the common man is the implication that mediocrity is an ideal, that the uncommon man is to be discredited or discarded.

Let us remember that the great advances have not been brought about by mediocre men and women. Rather they were brought about by distinctly uncommon men and women with vital sparks of leadership—men and women like St. Francis of Assisi, and Florence Nightingale and Abraham Lincoln. Many of these great leaders were, it is true, of humble origin, but that was not their greatness.

The most gigantic experiment of this cult of all history was the dictatorship of the proletariat in Russia. It is from the fumes of this cauldron that we mostly get these ideas. But one of the humors of sociology—if there is humor in it—is that the most recent phase of the revolution in Russia is a frantic search for the uncommon man. And he is given privileges and payment relatively to other citizens far more than America offers today.

There is no identity whatever between mediocrity and popular government—although that is what many of our bubble blowers are trying to put over on the American people.

The essence of our American system is that the best are to be selected for public responsibility and public service. It is also the essence of our economic life, our spiritual life, our educational institutions.

We have a recent and powerful example. In the command of our military forces and our scientific forces during the war we searched and found the uncommon men and women. They proved that they could give leadership without being dictators or fascists or endangering popular government.

Despite this curious cult who erect antagonisms to the uncommon man, I am confident it will not confuse our educational institutions. Our sure hope of recovery in the moral and spiritual world is the wealth of uncommon men and women among our people. And it is our educational institutions that will promote and train them.

CONCLUSION

To sum up, may I say that the colleges have a great obligation courageously to restore our moral and spiritual losses from the war, to renew our ideals of freedom, to regain our sensitiveness to wrong, and to provide the nation with renewed supply of trained leadership. Unless we rebuild this new era on these foundations, it means the war has been lost. It means more. It means that civilization is lost. I am convinced that our educational institutions are equal to this, the greatest of tasks.

An Extemporaneous Address Closing the Yama Conference of 1945

ABSECON, NEW JERSEY
[*November 10, 1945*]

W E MEET in a time of great confusion, much discouragement, even fear and despair. The discussions we have heard here have not added much cheer. My purpose is not to add to those confusions, this discouragement and this despair, but to point to some of the breaks of sunlight which still come from the skies.

Our fears of the great slave state of Russia are not so much brought on by political activity as by their systematic spread of a disintegrating ideology. I can illustrate my point of view on the approach of our Government to that country's political action.

A friend, recently up from the Congo, related to me a new method of catching elephants. He said you get a horn, a pair of field glasses, a pair of tweezers and a mason jar. You get up in a tree; blow the horn; an elephant comes. You look at him through the wrong end of the field glasses; he gets smaller and smaller the nearer he gets. Finally you take the tweezers, pick him up and put him in the mason jar. That seems to be the way our Government has been trying to catch the Russian bear.

However, we are confronted by a world-wide conflict in fundamental thought. That conflict is collectivism vs. free men, and collectivism receives constant refreshment from Russia. I have no fear of the sweep of extreme collectivism in the form of Communism over the American people. But we will be plagued and slowed down by experiments in collectivism by our woolly-minded intellectuals. Also sometimes I feel that our dangers in government are greater from mediocrity than ideologies.

There are many forms of collectivism—the Communism of Russia, the National Socialism of Germany, the Socialism of Britain, the Planned Economy of the New Deal—and they all have two fundamentals in common. They all require vast centralization of government and huge bureaucracies. Bureaucracy and power are not the foundations of liberty. The other common ground of all collectivism is that the state can conduct economic life better than free men. And that reaches to the heart of freedom itself, for there can be no freedom of mind and spirit unless there also be economic freedom. None of us who hold to economic freedom believe in the long dead laissez-faire type of economic life. We know free men must be as much protected from business tyranny as from political tyranny. We know there must be constant social reform as we grow in complexity and understanding. We—America—have held from our beginnings that we are not only the keeper of our brother in distress but that the state has a responsibility to the unfortunate. Nor can we remain a free country alone in a collectivist world, unless we cut off all communications. I am not prepared to admit that the battle against collectivism is lost in the outside world. Men who have tasted freedom of mind and spirit will struggle back to that ideal even through blood. Nor do the economic impulses to freedom ever die. Peoples will find that no collectivist state can lift the standard of living and prosperity of its citizens to the heights of a free economy.

We must realize that with the recession of liberty all over the world our country is today the world's greatest reservoir of the free spirit. And it is the deepest reservoir because the freedom lies deepest in the American heart. While freedom appears lost in much of the world, yet there are great areas where it still survives in the hearts of men. They include the British Empire, Western Europe, Latin America and even Eastern Europe, despite its repressions. Our foreign political policies and our foreign economic policies must be directed to strengthening and regenerating the forces of freedom. We must not engage in reprisals, but in help. In this field we confront a hungry world and we alone must save it from starvation. We must give economic strength to Britain, to Europe and to Asia that they shall recover in their productivity. Nations which have been free are today drifting to collectivism because of their miseries; the surest way to the recovery of their freedoms is by economic recovery. If we are not afraid, if we have courage, I believe that the lamps of free men can be relighted in the world.

Many of our speakers here have pointed out the reasons to fear inflation. That could bring the extinction of most of our liberties for a long time to come. There is no need for American inflation in the dangerous sense as it is now sweeping over the vanquished countries and many of the victors. The enormous productive capacity of our country which can satisfy any buying panic is our first defense.

If we lift our vision from our immediate problems, we can see that we still have our factories, our railways, our farms, our homes; we have the most efficient labor and farmers, the most able managers and technologists in the world. Our immediate plague is the mass of Government paper which we have created to win the war. But if we are intelligent enough it can be carried along and cured by our gigantic forces of production.

And we have new forces of production which will increase our efficiency, our productivity, and will enable us to pay off this huge burden of war losses. I can well repeat to you part of a statement I recently made to a technical college where I said:

It is exactly from great increases in national efficiency and consequently in production that the world has in the past received its major aid in recuperation from devastating wars.

After the Napoleonic wars the plight of Britain seemed hopeless. But the application of the steam engine so increased the productivity of her people that in time the burden of huge debt became easy, the standard of living increased and employment expanded. After our war of revolution it was the expansion of our agriculture and our ships that brought us through.

After our Civil War the expansion of railway transportation stimulated the productivity of the fertile Mid-West. It opened the mines of the Far West. With these aids, in a few years the United States overcame the economic losses of that war and was again on the march of progress.

After World War I there blossomed a great advance in scientific knowledge and technical skills. It brought expansion in electric power, radio, telephone, motor transportation and the application of a thousand labor-saving devices and improved methods. Again we increased our productivity until the losses of that war were soon overcome. A great advance in the standards of living and comfort were again on the march. . . .

Now do not get the idea into your heads that these surges of efficiency were the product of war. They have occurred in peace. No doubt their suspension during the war cumulates their force when peace comes.

From scientific discovery and invention we have today a host of potential new expansions—many of them suspended by war, others stimulated by the war. None of them are immediately revolutionary, but of great cumulative effect. Indeed the whole gamut of science and its application has opened a new frontier to the expansion of American life.

We shall see a great expansion in air transport as a result of improvements we now know.

There will be great expansion in the application of diesel and turbine gas engines. Among other services, they will expedite and cheapen railway and highway transport.

We shall see a great expansion in the new art which we now call electronics with its multitude of new gadgets. The radar and electronic microscope are new to industry and research.

There will be great improvements in synthetic or chemical materials, such as plastics, specialized rubber, glass and chemicalized wood. There will be a great expansion in synthetic textiles.

There will be much wider use of light materials.

We have developed better seeds, many improvements in farm machinery and larger industrial uses of farm products.

We will save great wastes by the improvements in weather forecasting.

We have seen the development of a host of labor-saving machine tools, big and little, during the past ten years. There is a great improvement in "know how" in the use of these tools and methods.

There are a host of new openings for reduction of waste by standardization and simplification of industrial methods and products through cooperation in industry and distribution.

We have seen startling discoveries in medicine, the sulfa drugs, penicillin, blood plasma, vitamins, D.D.T. and a host of others which will reduce the waste of sickness and prolong skilled lives.

We have made great advances in manipulation of the molecular structure of hydro-carbons, among them improved gasoline and a new host of hydro-carbon products.

. . . The atomic bomb has awakened high hopes of application of such power to industrial purposes. There is danger of too high hopes. Up to now there is no reason to believe the explosive qualities of these elements can be tamed down so that they run an engine directly with the amiability of the explosion of gasoline. . . . There are intermediate and controllable steps in the transformation of Uranium 235, or 238, where a great volume of heat is generated. We are likely to see this indirect application to some power purposes within the next ten years. That, however, would produce no great industrial revolution. The fuel element in the cost of modern services and manufactured articles is a very small percentage. If all of these per cents were saved, it would not be a revolution. It may be a contribution.

And when we look at the last dozen years' march of scientific thought on the atom we can expect more from such great minds as Lawrence, Oppenheimer, Bush, Millikan, Compton and their host of young colleagues, perhaps much more than even they now know.

We have had a great expansion of our scientific and industrial laboratories which will daily add to these forces of greater productivity.

And to give impulse to all these forces we have a vast vacuum of goods to fill.

The sum of all these possibilities is not only recovery but a renewed march in progress.

The Obligation of the Republican Party

Lincoln Day Dinner, National Republican Club

New York City

[February 12, 1946]

NINETY years ago the great issue before the American people was free men. The Whig Party refused to accept that issue. Even worse, it sought compromises, middle courses and evasions. The young Republican Party, under Abraham Lincoln, met the issue squarely, and its strength and vitality grew from its brave and uncompromising struggle in behalf of freedom and dignity for all men. The Whig Party died.

Today the great issue before the American people is free men against the tide of Statism which is sweeping three-quarters of the world—whether it be called Communism, Fascism, Socialism or the disguised American mixture of Fascism and Socialism called "Managed Economy" now being transformed into a further ambiguity, the "Welfare State." This growth of statism has been nourished by the confusion of a great war. And it can grow still more by continued excessive taxation and by creeping inflation.

Once more, we face a crisis in free men. As in Lincoln's time there are other issues, but again this issue dominates and underlies all others.

The question now is, will the Republican Party take this issue or will it seek to straddle, as did the Whigs 90 years ago?

Two-party government is essential to the democratic process. But the high purpose of two-party government is not to gain public office. The purpose is to give the people an opportunity to determine fundamental issues at the ballot box rather than elsewhere.

The American people do not have that opportunity offered to them by the political parties today. Both parties have straddled.

What the Republican Party needs, what the Nation needs from the Republican Party is a fundamental and constructive philosophy of government with the principles which flow from it. And that philosophy must reach far deeper than the froth of slogans or platform planks designed to appease every pressure group. This fundamental philosophy cannot be defined in the old terms of Conservative, Liberal, or Progressive. Lenin's direction to his Communist supporters was everywhere to distort, to bore within, words and terms. That pollution has gone on apace in the United States until many Americans think that a conservative is a Reactionary; that a Liberal is a left-winger equipped with mixed European ideologies; and that a progressive is a nut.

The Republican Party need not waste time disputing over terms. It needs to assert its own philosophy and its own principles under the term American and resolutely defend them.

What is that philosophy? It, of course, includes fidelity to the concepts underlying the Declaration of Independence and the Constitution with its bill of unalienable rights. But since these fundamental liberties were established two things have happened which require new concepts of freedom and new protections to freedom. The first is the Industrial Revolution. The second is our gigantic growth in area and population.

The Industrial Revolution, despite its fabulous gains in living standards, threatened us with a host of new dangers to free men. The imagination of free men had stretched new invention across a continent; we had big business. Some big business undertook extra-curricular activities in special privilege and vicious interference in the politics of free government. That was a new tyranny over free men. That battle for free men from outmoded *laissez-faire* was first fought out in the anti-trust acts and the public regulation of utilities and corporations.

Today we see a gigantic growth of labor unions paralleling big business. And out of the extra-curricular activities of some C. I. O. unions under radical leaders, we have another form of special privilege and vicious interference in the politics of free government. That is again tyranny. Free men cannot permit economic tyranny, whether by capital or labor, any more than they can tolerate political tyranny.

Therefore, the concept of freedom must include government regulation of economic life. But if men are to remain free, then government must not dictate or operate economic life any more than it may dictate or operate spiritual life. It must remain umpire and mediator.

And this gigantic growth in area and population projects a thousand problems in government, economics, public works, health and education. Moreover, being born of the religious faith, our philosophy insists that as men are their brothers' keepers they must care for the aged, the ill and the destitute.

But if we are to maintain free men in this gigantic population and solve these problems, our philosophy must fully embrace the concept that man can accomplish more by cooperation outside the government than by coercion from the government. It is this cooperation among free men aligned to public interest that releases the energies of the people for creative achievement and abundant production. The tens of thousands of community committees, local governments, labor unions, commercial associations, farm organizations and our host of other free institutions can do a million services in the public interest every year which Statism will wither on the vine.

There are fields where cooperation can be properly aided by government, but government swollen with power and laden with burdens becomes something above and apart from the governed. It becomes the enemy of the governed increasing its prerogatives with fanatical zeal.

To delineate the appropriate boundaries of the government

which preserve such a philosophy and principles is the task of the statesmanship for which this country is waiting.

One test of government is—does it provide a climate which stimulates the proper initiative of men? Does it strengthen the moral rectitude of the people? Does it stiffen their self-reliance? Does it create a climate in which righteous cooperation can thrive? With such tests the right and constructive answers to our problems will be found.

But by Statism it strangles them with uncertainties, fears and intellectual dishonesties which undermine their morals, their self-reliance, their confidence, their judgments, their energies and their cooperation.

Such a philosophy and such tests would mean a huge house-cleaning of Statism from our government.

We are told we must have a constructive program. What more constructive program is there in the world today than that of free men? From free men comes a dynamic, not a static, philosophy of life. Free men generate new ideas, new inventions. From them comes change, reform and progress. But there can be no change in the principles of free men or there will be no progress.

A society built on these foundations and undefiled by special interest can command by moral force the confidence of all. It is only a nation rooted in this philosophy that can be a sanctuary for the oppressed, the protector of the exploited, the calm tribunal before which men may articulate their differences and perfect their agreements. Reaction is foreign to it, for its motive and inspiration are to explore the illimitable means by which men can enrich the civilization to which they belong. It is liberalism in the true meaning of expanding freedom of men. It is conservatism in that it would conserve the freedoms we have won.

The Republican Party owes it to the American people to give them the opportunity to express themselves flatly on this issue as they did against slavery in 1860 under Mr. Lincoln. I have no fear that they would not declare for free men rather than for the world-wide reaction today toward economic serf-dom.

The dangers to freedom do not lie wholly in our domestic life, they lie also in our attitudes toward freedom in the world today. Freedom has shrunk in the world as a result of our own policies born of our own drift toward Statism. Here in America alone remains the chance to preserve the concepts and practices of free men.

Great as are the confusions and difficulties of the day, they can be overcome. The history of civilization shows that in many a crisis and time of confusion some men and women stood solid against error, firm for their principles and beliefs. They may not have known all the solutions or all the answers, yet if they stood firm until the furies had passed, they won. And to them rallied the spiritual forces which lie deep in the human experience and the human heart. It was such steadfast American men and women who carried the torch of free men through the confusions of the Revolutionary War. Again such groups stood firm and brought freedom through the confusions of war in Lincoln's time.

Have we any less faith?

On Congressional Election

Press Statement, New York City
[November 5, 1946]

THIS has been much more than just another Congressional election. The whole world, including the United States, has been for years driving to the left on the totalitarian road of "planned economy," or Socialism or Communism. America is by this election the first country to repudiate this road. And it defines that the Republican Party is the party of the right. We are again moving to the goal of free men. This decision of the United States will have a profound effect on nations who have been following along the road to the left.

The Right to Strike

This Week Magazine
[*December 29, 1946*]

B ECAUSE everybody has more cash in his pocket and in the bank, there is an illusion which always comes with the ending of war and its inevitable inflation. That illusion is that we have grown richer and more prosperous. The contrary is the case. The fact is, the American people have been terribly impoverished. That impoverishment will develop later and recovery from it depends upon two things.

First, on whether our people are willing, at least for a few years, to work more efficiently than ever before and thus restore their lost wealth.

Second, recovery depends on what progress we can make in the application of labor-saving devices, new methods, new inventions and scientific discoveries, which increase the productivity of each individual and of the nation. These being the facts, some blunt words are needed.

At the desk, the bench, and on the farm, men and women must give the best that is in them during reasonable and healthy work hours without artificial limitations on effort.

The initiative of men must be restored and encouraged so that labor-saving devices, scientific discovery, invention and new enterprise may have full development.

EXCEEDING THE LIMITS

Widespread strikes which paralyze production defeat this course. We cannot make economic or social recovery if we are to have a repetition of the unparalleled industrial conflict of 1946.

Nobody denies that there is a "right" to strike. But there are extremes at which any "right" becomes an oppression. There are legal limits even to the right of free speech. When the "right to strike" was fully accepted, strikes were believed to be solely pressures on employers to improve working conditions and wages. But a new idea has now grown up around the use of the strike: that this weapon can be employed for political and ideological purposes and that it can be used so to injure and endanger the people at large that in their misery they or the government will be forced to do the strikers' bidding. It is the people who suffer.

By the use of this tactic there have arisen in the United States a dozen men who now wield power over the life and living of the people greater than the government. They have never been elected by the people. Years of battle by the people finally eliminated such oppressions by arrogant business leaders.

POWERS NEEDED

The time is now here when strikes which endanger the life and living of hosts of people not party to the dispute must have prompt settlement. We must have more effective methods of collective bargaining and mediation before a strike is resorted to. In addition, the judicial machinery of the country should be given power and penalties to end any strike which the President, through the Attorney General, declares constitutes a danger to large numbers of innocent people.

But in order that justice be done, there must be further provision for arbitration conducted by delegates from both sides, together with independent members. The decisions of this group, arrived at by majority vote, should be final. I have always opposed compulsory arbitration as a limitation on the right to strike, but that right has now been carried to extremes. It is necessary to check this destruction if the people are to be masters in their own houses.

There is a heavy responsibility on all of us as we move into the new year. We must master the difficult art of working together. No country can move forward when its machinery stands idle. Only through production can we recover from the war, and keep America strong, prosperous and free.

Address before the
Holland Society of New York

Waldorf-Astoria Hotel, New York City
[November 20, 1947]

N O MAN could fail to deeply appreciate so graceful a mark of distinction as you have conferred upon me— and in its background have been the problems of war. The hideous aftermaths from war are not so much from the destruction of life and property as the evil political, social, economic and moral storms which sweep over the world. The appalling dangers to civilization haunt us hourly in the press, over the radio, and from the platform. These dangers are indeed so great that it is easier to sink into defeatism than to prove there is hope of remedy for the evils which beset us.

I could talk for hours upon these malign forces. But at the risk of being called a Pollyanna, I am going to give a moment to the brighter hopes for the future. I could even justify an occasional outbreak of Polly's excessive rejoicing and gladness in this lugubrious world—for faith comes from hope.

With this guarded fashion of rejoicing let me say at once that considering the destructive forces let loose during the past ten years, we can be grateful that so much of Western Civilization survives. It has proved to be tough.

There is no more inspiring example since this war than the courage and enduring moral fibre shown by the Dutch people. In the last moments of their five years of dreadful destruction, pillage and oppression, their land was swept over again by the final battles of the war. Yet within days they were uncomplainingly digging out the rubble of their cities, their homes and factories; reconstructing their schools and churches, and re-establishing their institutions of century-old freedom. With but little help from the outside world, they have today restored much of their productivity and they have re-established their way of life.

We should deplore some of the moral consequences of war among the American people—but we do see them pouring out their substances to save the hungry and cold all over the world. We see them even depriving themselves to save life among our conquered enemies. Moreover, they retain the stamina constantly to protest and act against the forces which would enslave mankind.

With fifty other nations we are struggling to erect a world institution to prevent future wars. Its accomplishments may not be great but the very fact that it meets and debates is something gained.

We in the Western Hemisphere are demonstrating every day not only that personal liberty and representative government are the only hope for moral and spiritual progress. We are also demonstrating that free enterprise is the only road to productivity. Today only the free-enterprise countries are free of starvation and cold. Moreover 95 per cent of all the goods being sent overseas in an effort to keep Europe and Asia alive are coming from the huge productivity of free-enterprise countries. Had we in this hemisphere yielded to the economic Utopias of either eastern or western Europe, I venture to say that hardly a ton of food or fuel would be moving overseas. Sooner or later the Utopia-seeking nations will notice these facts and their peoples will resume the only road to freedom from hunger and cold.

Obviously the great shadow which hangs over the future of the world is Russian Communism. We are now divided into two worlds, the one which holds to agnosticism and human slavery, the other that holds to faith and free men. I cannot but believe that the Communist-ridden peoples will sooner or later throw off their chains. That there are some rumblings is indicated by their repeated purges. It is certain that fifth columns are active all over the world and that they must be unceasingly combated, but as time goes on they are having less success. A year ago there were Communist ministers in the Cabinets of seven or eight governments outside the Iron Curtain; now they remain in only one or two such countries. In our own country their constant exposure is destroying the hopes they may have once had. Above all, we are realizing that we must aid other countries to combat their conspiracies.

Our task is to avoid war between these two worlds. Every year we gain brings us nearer to the day when these monstrous regimes, like all their predecessors in history, will fall.

Because I find this much hope and have this much faith, do not believe I am less aware of the dangers. You remember that the Apostle Paul remarked upon the potency of faith, hope and charity as a cure for the world's ills. He thought that the greatest of these was charity. Surely the United States Congress is taking care of this avenue to salvation. We citizens are thus able for the moment at least, to devote ourselves (outside of taxes) to faith and hope. There is hope. We Americans, jointly with the people of Holland, hold to faith.

Address before the
Sons of the Revolution

Washington's Birthday Banquet,
Waldorf-Astoria Hotel
New York City
[February 23, 1948]

AT THE outset, I wish to express my deep appreciation for the honor you have conferred upon me by awarding me the gold medal of this great patriotic society. This on his birthday is the great occasion of the year when we renew tribute to George Washington. The monuments our people have built to him, the naming after him of a great State, of our Capitol city, innumerable counties, towns and streets—all are our mute tributes. But it is on the occasion of his birthday that we express afresh each year the gratitude which lies in our hearts.

The task of saying something new or more eloquent about our greatest American has long since been exhausted. Everything has been said in the millions of orations delivered by every school child, every President, and every member of Congress—since Washington's term as President expired.

SOME MODERN DIFFICULTIES WITH WASHINGTON'S POLICIES

It is customary on these occasions to recall Washington's great deeds and his wise advice to his countrymen. The task of using this vehicle for discussion has become somewhat more difficult in these recent years.

61

Seeking some light on our own problems, I turned first to economic questions. But I found the first legislative act signed by the first President was a protective tariff bill. There seemed to be some elements of partisanship in that subject so I cannot use that text.

I thought perhaps Washington, who became President amid a postwar depression and inflation, might have some views on that subject. But I was unable to find that he had any remedy for postwar booms and slumps. I might mention, however, that in those primitive times, Presidents were not supposed to keep this kind of medicine. He seemed to think that stable currency, free markets and greater productivity were the answer. As this also involves some controversial aspects, I dropped that subject.

I also searched for some light on the organization of our government. I have recently been appointed to find some method for the Federal Government to get along with less than two million civil employees. I found that Washington conducted the government with less than one employee to every 4000 of the population. Today it runs about one employee to every 70 of the population. Such a reduction seemed too extreme, so that I must drop this discussion also.

When we come to foreign relations, any discourse on Washington's advice becomes still more difficult. For instance, on one occasion, he said: "The great rule of conduct for us in regard to foreign nations, is, in extending our commercial relations, to have with them as little political relations as possible." That did not seem to fit the proposed method of administering the Marshall Plan, and as I am not here engaged in controversy, I cannot pursue that subject.

There was a George Washington Plan, which he propounded over 150 years ago. He was emphatic on what he termed "our detached and distant situation." He framed it in these pungent questions: "Why forego the advantages of so peculiar a situation? Why quit our own to stand on foreign ground? Why by interweaving our destiny with any part of Europe entangle our peace and prosperity in the toils of European ambition, rivalship, interest, humor or caprice?" You will realize that some of us have had leanings toward the George Washington Plan in times gone by. He was not only the Father of his country but the ancestor of all isolationists. However, that is an unfriendly word in these days so I will not amplify on this line.

I looked to see if Washington offered any advice to his countrymen as to what to do afterwards if they did get entangled with foreign nations. He left no advice, whatever, on this subject.

But to be serious Washington was a practical soul who met new situations as they arose. His views on many questions might be modified by railroads, automobiles, steamships, airplanes, electronics, and juke boxes. We might also add ideologies, threats of war and economic forecasters.

Our present entanglements are appeals to our compassion for the hungry people from parts of Europe and Asia and an obnoxious desire of another part of Europe to interfere in our peace and our way of life. I am sure Washington, being a generous man, would today have responded to the human appeal. I am equally sure that Washington's immutable principles as declared by him in the Declaration and the Bill of Rights, would have led him to take measures of defense against those who would destroy those freedoms of men.

THE WORLD SITUATION

Truly the world situation in which we find ourselves today is not one in which we can find much satisfaction. That is an understatement. We are now three years after our last war to bring world peace, and every road to peace and disarmament seems closed. The United Nations which was to assure lasting peace seems frustrated. Nevertheless, I believe we are only at Valley Forge in the struggle for peace and disarmament. Just as Washington held to a great faith so we also today must hold to the United Nations as the hope of mankind.

FEDERATION OF WESTERN EUROPE

Today we are not only compelled to remain armed on what amounts to a gigantic-war footing, but we must realize that in case some one would make war upon us we have no certainty of military allies in the world. At the moment Britain and Western Europe might remain neutral. This is not an accusation as to their good faith or their gratitude for our having spent so much American treasure and blood in their liberation from Hitler. It is the bare stark fact of divided and weakened European nations in the face of Red Armies of 2,500,000 men along the Iron Curtain.

However, there is hope of some sort of federation of Western Europe, which would strengthen the forces of peace and defense. Enlightened statesmen have advocated for many years various forms of such economic, political and military unity. The Marshall Plan has been proposed as a method of stimulating such action. Certainly, unless some form of economic and political unity is attained that plan will have fallen far short of a return for our sacrifices.

A SUGGESTION IN WORLD ORGANIZATION

It has been suggested that we enter into a military alliance with such a federation if it were formed.

Here I wish to make a suggestion as to the defense part of such a union. Such a purpose might be more effectively accomplished if we examine a possibility of strengthening the United Nations.

There is perhaps a forgotten phase of the Charter of the United Nations which could now be summoned into being. Chapter VII of that document authorizes and encourages the organization of regional grouping of nations for defense and for consultation and action in the maintenance of peace.

By the Inter-American Treaty at Rio de Janeiro, we have already created, under the Charter, such an organization on this side of the Atlantic. It provides for mutual defense and preservation of peace in the Western Hemisphere. Whatever form of unification may be developed in Western Europe could also include their creation of such a regional organization under the Charter. That would enable them to better cooperate with all the Western Hemisphere states, both inside and outside of the United Nations. Such an action would bring more vitality and strength into the United Nations. It would avoid the United States' being involved in military alliances. That would seem an easier method for Western Europe than a purely military alliance. Such an approach would point toward peace rather than toward war which is the bane of military alliances. It could bring greater solidarity of action among all peace-loving nations.

Although the prospect is indeed very dim, perhaps sometime the Russian regional group might also cooperate for the common welfare of mankind. More especially is this possible if they witnessed the consolidation of strength of other great groups.

WASHINGTON ON UNITY

At this point, a word from George Washington's wisdom has a vital and lasting meaning. Washington came into office with the Federal Constitution. The 13 American States, like the 16 Western European States, had been through years of a fierce war with great physical destruction and economic demoralization. Their separate currencies, were depreciated; they were each burdened with debt. They maintained separate selfish economic and customs barriers. There was little unity in their foreign relations. Their military power had greatly weakened.

In urging continued unity upon the American States, Washington said: "All parts combined cannot fail to find in the united mass a means of greater strength, greater resource, greater security from external danger, a less interruption of their peace." If that could be applied to Western Europe they could look forward to 150 years of progress such as has been the fortune of our 48 federated states.

Finally, I may recall still another statement from Washington with which there can be no controversy. He said: ". . . The preservation of the sacred fire of liberty, and the destiny of the republican form of government, are justly considered as deeply, perhaps as *finally*, staked on the experiment entrusted to the hands of the American people."

That sacred fire of liberty lighted by Washington and his colleagues on this Continent still burns brightly. But the zeal and faith which will sustain that trust are no less imperative now than 150 years ago. Its maintenance is the one clear light in a confused and tormented world.

This Crisis in American Life

Address before the Republican National Convention at
Philadelphia

[*June 22, 1948*]

Republican Convention and your guests:

I T IS indeed difficult to express to you my appreciation for
your heart-warming welcome.

Those who have already addressed you in this Convention have emphasized the continuing grave crisis which envelops
our own country and the world. And this crisis is deeper than
some may think. Every important government including our
own has broken its promises to mankind. But civilization moves
forward only on promises that are kept. And from these disasters faith has been hurt; hope has been diminished; thinking
has been corrupted, and fear has been spread—all over the
world.

The problems which confront us far transcend partisan action
and I do not propose to speak in that sense tonight. I shall
speak but a few moments and that as an appraisal of the responsibilities you face.

What is done here, what *you* do here, will affect the destiny
of our country beyond any estimation of this moment. For you
are more than ever before, the trustees of a great cause, the
cause for which this party was founded, the cause of human
liberty.

THE WORLD PROBLEM OF FREE MEN

Liberty has been defeated in a score of nations. Those governments have revived slavery. They have revived mass guilt. They have revived government by hatred, by exile, by torture. Today the men in the Kremlin hold in their right hands the threat of military aggression against all civilization. With their left hands they work to weaken civilization by boring from within.

These tyrants have created a situation new in all human experience. We saved them from Hitler but they refuse to cooperate with us to establish good will or peace on earth. Thus today a powerful nation, dominated by men without conscience, finds it useful to have neither peace nor war in the world.

Whether some of us, who foresaw that danger and warned of it, were right or wrong, and whatever the terrible errors of American statesmanship that helped bring it about, we are today faced with a world situation in which there is little time for regrets.

The only obstacle to the annihilation of freedom has been the United States of America. Only as long as America is free and strong will human liberty survive in the world.

OUR AID TO FREE MEN ABROAD

It is in our interest and, above all, in the interest of liberty throughout the world, that we aid in giving strength and unity to the nations of Western Europe. It is only thus that we can restore a balance of power in the world able to resist the hordes from the Eurasian steppes who would ruin Western Civilization.

And we have also a huge burden of increased armament to assure that no hostile force will ever reach this hemisphere.

With all the good will in our hearts, our friends abroad should realize that our economy must not be exhausted or overstrained by these burdens, or the last hope of the world is lost. We should only be playing Stalin's game, for his expressed hope lies in our economic collapse for which his Fifth Columns are busily planning.

Our friends abroad should realize that we are today straining our American economy to the utmost. Warning signals already clang in our ears. Relief and defense will soon be costing us over 22 billion dollars a year. Our Federal budget threatens to increase to 50 billions a year, unless we delay many plans for internal social and economic improvement.

Even our present 40 odd billion taxes and the export of materials so drain the savings of our people that in the year 1947 we did not properly maintain and expand the great tools of production and distribution upon which our standard of living depends.

Nor is there any room for more taxes except by a cut in the standard of living of those who do the nation's work. Some will say that we can increase corporation taxes. That is easy to say. But any student of economics knows that, in the long run, such a tax will be passed on to the consumer—provided we want to maintain our real wages and great tools of production. Surely any American would seem to have the right to aspire to the income of a United States Senator—less taxes. However, if our remaining untaxed income above that level in the country were completely confiscated, the take would provide only $2\frac{1}{2}\%$ of the budget.

There are other warning signs. Our reputed prosperity has begun to walk on two stilts: one is the forced draft of exporting more than our surplus through relief; the other is a great armament program. We cannot go higher on these stilts, or we will break a leg getting down.

We should have no illusions. To the devasting Four Horsemen of the Apocalypse, modern civilization has added two more. Their names are High Taxes and Inflation. These are close by.

Therefore, with full compassion for those nations in difficulties, certain matters in aid to them must be recognized on both sides of the world.

The first is that our task is solely to aid their reconstruction.

We can provide only bare necessities. There is no room for non-essentials, for profligacy, or for inefficiency.

We must not create a perpetual dependence of Europe and Asia upon the United States. We must not soften their preparedness to meet their own dangers. Otherwise our sacrifices will only undermine their self-reliance and the contribution they must make themselves towards the saving of Western Civilization.

We must insist that reconstruction of Western Europe be as a whole. That must include the restoration of the productivity of Germany, or Europe will die. We need neither forget nor condone Nazi guilt, but a free world must not poison its concepts of life by accepting revenge and hatred as a guide. Otherwise, not only will our efforts fail, but the American taxpayer will be bled white supporting an idle and despairing German people.

GREAT STRIKES CAN DEFEAT ALL FREEDOM

And if we are to carry both these burdens of relief and armament, we must have uninterrupted operation of the major tools of production and distribution among all the participating nations.

We in America must face the fact that no citizen, or group of citizens, in this Republic can assure the power to endanger not only the health and welfare of our own people, but freedom of the world, by halting or paralyzing the economic life of this nation. Such men have not been elected by the people to have such powers. Representative government must be master in its own house, or it will perish. We fought that battle out once with arrogant business men. We can no more have economic tyranny, if freedom is to live, than we can have political tyranny. There are other ways for determining economic justice than war on our people.

THE BATTLE FOR LIBERTY AT HOME

Nor does the battle for freedom all lie beyond our own borders. We also have been infected with the European intermittent fever of creeping totalitarianism. It has been a mingling of germs from Karl Marx and Mussolini, with cheers from the Communists. This collectivism has slowly inserted its tentacles into our labor unions, our universities, our intelligentsia, and our Government.

Our difficulty lies not so much with obnoxious Communists in our midst as with the fuzzy-minded people who think we can have totalitarian economics in the hands of bureaucracy, and at the same time have personal liberty for the people and representative government in the nation. Their confused thinking convinces them that they are liberals—but if they are liberals, they have liberalism without liberty. Nor are they middle-of-the-roaders as they claim to be: they are a half-way house to totalitarianism.

They should take note that in every one of the countries of Europe where 400,000,000 people are now enslaved by the Communists, it has been the totalitarian liberals who provided the ladders upon which the Communist pirates have boarded the Ship of State.

The whole world was steadily moving along these collectivist roads until two years ago. Then in our Congressional elections, by their votes for both the Republican and Democratic candidates, the people showed the first turn from collectivism that has been made by any important nation in recent years.

The 300-year-old roots of freedom in America showed their resistance to the collectivist blight. The influence of our rebirth of liberty has now echoed throughout the world. But the battle is still on.

The deep soil of these 300-year-old roots is the spiritual concept that the rights of man to freedom are personal to him from his Creator—not from the State. That is our point of departure from all others. This spiritual concept, whatever our faults may be, has guided our people to a life, not only of material abundance, but far more glorious, to a life of human dignity.

Today the American people have reached an historic stage which has come to a few strong nations in their ability to contribute to moral leadership in the world. Few such nations have come upon that task with so few liabilities. In these 30 years of war we alone have taken no people's land; we have oppressed no race of man. We have faced all the world in friendship, with compassion, with a genuine love and helpfulness for our fellow men. In war, in peace, in disaster, we have aided those whom we believed to be in the right and to require our aid. At the end of wars, we have aided foe as well as ally; and in each instance, even the children of those who would do us hurt. We have hated war; we have loved peace.

What other nation has such a record?

It is these concepts of your country that this Party must bear high as the banner of a marching army. From this room free men and women will cheer free men and women the world over. You can say to them that the day is *not* done, that night has *not* come—that human liberty lives—and lives eternally here upon this continent.

THE RESPONSIBILITIES OF THIS CONVENTION

My fellow Republicans, from the inevitable passing of years, this is indicated as probably the last time I will meet with you in Convention. That does not mean I shall spend my days with less concern and less watchfulness of the deep currents which will determine the future of American life. But this does warrant my speaking from my heart of this great concern.

There may be some of you who believe that you have come here only to pass upon a platform and to select candidates for President and Vice President. Your greater task by far is to generate a spirit which will rekindle in every American a love not only for his country but a devotion to American civilization. You are here to feed the reviving fires of spiritual fervor which once made the word, American, a stirring description of a man who lived and died for human liberty, who knew no private interest, no personal ambition, no popular acclaim, no advantage of pride or place which overshadows the burning love for the freedom of man.

Great as your problems are, they are no greater than Americans have met before your time. You are no less able or courageous than they were.

Therefore, I repeat, what you say and do here and in this campaign, is of transcendent importance.

If you produce nothing but improvised platitudes, you will give no hope.

If you produce no leadership here, no virile fighter for the right, you will have done nothing of historic significance.

If you follow the counsel of those who believe that politics is only a game to be played for personal advantage, you are wasting your time and effort.

If here, or in this campaign, you calculate what will please this or that little segment of our population, and satisfy this or that pressure group or sectional interest, you will be betraying your opportunity, and tragically missing the call of your time.

If you temporize with collectivism in any form, you will stimulate its growth and make certain the defeat of free men.

If, on the other hand, in this campaign, as a mature and inspired political party, you face the truth that we are in a critical battle to safeguard our nation and civilization which, under God, have brought to us a life of liberty, then you will be guided step by step to restore the foundations of right thinking, of morals and of faith. If you choose your leadership with full recognition that only those can lead you who believe in your ideals, who seek not only victory but the opportunity to serve in this fight, then you will issue from this hall a clarion call, in as pure a note, in as full a tone as that call to arms which your political ancestors issued at Ripon, Wisconsin, when this party was born to make all men free.

And so I bespeak to you tonight to make yourselves worthy of the victory.

The Meaning of America

Homecoming Address at the Reception Tendered by
West Branch, Iowa, on the speaker's 74th Birthday
[August 10, 1948]

I AM deeply grateful for your generous welcome. I find it difficult to express my appreciation for the thousands of kindly acts and good wishes which have marked this day. They come from the thousands of you who do me the honor of coming here. They come in thousands of telegrams and letters from all States in the Union. They come in the magnificent gifts to the War Library at Stanford University. I wish I could personally acknowledge each of them but they are in so great a flood that I hope you will accept this expression of the gratitude that lies in my heart as acknowledgment of the honor you do me.

I was glad to have your invitation to come again to this Iowa village where I was born. Here I spent the first ten years of my boyhood. My parents and grandparents came to this village in the covered wagon—pioneers in this community. They lie buried over the hill. They broke the prairie into homes of independent living. They worshipped God; they did their duty to their neighbors. They toiled to bring to their children greater comfort, better education and to open to them wider opportunity than had been their own.

I am proud to have been born in Iowa. Through the eyes of a ten-year-old boy it was a place of adventure and daily discoveries—the wonder of the growing crops, the excitements of the harvest, the journeys to the woods for nuts and hunting, the joys of snowy winters, the comfort of the family fireside, of good food and tender care. And out of the excessive energy of all small boys there were evenings filled with accounts of defeat and victory over animate and inanimate things—so far as they were permitted in a Quaker community.

Indelible in those recollections was a widowed Mother, sitting with her needle, cheerfully supporting three children and at the same time ministering to her neighbors. After that came life with Uncle Allan on his farm near this village. With him there was the joy and sorrow which come to every small boy enroute to life's disciplines by way of farm chores. And among them was the unending making of provisions for the next winter. But in those primitive days, social security was had from the cellar, not from the Federal Government.

You may be surprised if I tell you that at an age somewhat under ten I began here my first national service. By my own efforts I furnished firecrackers required for the adequate celebration of the Independence of the United States on July 4th, 1882. To get those firecrackers, I entered into collective bargaining by which it was settled that I should receive one cent per hundred for picking potato bugs in a field in sight of this stand. My impression then, and now is, that it was an oppressive wage rate.

Also, I took part in the political issues of the day by walking beside a Garfield torchlight procession in the Presidential campaign of 1880. And by the village flags at half-mast, I learned of the assassination of Garfield, with some dim understanding that somewhere in the nation great men guarded its welfare.

One of the indelible impressions of memory was the original Quaker Meeting-house. Those recollections chiefly revolve around the stiff repression of the explosive energies of a small boy sitting during the long, long silences. One time, however, the silence was broken by the shrill voice of Aunt Hannah who was moved in meeting bitterly to denounce the modernistic tendencies of those times. She had firm views on any form of recreation, which included singing in Sunday-school. She closed with a peroration to the effect that if these tendencies persisted that edifice dedicated to God would some day become in fact that place of abomination—a "the-atre." And truly the old meeting-house in its decadent years, having made way for a better edifice, became a movie house. My view is that the abomination part depends on the choice of the film.

And among these recollections was that of a great lady who first taught me in school and remained my friend during her whole long and useful life, Mrs. Mollie Carran.

It was from her that I first heard something about the meaning of the word *American*. Many great writers and statesmen have attempted to express what we mean by that word. But there is an imponderable within it which reaches to the soul of our people and defies measure.

America means far more than a continent bounded by two oceans. It is more than pride of military power, glory in war, or in victory. It means more than vast expanse of farms, of great factories or mines, magnificent cities, or millions of automobiles and radios. It is more even than the traditions of the great tide westward from Europe which pioneered the conquest of this continent. It is more than our literature, our music, our poetry. Other nations have these things also.

Maybe the intangible we cannot describe lies in the personal experience and the living of each of us rather than in phrases, however inspiring.

Perhaps without immodesty I can claim to have had some experience in what *American* means. I have lived many kinds of American life. After my early boyhood in this Iowa village, I lived as the ward of a country doctor in Oregon. I lived among those to whom hard work was the price of existence. The opportunities of America opened out to me the public schools. They carried me to the professional training of an American university. I began by working with my own hands for my daily bread. I have tasted the despair of fruitless search for a job. I know the kindly encouragement of a humble boarding-house keeper. I know now that at that time there was an economic depression either coming or going. But nobody told me of it. So I did not have the modern worry of what the Federal Government would do about it.

I have conducted the administartion of great industries with their problems of production and the well-being of their employees.

I have seen America in contrast with many nations and many races. My profession took me into many foreign lands under many kinds of government. I have worked with their great spiritual leaders and their great statesmen. I have worked in governments of free men, of tyrannies, of Socialists and of Communists. I have met with princes, kings, despots and desperados.

I have seen the squalor of Asia, the frozen class barriers of Europe. And I was not a tourist. I was associated in their working lives and problems. I had to deal with their social systems and their governments. And outstanding everywhere to these great masses of people there was a hallowed word— *America*. To them, it was the hope of the world.

My every frequent homecoming has been a re-affirmation of the glory of America. Each time my soul was washed by the relief from grinding poverty of other nations, by the greater kindliness and frankness which comes from acceptance of equality and belief in wide-open opportunity to all who want a chance. It is more than that. It is a land of self-respect born alone of free men and women.

In later years I participated on behalf of America in a great war. I saw untold misery and revolution. I have seen liberty die and tyranny rise. I have seen human slavery again on the march.

I have been repeatedly placed by my countrymen where I had need to deal with the hurricanes of social and economic destruction which have swept the world. I have seen bitter famine and the worst misery that the brutality of war can produce.

I have had every honor to which any man could aspire. There is no place on the whole earth except here in America where all the sons of man can have this chance in life.

I recount all this in order that, in Quaker terms, I can give my own testimony.

The meaning of our word "America" flows from one pure source. Within the soul of America is freedom of mind and spirit in man. Here alone are the open windows through which pours the sunlight of the human spirit. Here alone is human dignity not a dream, but an accomplishment. Perhaps it is not perfect, but it is more full in realization here than any other place in the world.

Perhaps another etching of another meaning of America lies in this very community. It was largely settled by Quakers over 90 years ago. This small religious sect in England had declared 150 years before the Declaration of Independence, that certain freedoms of man came from the Creator and not from the State. They spent much time in British stocks and jails for their outburst of faith in the dignity of the individual man.

They first came in refuge to New England. But the Puritans cut off their ears by way of disapproval of their perhaps excessive religious individualism. Then came the great refuge of religious freedom which William Penn secured for them. From New England and Pennsylvania some of the ancestors of this community, before the Revolution, migrated first to Maryland, and after a generation they moved to the Piedmont of North Carolina. Then early in the last century slavery began to encroach upon them. Most of that community—5,000 of them—organized a concerted trek to Ohio and Indiana. This time they were seeking not religious freedom, but freedom from the stain of slavery on human liberty. Again after a generation they hitched their covered wagons and settled on the prairies hereabouts.

Everywhere along these treks there sprang up homes and farms. But more vital were the Schoolhouse and the Meetinghouse with their deep roots in religious faith, their tolerance and devotion to liberty of the individual. And in these people there was the will to serve their community and their country. Even this village was a station on the underground through which negroes were aided to the freedom of Canada. Sons of this community were in the then Red Cross of the Civil War. And despite their peaceloving faith, many of their sons were enrolled into the Union Army to battle for free men.

That imbedded individualism, that self-reliance, that sense of service, and above all those moral and spiritual foundations were not confined to the Quakers. They were but one atom in the mighty tide of many larger religious bodies where these qualities made up the intangibles in the word *American*.

At the time our ancestors were proclaiming that the Creator had endowed all mankind with rights of freedom as the children of God, with a free will, there was being proclaimed by Hegel, and later by Karl Marx, a satanic philosophy of agnosticism and that the rights of man came from the State. The greatness of America today comes from one philosophy, the despair of Europe from the other.

There are today fuzzy-minded people in our country who would compromise in these fundamental concepts. They scoff at these tested qualities in men. They never have understood and never will understand what the word *America* means. They explain that these qualities were good while there was a continent to conquer, and a nation to build. They say that time has passed. No doubt the land frontier has passed. But the frontiers of science and better understanding of human welfare are barely opening.

This new land with all its high promise cannot and will not be conquered except by men and women inspired from these same concepts of free spirit and free mind.

And it is those moral and spiritual qualities which arise alone in free men which will fulfill the meaning of the word *American*. And with them will come centuries of further greatness to America.

PART III

REPARATIONS AND ECONOMIC
SUPPORT TO THE WORLD

On the Necessary Steps for Promotion of German Exports, so as to Relieve American Taxpayers of the Burdens of Relief and for Economic Recovery of Europe

Report to the President
[March 18, 1947]

The President
The White House
Washington, D. C.

Dear Mr. President:

I am sending you herewith my conclusions upon the problems of reviving German industry and thus exports with which to relieve American and British taxpayers from their burden in preventing starvation in Germany. These problems also involve economic stability and peace in Europe.

Whatever may have been our policies in the past, I am convinced that the time has come to face the realities that have developed. The mission you assigned to me would be less than performed if I did not state the stark situation and make such recommendations as seem to me necessary.

I wish again to express my appreciation to you for your consideration, to my colleagues Mr. Hugh Gibson, Dr. Gustav Stolper, Dr. Dennis A. FitzGerald, Dr. William Sebrell, Jr., and Messrs. Louis Lochner, Frank Mason and Tracy Voorhees, and to our military and civil officials in Germany.

*   *   *   *   *

INTRODUCTION

Inquiry into the economic policies in Germany which would relieve financial support from the United States was one of the subjects assigned to my mission to that country. Aside from a mass of information and statistical material secured on this journey, I have been familiar with German economic problems over many years, including my experience before and after World War I. In view of the gravity of the crisis which confronts the world, it would be an ill service if I did not state my conclusions fully and frankly.

These conclusions are not the product of sentiment nor of feeling toward a nation which has brought such misery upon the whole earth. They are not given in condonement of the enormity of her crimes. They are the result of a desire to see the world look forward, get into production and establish a lasting peace. They are based upon the stern necessities of a world involved in the most dangerous economic crisis in all history.

At the present time the taxpayers of the United States and Britain are contributing nearly $600,000,000 a year to prevent starvation of the Germans in the American and British zones alone. The drain is likely to be even greater after peace unless the policies now in action are changed. Therefore, entirely aside from any humanitarian and political aspects, policies which will restore productivity in Germany and exports with which to buy their food and relieve this drain upon us are of primary importance.

But our economic interest is far wider than this. We desperately need recovery in all of Europe. We need it not only for economic reasons but as the first necessity to peace. The United States, through loans, lend-lease, surplus supplies, and relief, in the last two years, has spent, or pledged itself to spend, over fifteen billions of dollars in support of civilians in foreign countries. Even we do not have the resources for, nor can our taxpayers bear, a continuation of burdens at such a rate.

There is only one path to recovery in Europe. That is production. The whole economy of Europe is interlinked with German economy through the exchange of raw materials and manufactured goods. The productivity of Europe cannot be restored without the restoration of Germany as a contributor to that productivity.

SOME ASSUMPTIONS

In order to offer constructive conclusions as to economic policies which will relieve the American taxpayer and will promote economic recovery in Europe, I make six assumptions, which I believe will be accepted by sensible people. They necessarily include certain political aspects which underlie all these economic problems.

First. I assume that we wish to establish a unified federal state in Germany, embracing mainly the present American, British, Russian and French military occupation zones, with economic unity and free trade between the states. I shall refer to this area as the "New Germany."

Second. I assume that our objective must be to clear German life of the Nazi conspirators and to punish those who have contributed to this conspiracy, which murdered millions of people in cold blood and brought this appalling disaster upon the world.

Third. I assume that we will not make the major mistake of Versailles, but will complete absolute disarmament of the Germans so that they shall not be able again to engage in aggressions; that this disarmament will embrace destruction of all military arms, fortifications and direct arms factories, with certain control of industry; that the Germans will have *no* army, *no* navy, and *no* air forces, retaining only a constabulary in which no Nazi or previous army officer may be employed; that this disarmament must be continued for a generation or two, until Germany has lost the "know-how" of war and the descent of militarism through birth.

Fourth. I assume that these requirements must be safe-guarded by international guarantees and effective police service by the nations.

Fifth. I assume, in our own interest and that of Europe, that we wish to restore the productivity of the continent, that we wish to revive personal freedom, honest elections and gener-ally to reconstruct the German people into a peace-loving na-tion cooperating in the recovery of Western civilization.

Sixth. I assume that the United States will not join in such guarantees and policing unless the treaty with Germany is so concluded that it contributes to the restoration of productivity and lasting peace in Europe and promptly relieves us of drains upon our taxpayers.

THE GERMAN ECONOMIC PROBLEMS

The German economic problems have two aspects:

First, the long-view, broad economic policies toward the New Germany which alone can produce the reconstruction of Europe and peace.

Second, our immediate problems in the joint Anglo-Ameri-can military zones during the interregnum pending peace.

I therefore divide this discussion into these two parts.

PART I: THE LONG VIEW ECONOMIC PROBLEM

The long-view economic problems involved in the peace with the New Germany and its aftermaths are greatly affected by war destruction, the boundary settlements for the New Ger-many, the plant removals for reparations, and the policies with respect to "war potential" of industry.

These effects may be summarized:

1. There was considerable destruction of non-war industry from the air and otherwise during the war. The loss to peaceful

productivity has not been determined, but it is considerable.

2. The proposed annexations to Poland and Russia, and the possible annexation of the Saar Basin by France, will take from Germany, as compared to 1936,* about 25% of her food supply, about 30% of her bituminous coal and about 20% of her manufacturing capacity.

3. The population of Germany in 1936 was about 68,000,000. The population of the New Germany by 1949 will be about 71,000,000, due to the expulsion of Germans from the Polish and Russian annexations, from Czechoslovakia, Hungary, Austria, Yugoslavia, Roumania and the return of prisoners into this area.

4. The Allied economic policies toward Germany are of two categories: the first involves world safety, and the second, reparations for wrong done:

a. There has necessarily been, or will be, a demolition of all arms plants as part of disarmament. This destruction, however, has included some plants which might have been converted to peaceable production.

b. Reparations have been provided by assignment for removal to the different Allies of certain percentages of "usable and complete industrial equipment." What proportion of Germany's peaceable productive plant has been, or is, in the course of removal in the French and Russian zones is not known. Certainly they have been very large from the Russian zone. The total for all Germany amounts to an important segment of its peaceful productivity. These removals include a large amount of "light industry" (producing mostly consumers' goods) as well as "heavy industry" (producing mostly capital goods). The removal of plants from the American and British zones has been halted because of the refusal of Russia and France to cooperate in inter-zonal economic unity as provided for at Potsdam.

5. In addition to the above courses of action, there have been

---

* I have adopted 1936 as a basis for economic comparisons because it was a full year before German industry was distorted by her annexations and her most intensive armament activity.

general policies of destruction or limitation of possible peaceful productivity under the headings of "pastoral state" and "war potential." The original of these policies apparently expressed on September 15, 1944, at Quebec, aimed at:

> "converting Germany into a country principally agricultural and pastoral,"

and included,

> "The industries of the Ruhr and the Saar would therefore be put out of action, closed down. . . ."

This idea of a "pastoral state" partially survived in JCS Order 1067 of April, 1945 for the American zone. It was not accepted by the British. The "pastoral state" concept was not entirely absent in the Potsdam Declaration. It was partially ameliorated or its name changed for another concept, the "level of industry," developed by the agreement of March 26, 1946, and signed by Russia, Britain, France and the United States. This agreement was a compromise between the drastic terms proposed by Russia and France and the more liberal terms proposed by the other two nations.

One major theme of this "level of industry" concept is to destroy Germany's "war potential." Under this concept certain industries are to be blown up or prohibited, others are to be limited as to production. The emphasis was placed upon the limitation of "heavy industry" with the view that Germany could export enough goods from "light industry" to buy her food and necessary raw materials.

The absolute destruction or prohibition includes ocean-going ships, shipbuilding, aircraft, ball bearings, aluminum, magnesium, beryllium, vanadium and radio-transmitting equipment, together with synthetic oil, ammonia and rubber. Some of these provisions may be essential to disarmament. Such exceptions are not included in the discussion which follows.

Beyond these prohibitions, however, the "level of industry" concept provides elaborate restrictions, mostly on heavy industry. The following items are illustrative:

Iron and steel production to be reduced from 19 million tons (as in 1936) to a capacity of 7.5 million tons, with a maximum production of 5.8 million tons and only the "older plants" to be used.

Heavy machinery production to be . . . . 31% of 1938
Light machinery production to be . . . . 50% of 1938
Machine tools to be . . . . 38% of 1938
Electrical machinery to be . . . . from 30% to 50% of 1938
Agricultural implements to be . . . . 70% of 1936
Automobiles to be . . . . 10% of 1936
Trucks to be . . . . 67% of 1936
Basic chemicals, including nitrogen, calcium carbide,
    sulphuric acid, chlorine and alkali to be . . . . 40% of 1936
Cement to be . . . . 65% of 1936
Electric power produced to be . . . . 60% of 1936
No new locomotives until 1949.
Some "light industries" were also to be limited:
Textiles to be . . . . 77% of 1936
Paper to be . . . . 65% of 1936
Boots and shoes to be . . . . 70% of 1936
Precision instruments and optics to be . . . . 70% of 1936
Miscellaneous chemicals to be . . . . 70% of 1936
Pharmaceuticals to be . . . . 80% of 1936
Dyestuffs (export) to be . . . . 58% of 1936

THE CONSEQUENCES TO FOOD SUPPLY

We may first examine what has happened, and what will happen, to the German food supply under all the circumstances of annexation and industrial controls.

Germany in 1936 was, by most intensive cultivation, able to produce about 85% of her food supply. This 85% has now been reduced by 25% through the Russian and Polish annexations, or is down to about 64% because even a larger population is to be concentrated in the New Germany.

Her production, however, was greatly dependent upon intensive use of fertilizers. The New Germany will require at least 500,000 metric tons of nitrogen and 650,000 tons of phosphoric anhydride, she having sufficient potash.

Under the level of industry agreement, the domestic production of nitrogen eventually would be reduced to under 200,000 tons; the production of phosphoric anhydride, would be reduced to about 200,000 tons. A larger production of nitrogen is allowed pending an opportunity to import. Part of this reduction is due to the "level of industry" steel reduction from which some nitrogen and a large percentage of phosphoric anhydride requirements were obtained as by-products.

From these figures it is obvious that a great discrepancy exists between minimum agricultural needs and the possible fertilizer production under the "level of industry" plan. If we persist in these policies, unless there are large imports of fertilizer, Germany's food production is likely to drop under 60% of her requirements even with an austere diet.

New Germany, if there is to be a will to work, to maintain order and to aspire to peace, must have an average food supply of at least 2600 calories per person per day, with adequate fats and protein content. (The British average being 2800-2900 calories at present and prewar Germany about 3000 calories.)

Taking the above limitations into consideration and based upon actual experience in the American and British zones, and extending that experience with adaptations to the Russian and French zones, the indications are that New Germany would need, at present prices, to import over $1,250,000,000 annually in food and animal feed alone.

At the end of the war Germany had a very large nitrogen capacity. Despite losses from war destruction, its potential production was still about 700,000 tons per annum. This capacity, if it had been preserved, would have supplied not only her own needs but large exports to neighboring countries as well. Fertilizers are now sorely needed all over Europe for crop restoration. Therefore, through the fertilizer reduction Germany not only loses in her own food production but her export potential to pay for food, and the crops elsewhere in Europe are reduced.

CONSEQUENCES OF "LEVEL OF INDUSTRY" UPON "HEAVY INDUSTRY"

The effect of the agreed "level of industry" is stated in American official reports that "The 'heavy industry' products for which Germany was noted will virtually disappear from her exports."

I have exhaustively examined the production and exports of Germany over some years in the light of this "level of industry" and they amply confirm this statement. What the result may be is indicated by the fact that her exports during peace from now-restricted "heavy industries" comprised between 60% and 70% of the total German exports. In 1936, for instance, a generally prosperous year, they amounted to about $1,900,000,000 out of a total of about $2,700,000,000, both figures converted into present prices. Under the "level of industry" most of this 60-70% is to be abolished, and Germany must pay for most of her imports from exports of "light industry."

Germany must not alone import food and animal feed, but also reduced amounts of copper, lead, zinc, iron ore, leather, cotton, wool, and other raw materials. Due to the prohibitions, she must import all of her oil and rubber, and considerable nitrogen for fertilizers.

It is indeed a cynical fact that today we are supplying Germany with oil and nitrogen at the expense of the American and British taxpayer, at a rate of $70,000,000 per annum, which, except for the "level of industry" and the Russian refusal of zonal cooperation, Germany could have produced herself.

CONSEQUENCES UPON LIGHT INDUSTRY

As I have said, the assumption is that exports from the German "light industry," from coal and native raw materials, such as potash, can pay for her imports of food and other necessities. There are two reasons for believing this assumption to be completely invalid.

Had there been no loss of "light industry" plants by annexation, had there been no destruction of them by war, had there been no removals for reparations, they could not have produced enough exports to pay the food bill alone. And the situation is made doubly impossible by the restrictions now imposed on what "light industry" is left, as for instance, on textiles.

If Germany is to buy food and the necessary imports of raw material for the "light industry," she would require not only complete restoration to pre-war level in "light industry" but a much larger equipment than she had even before the war.

Then Germany, with the expansion of these industries, would be in a competitive field of consumers' goods with all the rest of the world whose "light industries" have been little damaged by war.

SOME ECONOMIC ILLUSIONS

There are several illusions in all this "war potential" attitude.

a. There is the illusion that the New Germany left after the annexations can be reduced to a "pastoral state." It cannot be done unless we exterminate or move 25,000,000 people out of it. This would approximately reduce Germany to the density of the population of France.

b. There is an illusion in "war potential." Almost every industry on earth is a "war potential" in modern war. No industry (except direct arms manufacture) is a war potential if the energies of a people are confined to the paths of peace. If Germany be disarmed in the way I have assumed above, there must be a control commission to see that they do not have any army or any navy. And two score of intelligent men, as part of that commission, could see that there is no arms production and that no industry is manufacturing or storing materials for evil purposes. Moreover, industry is not likely to waste its substance, either by storing or manufacturing for war, when there is no army or navy to use it.

The question here is not "level of industry." The real question is whether the Allied nations will stick to their abolition of militarism itself in Germany. If they do that, there is little danger from "war potential" in industry.

c. Another illusion is that the "light industry" in Germany can be expanded to a point where she will be able to pay for her imports. In my view, it cannot be done for years, and even then it is doubtful in the face of competition with the "light industries" of other parts of the world.

d. The over-all illusion is that Germany can ever become self-supporting under the "levels of industry" plan within the borders envisioned at present for New Germany.

e. A still further illusion is that Europe as a whole can recover without the economic recovery of Germany.

CONSEQUENCES TO EUROPE GENERALLY

Thus there is a still wider aspect of this "level of industry"—the needs of the rest of Europe. Germany had been for a century one of the great European centers of production of capital goods—"heavy industry," which I may repeat are construction materials, factory equipment, railway equipment, electrical and heavy machinery. The other nations of Europe are in desperate need of such goods for reconstruction from war damage. Moreover, a considerable part of the European equipment on these lines is German-made, and today, they cannot even get replacements and spare parts, in consequence of which their productivity lags.

From the standpoint of other nations, the expansion of "light industry" to a point of self-support for Germany will, by competition, injure these industries in the rest of Europe. On the other hand, the products of "heavy industry" is Europe's first necessity for recovery.

It must not be overlooked that Germany was the market for every nation in Europe and such a reduction of her economy will tend to demoralize the industries and employment in those countries. For instance, Germany was the market for over half the exports of Turkey and over one-third those of Greece. In consequence, their loss of this market contributes to increase the relief they seek from us now.

Another illustration is the proposed limits on steel. Large and efficient steel and iron plants, undamaged or only partly damaged, are standing idle in Germany. Formerly the Germans imported millions of tons of iron ore from France and Sweden. These mines, under the "level of industry," must remain idle until a new steel industry is built elsewhere. That will require years and an amount of capital that is not in sight. In the meantime, Europe needs steel for reconstruction as she never did before.

To indicate the anxiety of surrounding states a memorandum of the Netherlands Government of January 1947, in presenting the absolute necessity to the surrounding nations that a productive economic state be created in Germany, said: "The provisions of the plan for reparations and the level of German economy of March 1946 require to be revised . . . it is inadvisable to lay down maximum quota for production of German industries including the iron and steel industries."

The sum of all of this is: Germany, under the "level of industry" concept, unless she is to be allowed to starve, will be a drain on the taxpayers of other nations for years and years to come. In the meantime, if her light industries were built to become self-supporting, she would become an economic menace to Europe; if her heavy industries are allowed to function, she has an ability to export and would become an asset in Europe's recovery. To persist in the present policies will create, sooner or later, a cesspool of unemployment or pauper labor in the center of Europe which is bound to infect her neighbors.

We can keep Germany in these economic chains but it will also keep Europe in rags.

A NEW ECONOMIC POLICY

Therefore, I suggest that we adopt at once a new economic concept in peace with New Germany.

(1) We should free German industry, subject to a control

commission, which will see that she does no evil in industry, just as we see that she does not move into militarism through armies and navies.

The difference between this concept and the "level of industry" concept is the saving of several hundred millions of dollars a year to the American and British taxpayers. It is the difference between the regeneration and a further degeneration of Europe.

(2) The removal and destruction of plants (except direct arms plants) should stop.

(3) A further obstacle to building Germany as an essential unit of European economy arises from the Russian Government's acquiring a large part of the key operating industries in their zone. Germany in peace must be free from ownership of industry by a foreign government. Such ownership can thwart every action of control or of up-building by joint action of other nations. German industry must be operated by Germans if any international control is to work, if she is to recover production and is to serve all nations equally.

(4) There can be no separation or different regime of the Ruhr or Rhineland from the New Germany. That is the heart of her industrial economy. Any control commission can dictate the destination of coal or other exports from that area and even such control would not be needed after the era of scarcity passes from Europe.

PART II: THE INTERREGNUM BEFORE PEACE

How long it may be before there is such a constructive peace with Germany, no one can tell. It may be long delayed. In the meantime, we are faced with the feeding of the people in the Anglo-American zones on a level just above starvation until we can develop enough export goods from these zones so that the Germans may pay for their food. I have said, American and British taxpayers are called upon for about $600,000,000 a year for relief.

We have an admirable staff in Military Government of Germany under Generals Clay and Draper but their administration is constantly frustrated in building up the needed exports to pay for food and minimum raw material imports. A large part of these delays is due to the following:

a. The Russians and the French have failed to carry out the provisions of the Potsdam agreement for economic unity in the four zones. The Russian zone ordinarily produces a surplus of food but that surplus is used elsewhere, thus increasing the burden of imports on the Anglo-American zones. Both the Russian and French zones are producing industrial commodities which would relieve necessities in the Anglo-American zones and could contribute to exports with which to pay for food. The net effect is that the United States and Britain through relief are paying Russian and French reparations.

b. The inability to determine what specific plants are to be the victims of "level of industry," or destruction or the removal for reparations, produces stagnation because the Germans do not know where to begin work.

c. There is lack of working capital with which to import raw materials for such industries as are allowed to function.

d. An inflated currency and no adequate banking system hampers all forward movement in such industry as is left.

e. While de-Nazification and de-cartelization are necessary and important certain phases of them limit recovery. They are so involved as not to warrant description here.

CONCLUSION AS TO THE BI-ZONAL ADMINISTRATION

If, however, we cannot get a quick and sound peace on the lines I have recounted, the Anglo-American zones should abandon the destruction of plants, the transfer of plants for reparations and the "level of industry" concept, and start every plant, "heavy" as well as "light," which can produce non-arms goods. This will relieve far more rapidly great costs to our taxpayers; it will do infinitely more for Europe than American loans and charity.

Indeed the Congressional Committee on Postwar Economic

Policy urged, on December 30, 1946, that the "levels of industry" be ignored wherever they conflict with exports so that there may be earlier recovery and payment for food.

The violation by Russia and France of the agreement for economic unification of the four zones of military occupation and the additional burdens this imposed upon us in consequence certainly warrant our ignoring all agreements for "level of industry," transfer and destruction of non-arms plants.

If this interregnum is to endure for long, we could build a self-sustaining economic community out of the Anglo-American zones alone. This could be only a temporary expedient, not a final solution. Building a lasting peace in Europe should be our objective.

On Japanese Reparations

Letter to the Honorable Robert Patterson,

Secretary of War

[May 7, 1947]

New York City

The Honorable Robert Patterson
Secretary of War
War Department
Washington, D. C.

Dear Mr. Secretary:

You and Mr. Clifford Strike did the honor to consult with me on measures proposed to end the industrial paralysis in Japan. You presented me with a proposed new level of industry (which I refer to as the "new level").

Since our discussion, I have re-examined my notes upon this subject made during my visit to Japan in May 1946. I have re-read the various agreements and reports on reparations, war potential, the "original" level of industry and other regulations. I have now had time to digest more fully the very able Strike report and to include in my thinking the constructive report of the recent Food Commission under Colonel R. L. Harrison.

At the outset I wish to say that when I think of the white crosses over tens of thousands of American boys in the Pacific and the millions of butchered Chinese, I sympathize emotionally with Draconic measures of punishment. But when we look to the real interest of the United States and the future peace of the world, we must confine punishment to the war leaders and realize that we must live with this 80,000,000 people.

I had prepared an elaborate analysis of the economic and reparations situation in Japan. However, the only matters of interest are my conclusions.

I am convinced that there must be a revolutionary change in the whole concept of "levels of industry," "plant removals" for reparations and destruction of peace industry plants, if the Japanese people are to produce enough exports with which to pay for their food and other necessary imports, or become a stable and peaceable state. That drastic change is necessary must be evident by now from the fact that the American tax-payer is called upon to furnish upwards of $400,000,000 in the next fiscal year to keep the people barely alive; and unless there are revolutionary changes, it will continue indefinitely.

The "original" concepts in economic and military policy which contributed to this situation arise partly from the inadequate data at the time upon which the policies were based and upon several illusions.

As to the data, I may point out just two instances as illustrative. The food deficiency in Japan was under-estimated. The estimate of Japan's foreign trade deficit under these regulations showed a deficit for 1947 of under $20,000,000, whereas experience proves the deficit to be over $400,000,-000.

Without giving more instances, it is safe to say that there was an underestimate of the thin margins of the Japanese economy and the destruction to it from war and her territorial separations.

Of the illusions, the first is that to demilitarize Japan it is necessary to do little more than to destroy or remove all arms fortifications and direct arms factories and to prevent *any* army, *any* navy, *any* air force, *any* munitions or aircraft manufacture, and to enforce such a regime over a generation or two until Japan loses the know-how of war.

The second illusion is the whole concept of control of "war

potential" in industry of the type which can contribute to peace economy. All industry is "war potential" in total war. Very little industry is war potential (except arms manufacture) if a country has a forced demilitarization such as I assume above. Another part of this illusion is that these major "levels of industry" can be enforced and a nation function without a complete "planned economy" directed by foreign agents. On the other hand, to watch a major free economy, to see it is directed to no evil, is a simple problem of inspection. People are not going to manufacture for war where there is compulsory elimination of militarism.

The third illusion is that Japan can ever be self-supporting in food. That is impossible with only 15% of arable land in a state the size of California with 80,000,000 people; all her modern history she has imported 15 to 20% of her food and now the population has been increased by six or seven million expellees. One third of the population of Japan must live by export industry.

The fourth illusion is that there are any consequential reparations to be had from the removal of industrial plants overseas. The buildings, foundations, water, electrical and other connections in such plants have no value for removal. All that is removable of any use is motive power and machine tools, all second hand. The cost of tearing them out, crating them, shipping them to some area where there is neither skilled labor nor skilled management and to build new foundations, buildings and connections, leaves even these values comparatively trivial.

These ideas in action or threat of action have created the present economic paralysis.

I may say from my knowledge that General MacArthur has long sought the remedy to these matters. The engineering Committee under Mr. Strike, which you appointed, in its able report of February 22nd, recommends radical changes in "level of industry" and plant removal plans. General MacArthur strongly supported their recommendations. But the "new level" of industry submitted to me does not even fulfill the urgent Strike recommendations. In my opinion the Strike recommendations did not go nearly far enough.

My suggestions are:

First. Allow the removal to claimants of machine tools and equipment from such munitions factories as cannot be converted into peace-time production. Assess by independent engineers the actual value to any proposed recipient of peace-time plants, deducting the cost of removal and shipment, and then call upon Japan to pay such a sum over the years and to retain the plants.

Second. Do away with the whole concept of "level of industry," both "original" and "new." Establish a few absolute prohibitions such as monopolies, arms manufacture, aircraft construction, speed (but not size) of ships, and install a general watch to see that industry is devoted to peace-time production.

The sum of my reasons are:

(a) No further industrial repressions are necessary to preserve peace in a perpetually demilitarized country.

(b) The continued uncertainty of plant removals and the present proposed levels of industry are bound to continue the paralysis of export industry.

(c) We cannot find competent American men over the years to competently direct the kind of planned economy for Japan which either the "original" or "new" limit of industry plus the export-import controls amount to. We could find the minor inspection staff to see that Japanese industry does no evil.

(d) The development of de-monopolized private enterprise is the only hope of increasing the standards of living in Japan. Thereby is the only possibility of holding her people as a bulwark against the Communist invasion of Asia.

(e) Japan's full productivity (except arms) aids in the recovery of her neighbors.

(f) It is the only way Japan can be gotten off the back of the American taxpayer.

Finally, may I say that what the world needs today above all things is recovered peace-purpose productivity. The United

States does not possess the strength to bear the deficient productivity which now dominates industry all over the world. Chains on any productive area are chains on the whole world. We need a larger vision of the primary basis of world peace which is productivity. Otherwise there would be a disintegration of Western Civilization everywhere.

We Must Speed Peace

(On Food and Relief Requirements for Germany, Japan and Korea) Letter to Congressman John Taber
[*May 26, 1947*]

New York City

Honorable John Taber
Chairman, Committee on Appropriations
House of Representatives
Washington, D. C.

Dear Mr. Taber:

I have your request for a memorandum on my views upon the recommendations of the War Department of $725,000,000 for food and collateral relief requirements for Germany, Japan and Korea for the next fiscal year.

You have also requested that I should furnish you a memorandum upon the causes of these continuing demands upon us, measures which might ameliorate these demands upon our taxpayers and generally upon our foreign relief and reconstruction policies. I shall, as you requested, attend the Committee hearing on Tuesday to give any further information they desire.

For clarity, I have throughout this text numbered my specific recommendations.

1. As matters stand this appropriation of $725,000,000 should be made. In addition to this proposed American appropriation the British are also to contribute their share of bi-zonal

relief in Germany. These enormous sums are inescapable for the next year unless millions of people under our flags are to die of starvation. They are about the same as during the present fiscal year and this year's experience demonstrates how near starvation is in these countries.

Surely we must take steps to bring these burdens upon our taxpayers to an end.

We are now providing relief for the third year after the war.

The delay by Russia in making peace with Germany and Japan together with the Allied policies of reparations and industrial demilitarization have paralyzed the industrial productivity of these countries. They are unable to make substantial exports and are not contributing, as they otherwise could, to their own support.

General Marshall, in Moscow, ably urged the immediate necessity for Russia and France to comply with the Potsdam agreement, which provided for economic unification of the four zones; for the revision of the plant transfers for reparations; and the revision of so-called "levels of industry." Meanwhile, Russia and France are taking industrial exports from their zones which, under the Potsdam agreement, would contribute to paying the food bill in the American and British zones. Thus we are paying reparations. We are shipping fertilizers for relief which could be supplied from the French zone. We are supplying France with Ruhr coal which could be used for the manufacturing of exports in Germany with which to pay for food.

2. In view of the Russian refusal to General Marshall's able presentation at Moscow, and the continued violation of the Potsdam agreement to unify German economy in both Russia and France, we are surely no longer bound by that agreement as to reparations and industrial policies.

In the bizonal area of Germany, after two years since V-E Day, the agricultural production is about 75 per cent of prewar and the industrial production is only at 33 per cent of 1936, and exports are only 3 per cent. In Japan, there has been about 80 per cent recovery in agricultural production but industrial production is only 30 per cent of prewar, with exports about 4 per cent.

To understand the situation in the German area, we might visualize what would happen if the present policies were imposed on the United States. Suppose America were divided into four zones with little interchange of economic life or food surpluses; with an obligation to tear down and ship abroad 25 per cent of our peace-production plants, and with a restricted "level of industry" which would destroy 60 per cent of our possible export trade. Then add to this the failure even to designate the plants that are to be removed, so that all initiative to operate the remaining plants is destroyed by uncertainty as to whom the victims will be. Suppose also we were not allowed to produce oil, and were limited in fertilizer production. Without relief from some humanitarian country millions of our people would die.

Unless there are revolutionary changes in our policies as to Germany and Japan, the burdens upon our taxpayers are not likely to lessen and are more likely to increase. There are three alternatives before us in our occupied territories: to wash our hands of the whole business and then let the conquered countries drag the whole world to final chaos; or, for humanitarian reasons, merely to carry these people on a food subsistence level, hoping for improvement in the attitudes of other nations; or to act at once to free ourselves from their hindrances as far as possible.

3. The time has come when we should issue a last call to Russia and France to comply with the Potsdam agreement. If they do not at once respond, we and the British should immediately take the steps to set up the economy of the bizonal areas so as to restore their industrial production and exports.

4. An effort should be made to consolidate the French zone (except the Saar) into the bizonal area. In this we have a right to expect French cooperation in view of the great sacrifices the American people are now making on behalf of France.

5. In any event, we should immediately carry out the present project of a temporary centralized German government

over the American and British zones subject to our military direction. We might even contemplate a separate peace with this government if the next conference of Foreign Ministers does not succeed in more constructive policies.

6. If we are to secure adequate exports with which they can pay for food, it is urgent that we at once revise the reparations and industrial demilitarization policies imposed upon these zones by various Allied agreements. These latter policies are identical in Japan where they must likewise be revised.

7. We should, in our German zones and in Japan, suspend the whole concept of "levels of industry," placing restrictions upon only a few specified industries, such as shipping and aviation.

8. We should at once abolish for good the destruction or removal of all industrial plants which can make peacetime goods or services. The heavy burden now borne by our taxpayers is ample proof of the folly of these policies. It is an illusion that there are any consequential reparations to be had by removal of peace-time industrial plants. The buildings, foundations, water, electrical and other connections in such plants have no value for removal. All that is removable of any use are machines, all second-hand and many obsolete. The cost of tearing them out, shipping them to some area where there is neither skilled labor nor skilled management, and of building new foundations, buildings and connections, leave even these values comparatively trivial. We should allow the removal of equipment from such munitions factories which cannot be converted into peace-time production. We should assess by independent engineers the actual value to any proposed recipient of peace-time plants, deducting the cost of dismantling, and then call upon Germany or Japan to pay such a sum over the years and retain the plants. With such action, the uncertainties which now paralyze German and Japanese initiative would quickly revive many industries and gradually provide exports to pay for their food. The drain upon our taxpayers would gradually disappear. Unless this is done, Germany and Japan will not be self-supporting in our time.

Such policies have no practical relation to the demilitarization of either Germany or Japan. I assume we are not going to make the major mistake of Versailles of leaving these countries the nuclei of militarism by granting them any armies or navies. It seems generally agreed that we will absolutely disarm these peoples so that they shall not again be able to engage in aggressions; that this disarmament will embrace destruction of all military arms, fortifications and arms factories; that they will have no army, no navy, and no air force; that they will retain only a constabulary in which no previous officer may be employed; that no militarist officials can hold public office; that this disarmament must be continued for a generation or two, until they have lost the "know-how" of war, and the descent of militarism through birth. We have already offered to join in guarantees which will make these prohibitions effective.

9. With such a policy of demilitarization, the chains on production and export of peace-purpose goods should be removed and a simple check maintained to assure that industry does no evil.

The situation in Japan is not complicated by zonal occupation of other armies, and we are more free to act. Also, the United States is paying the entire food bill. The world has had the service of a great administrator in General MacArthur under whose guidance the Japanese have adopted a constitution approved by us; they have freely elected a government and are determined upon democratic processes.

10. We should at once summon the peace conference with Japan and make a peace with her by as many nations as wish to adhere.

Such policies as I have outlined are of a vast importance to the nations outside of Germany and Japan. The whole world is suffering from delay in restoration of productivity. The whole world is an interlocked economy, and paralysis in two great centers of production is a world disaster. There is greater opportunity to speed recovery in the world by such action as I outline than by any amount of gifts and loans from the United States.

There has been announced an American policy of defending

the frontiers of Western Civilization. The most vital of these frontiers are Germany and Japan. If they are lost, all Europe and the Far East are lost.

The reasons for continuous obstruction by Russia to every effort which would restore production have at least some expression in the Russian press as a method by which the United States can be bled white by relief measures. We should wait no longer. Russia will not make war about it.

COORDINATION OF AMERICAN POLICIES

11. The problems of relief I have been discussing are involved in a much wider action. That is the coordination of all aid which we are extending for relief and reconstruction abroad. The resources of the United States are not unlimited and we are carrying over 90 per cent of these burdens. In the two years since the war the United States has spent upwards of fourteen billions in free relief, government loans or loans from agencies dependent upon the United States for their survival. Already we are practically committed to five billion during the next fiscal year. These activities are divided among five or six agencies directed from Washington that are extending aid to a score of nations. Their policies are not coordinated so as to secure cooperation among nations which would save large sums to the American taxpayers and would produce more rapid restoration of recovery abroad. The purpose of these activities is to save life and restore productivity. The restoration of production in the world is of mutual interest to all nations. I have in this memorandum cited instances of a lack of cooperation among nations. To state it bluntly, we cannot get such cooperation unless there is coordination of our own organization at home so as to make American aid to other nations conditional upon their cooperation to the common end. I am talking about the American taxpayer, about mutual economic action and not about dollar diplomacy.

The Limits of American Aid to Foreign Countries

Letter to Senator Styles Bridges
[June 13, 1947]

New York City

The Honorable Styles Bridges, Chairman
Committee on Appropriations
United States Senate
Washington, D. C.

My dear Senator:

I have your letter asking me to give you and your associates my views upon the following points:

1. What are the limits of relief and loans that we can reasonably give to foreign nations annually without seriously impairing our resources in a free economy?

2. Are there methods by which we could increase our gifts and loans above those now available from our present production?

3. What policies should be adopted to make our resources more effective in world rehabilitation?

THE PROBLEM

As a background to this appraisal I wish at the outset to state:

Upwards of a billion people in the war-torn areas of Western Europe and Asia are asking for help. In these nations some have not recovered one-third of their prewar industrial production; most of them have not recovered over 75 per cent of their prewar food production.

There is greater danger of political and economic chaos in the world today than at any time since the war ended. There is more hunger and want today than there was during the war.

In the face of this threatening situation the American people must continue to do the utmost to prevent starvation in the world. We must do our utmost to aid nations in the recovery of their own productivity. That underlies peace and progress on earth.

But the greatest danger to all civilization is for us to impair our economy by drains which cripple our own productivity. Unless this one remaining Gibraltar of economic strength is maintained, chaos will be inevitable over the whole world.

To discover the common sense course requires clear objectives and organization on our part. The burden is beyond our resources unless there is immediate unity and cooperation among other nations to lessen our unnecessary burdens and thus enable the application of our resources to the most effective use.

THE ECONOMICS OF THE PROBLEM

Too often gifts and loans to foreign peoples are visualized as just money transactions. The only way money of important volume can be transferred from one nation to another is by goods (including gold) and services. Therefore, when we make a gift, credit, or loan, it is not money that we transfer; it is goods and services. There is thus a direct relationship of exports to the volume of loans and gifts.

While exports to pay for our imports cause us no difficulty, it must be recognized that we cannot safely, through gifts and loans, export more goods than our surplus. And the surplus applies to specific commodities, for we do not produce a surplus in all kinds of goods. If we ship more than our surplus we are taking it from the standard of living of the American people. Further, the immediate result of exporting more than a surplus in our free economy is to raise prices. From that we get a dangerous spiral of increased costs of living and wages.

OUR PRESENT ECONOMIC SITUATION

To appraise our present national situation, it is necessary to examine our experience in the two years since the war. In so doing, many debit and credit items must be estimated. We must estimate the exports, including army supplies to foreign civilians, and we must estimate imports of the last months of the present fiscal year. Until full data are available many months hence, the sums given must be considered as illustrative of the situation.

Our exports of goods and services in dollars were about as follows:

	1945-46	1946-47
Exports	$13.5 billion	$15.5 billion
Imports	$ 7.2 billion	$ 7.7 billion
Excess of Exports over Imports	$ 6.3 billion	$ 7.8 billion

We have provided for the excess of exports over imports by loans or gifts.

An examination of the sources and amounts of these loans and gifts for the combined two years since the war were about as follows:

We have provided about $4.5 billion in gifts from our government through relief; We have provided about $1.5 billion in gifts by our citizens for relief and by way of remittances to relatives abroad;

We have provided about $5.5 billion in credits by government agencies including the Export-Import Bank loans, subscription to the World Bank and the Stabilization Fund. Loans by these institutions are, in the final analysis, largely drafts on American dollars and are dependent upon us for resources to maintain their operations. We have provided about $1.5 billion in private credits and loans.

Thus we have provided in the last two years about $6 billion in relief and gifts together with about $7 billion in loans or credits, or a total of $13 billion. The differences between these amounts and the trade deficits given above are no doubt accounted for by drawing upon previous foreign dollar balances in the United States.

OUR COMMITMENTS FOR THE NEXT 12 MONTHS

The estimated unexpended balances of appropriations and various credit commitments to foreign nations on July 1, 1947, are not included in the above. They already amount to over $5 billion. We should add further probable loans and expected private gifts of $1 billion. And we must add unknown further calls from the World Bank and Stabilization Funds.

There is also a further liability of the United States in the shape of the foreign deposits in American banks, including earmarked gold and foreign ownership of American securities. These aggregate at least $14 billion. We must at all times be prepared to meet their withdrawal. Some withdrawals are likely to be used to pay for exports during next year, thus increasing the total volume of exports required from us. And to all these commitments and liabilities we must add the exports necessary to pay for our imports amounting to probably $7.5 billion.

Any study of our international balance sheet, taking into account, on one hand, our commitments in loans, foreign deposits, and investments in the United States, etc., and on the other hand, probable returns from previous loans and lend-lease, including our citizens' greatly impaired foreign investments, will likely discover that the United States is today a debtor rather than a creditor nation.

There is another angle to our national situation that we cannot ignore. These gifts and loans to foreign nations are spent in current purchase of goods. These gifts are an immediate burden on the taxpayer. The goods furnished under loans also must be paid for immediately while the repayment is deferred for years. This has a bearing upon our tax burdens. Including local government expenditures, they now amount to about 35 per cent of our national income. No free nation can continue at that rate for long without impairing its productivity.

To pay for our imports and to satisfy the probable gift and loan commitments already made for the next fiscal year, and assuming present prices, we would need export at about the same ratio as during the past two years $14 to $16 billion annually of goods and services.

A TEST OF THE LIMITS OF LOANS AND RELIEF

The most definite test of the extent of our ability to aid foreign nations is whether we have been over-exporting our resources during the past two years, and thus unduly straining our economy. For example, we have exported gigantic amounts of agricultural products. During the past 12 months the index of our cost of living has advanced more than 20 per cent. Increases in the cost of agricultural products were responsible for about 70 per cent of this increase. This has contributed greatly to set in motion the inflation spiral of increasing wages with more increases in prices. A good deal of economic disorder and waste was created by interruptions in production in making these adjustments.

Other examples could be cited. Some of our exports have been taken from our own possible railway, factory and housing reconstruction. Some part of the rise in prices of these materials is due to exports. So much have prices risen in the construction industries with the accompanying wage spiral and costs, that we now have considerable unemployment in these trades while at the same time, the country is crying for homes and buildings.

I would not contend that the whole rise in living costs, with its inflation spiral has been due to our large exports. But it cannot be denied that with fewer exports that increase would not have been so great.

The conclusion seems to me irrefutable that as the result of our rate of giving and lending we are over-exporting goods and cannot continue at such a rate with our present production and consumption without further evil consequences to our stability.

We cannot estimate how much the curtailment in exports, and hence in giving and lending to finance the trade deficit, might be for the next year until we are able to estimate our next year's surplus in agriculture and other major commodities.

While the world situation requires that we do our best, my own view is that, unless we can undertake to increase our productivity or decrease our consumption of goods, we must seriously reduce the volume of exports below the rate of the last two years with a corresponding reduction in the gifts and loans for which we supply goods.

Various proposals have been made for expansion of loans by fifty or more billion dollars. The impracticability of these ideas with our present rate of production must be obvious.

STRAIN ON OUR NATURAL RESOURCES

There is a further question of the impairment of our natural resources involved in the export of such materials as iron, oil, metals, lumber and some other items. As our resources in this sort of commodities are not renewable, their shipment abroad is a depletion of our resources and a charge against our future economy. While such exports may be necessary to restore the world, we cannot ignore the consequences.

POSSIBILITIES OF INCREASING OUR AIDS AND MAKING THEM MORE EFFECTIVE

There are certain measures which have been suggested as enabling us to better bear the load or to increase our exports and to make more effective our aid to foreign countries.

EXPORTING GOLD

1. It has been suggested that we can export gold from our seeming large stocks and thus enable other nations to buy elsewhere than in the United States. With our present requirements for currency and bank reserves, and to cover the very large foreign demand deposits in our banks, it is necessary that we hold a large stock in reserve. The amount of gold that we have free of such necessities is not material in this situation.

INCREASING IMPORTS BY STOCKPILING

2. One proposal is that we at once import more goods and thus diminish the amount of gifts and loans necessary to furnish. This is a very minor help in the immediate world situation. It would be no help to the world to import materials into the United States which are needed elsewhere. Nor would it help to import goods which we ourselves produce economically. That would create unemployment in the United States and weaken our productivity.

There is, however, a method of increasing our imports which should have serious consideration. We could import and stockpile for national defense many commodities, both those we do not produce and those in which our natural resources are being depleted. We do not have enough of such resources to assure our national defense. Commodities of this kind are tin, manganese, iron ore, mercury, copper, lead, zinc, tungsten, chromite, nickel, and rubber. There are few immediate surpluses of these commodities abroad, but such surpluses will be available within a reasonable time. It happens that few of such commodities are produced by our direct debtors, but our purchase of them would, through multilateral trade, strengthen the whole international financial structure and we would be receiving commodities instead of obligations.

RE-ESTABLISHMENT OF WAR-TIME CONTROL MEASURES

3. Another proposal is that we re-establish war-time control measures to increase our productivity or reduce our consumption and thus increase our ability to export more goods. The seeming warranty of this idea arises out of the fact that we exported in goods and services over $15 billion in some war years in addition to many billions in supplies to our armies. But we must remember that war-purpose production was greatly expanded and consumption restricted through war-inspired patriotic impulses.

The restoration of these controls would require again the abolition of the production of important commodities; the restoration of longer work hours in labor; the return of women to industry and agriculture, rationing of most commodities, and total government control of all economic activities. That is a form of totalitarian economy which the American people are not likely to accept in peace for it would do violence to our whole concept of freedom. Moreover, without emotional background of fighting for national defense, such measures would more likely decrease than increase our productivity.

A METHOD OF INCREASING FOOD EXPORTS

4. Should the next world harvest indicate dangerous shortages, it is possible to increase our food exports for limited periods by voluntarily reducing our own food consumption and altering certain food manufacturing practices. We have here a great spiritual impulse to save starving people. And we may be called upon to do it again unless there is a world increase in food production.

COOPERATION OF OTHER NATIONS VITAL TO SALVATION

5. A most productive field of action by which the limited American economic resources can be made more effective for world reconstruction lies in cooperation of foreign nations in the political field.

The obstruction of the Soviet Government to peace has, during the past two years, imposed billions in expenditures upon us through support of occupation armies and relief to starvation which would not otherwise have been required. However, we can apparently expect little cooperation from that quarter.

But if there were full mutual cooperation from the other nations, it would lessen our burdens and divert much of our dead loss expenditures to more constructive channels abroad.

For instance, cooperation in the three western zones in Germany and in Japan to abolish the inhibitions on their productivity due to wrong concepts of reparations, and levels of industry, would increase their productivity and exports, and thus would greatly reduce the drains upon us for food and other supplies. Restoration of their productivity would aid all other nations. Cooperative action to speed peace, such as I recently outlined in a letter to Congressman Taber would greatly reduce demands upon us.

Such cooperation would allow our resources to flow into channels more beneficial to all the world.

POLICIES TO BE ADOPTED

In my view we need to develop or expand the following policies, some of which are already partially in action.

1. We must have in our own foreign economic relations single, coordinated action in all direct and indirect agencies of government—the relief funds, the Export-Import Bank, the World Bank, the Stabilization Fund, the Federal Reserve system, and all those agencies which administer our exports. We must consolidate our front if we are to succeed in our policies.

2. We must prevent excessive exports and by so doing reduce excessive prices. In the matter of food we should begin about August 1st with the new harvest.

3. If necessary to prevent starvation we should increase our available export surplus volume by voluntary reduction of consumption by the public and alteration of some trade practices.

4. We should periodically estimate the goods and services

which we can safely export and limit purchases of our commodities by limiting gifts and loans.

5. We should prepare to stockpile for national defense certain commodities from abroad when they are available in surplus.

6. We should bluntly insist that in return for our sacrifices, which are inherent in all loans and gifts that all nations recipient of our economic aid cooperate with us in measures to reduce the burdens upon us, to promote productivity and bring peace for the world at large.

7. We should insist upon certain principles in operation of gifts and loans, whether directly from our government or through government-supported agencies. These principles involve important questions of security, inspection of use, and application to the utmost in increase of productivity.

8. We should concentrate our limited resources in the areas in which Western Civilization can be preserved.

This problem can be solved if there is prompt unity and mutual aid between other nations, resolution on their part to build back their productivity, and if we act, on our side, with sense and devotion in this great crisis of mankind.

Destruction at Our Expense

Foreword Written for Common Cause, Inc. Magazine
[December 27, 1947]

A T A time when the world is crying, and even dying, from lack of industrial production we apparently pursue the policy of destruction of the gigantic productive equipment in the Western zones of Germany. It means less essential goods to all Europe, greater delay in recovery of the world and larger drains on the American taxpayer. I can only repeat a statement in my report of ten months ago: "The removal and destruction of plants (except arms plants) should stop . . . we can keep Germany in economic chains but it will also keep Europe in rags." And, I would add, it will keep food scarcity and high taxes in America as we vainly spend a billion a year to keep alive these millions of idle Germans.

The Marshall Plan

Statement to Senator Arthur H. Vandenberg, Committee on Foreign Relations, United States Senate

[January 18, 1948]

Senator Arthur H. Vanderberg, Chairman.
Committee on Foreign Relations
United States Senate
Washington, D. C.

January 18, 1948

My dear Senator:

I have your request that I should present to the Foreign Relations Committee my views on the proposed "Economic Cooperation Administration" for aid to 16 Western European countries.

First of all I wish to make clear my conviction that we should help to the full extent which does not weaken our own economy and thus defeat all world recovery.

There are three dominant reasons why we should do so:

First, the spiritual character of the American people has always led them, and will for all time compel them, to prevent hunger and cold to the full extent of their surplus, and even to the extent of personal self-denial.

Second, while the defeat of Communism in Western Europe is of vital importance to the preservation of moral and spiritual values for which we stand, it is also of vital importance to us that the economic and political unity of Western Europe should be stimulated.

Third, the project builds for peace in the world.

The dangers inherent in the project are very great. On one side is the possible failure of Western Europe, now engaged in wide-spread experiments in socialization of industry, to secure the restoration of productivity; their possible failure to secure domestic fiscal and currency stability; their possible failure to secure economic and political cooperation with each other; and their possible failure to defeat the destructive politico-economic forces in their midst.

On the American side, dangers are that the volume of exports and finance proposed may accelerate an already serious inflation; that it further delays our recuperation from the war; that it drains our natural resources and continues excessive taxation: all of which might bring depression and thus destroy the strength of the one remaining source of aid to a world in chaos.

We must take some risks, and I should have liked to be able to give unqualified endorsement of the E.C.A. as presented to the Congress. I am compelled, however, by conscience to say that the plan as presented should have certain constructive modifications and more safeguards.

I suggest six directions of such action:

First, as to its organization.

Second, as to the scope of the plan.

Third, as to positive conditions to which the recipient countries should agree.

Fourth, as to the period to which we are committed.

Fifth, as to limits of burden upon the United States.

Sixth, as to some suggestions for lightening the burden to the American taxpayer and upon our economy, and yet preserve our purpose.

ORGANIZATION OF E.C.A.

No one would contend that the political relations involved in this plan should not be controlled by the foreign policy branch of the Government. But this plan is far more business and economic than political.

By this proposal, together with other authorities, and our other foreign aid projects, we are placing the control of the whole American economy in the hands of the organization which directs these operations. Its policies can determine the volume of exports, and thus prices, wages, rationing, inflation, and the progress of the incomplete reconstruction in the United States.

Beyond domestic questions, there are momentous foreign economic policies to be decided by the administrators of these powers. The need, finance and source of supply must be determined for each recipient country. These operations must be coordinated with our exports to all other countries and with our other relief operations. Above all there must be continuous evaluation to determine whether the economic and social policies of the constituent countries are contributing to success.

Such power should not be placed in the hands of any one man or any one department of our government. Obviously the administrative work involved should be conducted by one man. But its policies should be directed by a group, no doubt including department heads, but also including non-official citizens. The proposals of Congressman Christian Herter insofar as they imply group conclusions come nearer to meeting this requirement.

I assume it is intended to carry out this operation as a bi-partisan enterprise, for only thus can we hope for success. There is far too much at stake to permit partisan approach. If these policies are to be bi-partisan, then the members of this board or commission should be selected by prior consultation with the Congressional leaders.

SCOPE OF RESPONSIBILITIES SHOULD NOT BE LIMITED TO THE 16 COUNTRIES

Even if administration of these funds is limited to the 16 countries, the scope of policy determination must be far wider. The front against Communism lies not alone in Europe; it stretches through Latin America and Asia. We have to bear in mind that the exports of the United States include also very necessary exports to those countries which supply us with essential imports and whose economies are positively linked with our own as, for instance, the Latin-American states.

We must, if we pursue this national policy, include aid to China and other nations, together with the occupied territories of Germany, Japan and Korea. There are thus not 16 countries directly under relief, but 20, and possibly more.

The food supply and reconstruction of industry in Germany, Japan, Korea and China are inseparable from the 16 countries. Both logic and administrative management suggest that they be placed in the hands of this commission.

We cannot separate a 20-nation segment of the world from the other 20 friendly nations and give it priority over them. Any undertaking to use American resources to the full extent to bring about stability of the world implies coordination with other countries.

CERTAIN CONDITIONS WHICH SHOULD BE AGREED TO BY RECIPIENTS OF E.C.A.

The plan presupposes certain basic conditions of cooperation between the countries to be aided which are essential to the success of our efforts.

One of the hopes of the world is economic and political solidarity of Western Europe.

Internally in each country the plan envisages an increase in productivity by abandonment of restraints upon enterprise and economy. It envisages balanced budgets and checks on inflation. Above all there need be abandonment of their wholly fictitious basis of foreign exchange. Were these things assured and were exchange based upon realities, private Western Hemisphere funds would pour into those areas; their domestic hoards of gold and currency would begin to come out and the demand for their exports would increase. All of which would decrease the drains and strains upon the United States taxpayer.

Moreover, the reopening of German and Japanese industrial

plants is not only essential to provide needed materials in Europe and Asia, but the situation is at present an "operation rathole" to the extent of a billion and a half dollars for each year of charitable food from the United States to keep these people alive. With restoration of their production, and exports, that sum could be applied to reconstruction by E.C.A., not used to keep idle thousands of German and Japanese plants and workmen. Specifically, those of the 16 countries concerned should agree to the trizonal economic union of Western Germany; a peace with Japan; a cessation of plant destruction and removal; and abolition of or increase in "levels of industry" in these two countries.

No one expects all these things to happen overnight, but unless they are begun quickly our service toward world recovery will be largely in vain.

OUR COMMITMENTS SHOULD NOT BE EXTENDED
TO FOUR YEARS

The plan originally proposed an authorization to E.C.A. of 17 billion dollars and a four-year program. The first 15-months' appropriation is proposed at 6.8 billion. But in addition to this, we are committed to Western Germany, Japan, Korea, and possibly China, and perhaps others, for supplies amounting to about 2 billion in this same period of 15 months, or a total of nearly 9 billion dollars.

It was prudent not to require that commitments be made by the United States at the present time for more than the first 15 months, until July 1, 1949. We cannot even hazard what the export and financial possibilities of the United States will be for more than a year in advance. Food being the largest item in the whole program, we can only judge from harvest to harvest. Nor can we long forecast our industrial production. Furthermore, we cannot tell in advance the requirements of each of these countries to which it is proposed to extend aid. They, too, are dependent upon their harvests; they are dependent upon cooperation between governments, and upon their labor and many other elements for which we cannot fix a financial or commodity commitment.

Even a moral commitment to a four-year program is unwise. We cannot enforce ideas upon other self-governing peoples, and we should keep ourselves entirely free to end our efforts without recrimination. The United States will at all times aid against hunger and cold. The fact that we have already spent probably 20 billions upon this purpose since this war and over 5 billions after the last war should be sufficient assurance that we will continue to support right-thinking peoples in the future.

THE BURDEN UPON THE UNITED STATES

Whether the American economy can stand a burden of 9 billions of relief in this 15 months must arouse great anxiety.

It amounts to about 18% of our whole Federal tax income during such a period. It amounts to 36% of all the personal income taxes. Yet the country surely needs tax relief if its productivity and employment are to be sustained.

Another disturbing question is the effect upon prices, wages and inflation generally of the volume of exports and finance here proposed. In the fiscal year 1946 we exported 4.4 billion dollars more goods than we imported. In the fiscal year 1947 we exported 7 billion dollars worth of goods more than we imported. (In both cases services are omitted.)

These differences were represented by gifts and loans to foreign nations. They were bumper-crop years, yet the volume of exports in fiscal year 1947 and since have undoubtedly raised prices and started inflationary spirals. It seems difficult to believe that we can continue at the rate now proposed and not produce the same effect.

It is not an answer to say that under this plan large amounts of American money will be used for purchases of commodities in other countries on behalf of recipient nations and thus relieve export pressure upon the United States. These other countries thus receiving our money will wish to transform that money into goods from the United States. If we refuse export certificates for all or part of their demands because we do not have the goods, either our money will go to a discount, or we will necessarily enter obligations to pay those nations at some future date. Thus the United States will in effect be borrowing money abroad to finance this program.

It is an illusion that scarcity and thus increasing inflation can be more than temporarily retarded by compulsory fixing of wages, prices and rationing. Aside from the reduction of primary freedoms involved, history and our national experience prove that any such course sets up chain reactions which ultimately decrease production and defeat their very purpose. A part of Western Europe's present difficulties is due to these practices.

The only safe road for us is not to over-export. We can to some extent increase the amounts available for export and hold prices by adopting strong voluntary conservation measures; by using voluntary restraints on prices and wages; by doing more and harder work with uninterrupted production. Such voluntary organization, if vigorously and systematically administered, avoids most of the evils of the coercive system.

SOME SUGGESTIONS FOR LIGHTENING THE BURDEN UPON THE AMERICAN TAXPAYER AND UPON OUR ECONOMY

If some of the imported quantities scheduled be reexamined in the light of supplies, if certain principles were established by Congress, if certain requirements were fixed, and if an effective business organization were set up, I am confident that the burden upon the American taxpayer could be lessened and our essential purpose accomplished.

European proposals on which this plan is based have undoubtedly been formulated in good faith but some suggestions seem permissible.

First. The food programs when correlated to the needs of the rest of the world would appear greater than the world supply during the first period from April to June, 1948, and at the same time maintain rations in the occupied areas and some "plan" countries at an endurable level. Further, these programs seem to imply a dependence upon world harvests much greater next year than last.

Second. The program for agricultural reconstruction seems imperative, but the program for industrial production implies not alone a restoration of prewar productivity but a great increase in such production above prewar. That is indeed greatly to be desired, but whether Americans are able out of production and taxes at this time to provide more than a restoration to prewar levels is another question.

Third. The program calls for export of about $800,000,000 of capital goods including steel and machinery from the United States in the 15 months period. Both the Harriman and the House of Representatives Reports cast doubt upon our ability to supply this amount of steel production and to maintain our necessary exports to other vital quarters. A House report states that these demands are "a staggering deficit to impose upon steel in the United States . . . it is difficult to see how . . . it would be possible to fulfill this program without seriously weakening our economy." The capital goods programs of the 16 nations of necessity may need to be extended over a longer term.

In fact, our productive machine today is crippled by the insufficient railway equipment for the prompt delivery of goods; our food production is lessened by scarcity in agricultural machinery; we have sporadic oil famines due to lack of oil-well, refining and transport equipment; our automotive industry is short of raw materials; we are dreadfully short of building materials for veterans' homes. No further evidence of shortage is needed than the black market where steel is selling for over 100 per cent premiums.

It would seem that the possibilities of early steel and machinery production in Germany should be more vigorously undertaken, obviously with readily effective curbs as to any munitions diversion. With removal of the inhibitions on these German industries, with vigor and working capital, a large segment of this program could be supplied from that quarter, instead of by increasing scarcities and delaying reconstruction and increasing taxpayer costs in the United States. It may be said that Germany cannot do this and export coal to the 16 nations. Pending increase in Ruhr coal, some increase in United States coal exports might be found to be better. The same policies should be applied to fertilizers and to oil refining in Germany.

In any event, it would appear that the 15 months' capital goods program must be extended over a much longer period.

Fourth. The estimates of over $650,000,000 of petroleum supplies to the 16 nations for the next 15 months represent a considerable increase over the last 15 months and would seem to be greater than the supply. Pending development in the Persian Gulf, the world is already short of oil and there seems no source for any such an increase.

Fifth. Inquiry might be made into methods of relieving the United States Treasury of some of this cost through collateral loans by, say, the R.F.C. or by the Export-Import Bank.

There are citizens in some of these European states who have large private property in the United States and in other parts of the Western Hemisphere. Prior to the war, the British Government collected a group of such investments and borrowed money on them in the United States. There are large sums of this character still outstanding, and they could be collected by the various European governments, paying their citizens in their own bonds; these assets could then be pledged as security for loans in the United States. If there is protest that taking over these privately held resources is a hardship to the owners, it may be pointed out that the alternative is a far greater hardship for the American taxpayer. In the first instance, the owner would be reimbursed in full in his own currency; in the second, the American citizen would be taxed the full amount and never see it again.

Sixth. Some expansion of private enterprise in supplying of capital goods to the 16 nations, and thus relief to the United States Treasury, might be found in the use of foreign currencies realized from the sale by the recipient countries of United States goods coming to them as gifts or grants.

In April, 1947, I recommended to the Congress, in connection with the relief appropriations then before it, that it should specify that the currency received from the resale of American goods to the populations in each country be deposited in their national banks to the credit of the United States. We should then set up a commission which, in cooperation with the government concerned, would use this money to promote productivity within that country. A form of that proposal was incorporated in the European Aid Act of 1947 and is contemplated in the present legislation.

My suggestion here is that if these funds were to be used in the aided countries to pay for labor and domestic materials in productive works, there should be thus created an equity upon which American private enterprise could furnish the necessary imports of capital goods.

Seventh. It is proposed that this nearly $9 billion in 15 months shall be by grants which are gifts, as well as by loans. I suggest the Congress should define some general principles of distinction between gifts and loans.

We must disillusion ourselves that loans from the United States Government, except where secured by transferable property, or other specific security, are real loans. They are gifts. There are economic as well as political reasons why such "loans" will not, and cannot, be repaid. We will act more intelligently if within the minds of our own people and those of the recipient peoples we separate our gifts from our loans. We should separate charity from business.

That division can be made clear if we confine our gifts to the actual American surplus of consumption goods such as food, coal, fertilizers and cotton (not for re-export), which are essential to maintain life. I believe the American people are perfectly willing to give these commodities as a gift to those countries who cannot pay for them. While giving these away will be privation, yet we can reproduce the agricultural products and we have ample future resources in coal and some fertilizers. The total of such relief goods from the United States during this 15 months might amount to $3 billion. Such an amount of gifts would enable participating countries to use their exports to pay for other goods in their programs.

The relief exports to Germany, Japan and Korea should be a first charge on all reparations.

Eighth. I do not believe we should be called upon to make gifts or grants of steel and other capital goods. They can be paid for out of the increased productivity which they create.

In the program of proposed supplies to the 16 countries from the United States, nearly one billion dollars are capital goods. Aside from the portion which can be financed by private enterprise, such goods should be financed by the Export-Import Bank or the World Bank whose independence of decision should not be modified under the present set-up as they can continue to take specific and ultimately reliable securities payable from the increased production they create.

Ninth. I do not believe we should make gifts or grants of American money to pay for goods from other countries.

The program of supplies apparently calls for a large part of $3.5 billion of Western Hemisphere goods to be purchased with American money from Canada, Argentina and other Western Hemisphere states. Of this amount, under $200 million represents captial goods, the rest being mostly agricultural products. As the latter represents surplus production of the other Western Hemisphere countries, it would appear that they should be anxious to sell and, no doubt, to cooperate in creating world stability. It would seem, therefore, that these states should extend credits to the 16 countries for such goods. A partial guarantee, or advance, against such credits by the United States through the Export-Import Bank is the most that we should be asked to give.

CONCLUSION

With these various suggestions I believe it is possible considerably to reduce the burden upon our citizens and at the same time to assure the accomplishment of our national purpose.

The Marshall Plan Bill

Statement to Speaker Joseph W. Martin,
House of Representatives
[March 24, 1948]

Washington, D. C.

The Honorable Joseph W. Martin, Speaker
House of Representatives
Washington, D. C.

My dear Mr. Speaker:

I have your request that I give to you my views and recommendations upon the Marshall Plan Bill as reported out of the House Committee on Foreign Affairs.

On January 18th, at the request of Senator Arthur Vandenberg, I made an analysis of and recommendations as to the legislation originally presented by the Administration. Many members of the Congress, myself, and others urged its support in principle because of world conditions, but recommended that certain additional safeguards be introduced into the legislation. We believed these would make for more efficient administration, less drain upon the American taxpayer, less strain on our economy, and at the same time deliver the same volume of commodities to the Marshall Plan countries.

I have now compared the bill as passed by the Senate and the House Foreign Affairs Committee; have had the advantage of the able reports of the Herter Committee and the discussions before the Congress and their Committee reports. While claiming no credit for amendments so ably perfected by the

Senate and by the House Committee, it seems to me that the most clear presentation of my personal views and recommendations as to the legislation would be:

First, to review the suggestions made in my letter to Senator Vandenberg (likewise made by others) which have been adopted or incorporated in part; and

Second, to suggest some further recommendations which I urge for adoption.

I: PREVIOUS RECOMMENDATIONS ALREADY ADOPTED BY BOTH SENATE AND HOUSE COMMITTEES OR INCORPORATED IN PART

1. We proposed that there be set up a business administration under a separate Administrator, yet coordinated with the State Department. This has been done effectively.

2. We urged that a non-partisan board of citizens be created to advise and consult with the Administrator with respect to basic policy matters. This has been done.

3. We suggested that there be an organization coordination in all government agencies involved in financial relations with the Marshall Plan countries. This has been accomplished, in effect, by enlarging the National Advisory Council on Monetary and Financial Problems to include the Administrator.

4. We recommended that all government relief organizations for the Marshall Plan countries be consolidated under the Administrator. This has been done by committing to the Administrator any remaining funds in other accounts.

5. We proposed that there must be protection against excessive exports which would injure American economy. The bills are intended to safeguard this.

6. We urged that private channels of trade be utilized to the fullest extent and that partial guarantees be given by the Export-Import Bank to private enterprise. This idea, apparently limited to Americans, was incorporated in the Senate bill and has been strengthened further by the House Committee.

7. I suggested that amounts equivalent to any relief to any

particular country be deposited in the currency of that country in a trust fund to be administered jointly by the Administrator and the country concerned for the internal benefit of that country. This has been done. And such sums arising out of previous relief activities have also been transferred to the new administration.

8. We urged that increased production and economic cooperation between countries receiving aid, with monetary and budgetary reforms were vital conditions of success of any plan. That has been made a prominent part of the Administrator's duties and an implied condition of continued support.

9. We recommended that as part payment the countries under aid furnish us, for stockpiling purposes, such commodities as we do not possess sufficiently for future defense. This has been made an implied condition of support in the House bill.

10. We suggested that the petroleum products provided under the original program could not be furnished from the world's present supplies. The act now provides that the world shortage makes undesirable the expansion of petroleum-consuming equipment in the Marshall Plan countries (which originally had been contemplated) where alternate fuel sources are practicable. This provision is most essential until Persian Gulf oil can flow freely to Europe. Thereafter it should be contemplated for many other sources of energy.

11. I proposed that the Congress define more clearly the areas of grants (gifts) from the areas of loans; that all capital goods provided from the United States be made as loans from the Export-Import Bank or private enterprise, that all consumption goods from the United States be made as gifts. The reasons were that the former could be repaid out of the increased productivity they create, and that the latter would never be paid because we cannot receive this volume of European goods in return without creating unemployment at home. The House Committee has effected this, to some extent, by dividing the aid into $1 billion of loans through the Export-Import Bank and $4.3 billion of unspecified grants and

loans. Both bills require consultation with the National Advisory Council in the determination between loans and grants.

12. We urged that no moral commitment be made to the proposed 4-year plan beyond the first period (now one year), with a view to giving complete freedom of review by the Congress at the end of that period. The plan still stands as a four-year program, but the standards of progress and of performance to be made by the Marshall Plan countries have been emphasized more strongly, and these, no doubt, will be taken into account by the Congress in determining the volume and kind of aid beyond the first year. The House Committee has strengthened the Congressional control of such extensions by an express statement that no implied commitment has been made to any country and a requirement that further assistance shall be authorized as well as simply appropriated as in the Senate bill.

13. We suggested that the Marshall Plan countries should participate in the cost of the program by using the assets of their private citizens in the United States, reimbursing those citizens in their own currencies. This has not been required, but the Administrator is directed to locate and implement such resources and to secure their use, as far as possible.

14. We recommended that definite action be taken to restore German production, particularly steel and machinery, so much needed by the Marshall Plan countries, and to stop removal and demolition of plants. This would relieve the drain upon the American taxpayers, which arises both from shipment of such goods from the United States and by necessary feeding of idle German workmen in the meantime at the expense of our taxpayers. The House bill makes partial provision looking to this end.

II: MY PRESENT RECOMMENDATIONS

1. I originally urged that all relief operations, not only to the Marshall Plan countries, but to China, Germany, Japan, Korea, Greece and Turkey, be consolidated under the Administrator. This would prevent overlap in procurement and enable

better coordination of policies. The House Committee has made such provisions as to Greece, Turkey and China. Relief to Germany, Korea and Japan should be incorporated when those appropriations are made later on.

2. I do not recommend a decrease in the authorized total in the House bill for the first year. No doubt the Appropriations Committees will review the effect of decreased prices; the effect of possible savings to be made by guaranteed loans through American citizens, through possible credits of other Western Hemisphere countries; the reduction in such estimated prices as Argentine wheat of over $4.50 per bushel; the reduction in amounts of proposed commodity shipments which cannot be provided now because of scarcity; etc.

3. Certain new provisions in the House Foreign Affairs Committee bill seem to me to be most advantageous. Chief among these are: (a) authority to the Administrator to create a corporation to facilitate operations; (b) assistance to Trieste; (c) chartering American vessels to Marshall Plan countries when available; (d) equitable access of Americans to the development of strategic materials; (e) the encouragement of better use of manpower and displaced persons; (f) aid to Greece, Turkey and China; and (g) the appropriation to the International Children's Emergency Fund, which is reconstruction at its very base. I hope these will be adopted by the Congress.

4. It seems to me that Section 117 (d) is too strongly drawn. If the Marshall Plan countries are to become independent of relief, they must trade with the satellite countries. A provision against munition shipment would appear to be sufficient.

5. It would seem to me that the provision in the Senate bill for a committee of seven members each from the Senate and House to work in conjunction with the Administrator is much more effective than merely reports to the Chairman of Committees, as in the House bill, and should be restored.

6. I urged from the beginning that the other countries in the Western Hemisphere take part in these burdens. The President is authorized to make such a request in the legislation. To

bring this about more effectively, and to reduce the drain on the American taxpayers, I suggested that Western Hemisphere countries extend credits for, say, ten years to the Marshall Plan countries, and that the United States guarantee such credits up to 70 % and advance dollars to that amount to the credit-extending Western Hemisphere countries. A permissive authority to the Administrator to make such arrangements was included in the Senate bill. I regret this provision has been deleted from the House Committee bill. The provision in the legislation for guaranteed loans is apparently limited to United States citizens.

This plan is all the more feasible by reason of the fact that most American supplies (consumption goods supplied) must be gifts. The dollar exchange arising out of imports by the United States from the Marshall Plan countries would be free for their purchases in other Western Hemisphere states, thus minimizing the extent of such credit.

I am convinced that a number of countries in the Western Hemipshere are in a position to extend such credits. Because their natural trade is exchange of surplus agricultural products for manufactured goods, to and from Europe such credits can be repaid to them in the course of trade without hardship because they can absorb European manufactured goods without creating unemployment. The increased productivity in Europe would render this possible. As an example, under the State Department program of commodities to be shipped over the four years from other Western Hemisphere states, at the expense of the American taxpayer, is about one billion dollars worth of coffee. Coffee is a comfort, not a nutrient. It would seem that a country desirous of selling its coffee surplus would be willing to deal on a dollar-credit basis, especially if the United States guaranteed 70% of that credit.

I strongly urge the restoration of this guarantee provision, as it could save the American taxpayer a great deal.

IN CONCLUSION

I realize that many approach this gigantic experiment with great apprehension and a realization of the sacrifices it will mean to our people. All legislation must be the result of compromise. However, if it should produce economic, political and self-defense unity in Western Europe, and thus a major dam against Russian aggression, it would stem the tide now running so strongly against civilization and peace. The plan, if well devised and under a capable Administrator, stands a good chance of success. I believe it is worth taking the chance.

PART IV

EDUCATIONAL, SOCIAL AND SCIENTIFIC

On the Twenty-Fifth Anniversary
of Radio

Broadcast—Columbia Broadcasting System
[November 10, 1945]

I AM glad to be invited to take part in this program of celebration of the 25th anniversary of radio broadcasting. It has been suggested that I say a word on the origin of its regulation by government. I suppose the reason is because I was the first traffic cop of the broadcasting waves. Probably, it would be more accurate to say I was its first nurse.

A few months after broadcasting was born in 1920, I became Secretary of Commerce. There were then two infant experimental broadcasting stations with less than 50,000 receiving sets. The Secretary of Commerce had some years before been empowered by Congress with a very limited authority to prevent interference in sending Morse telegraphic signals by radio. Therefore it seemed my job to look after the new art of voice transmission in its governmental aspects. By the end of 1921, there were sixty broadcasting stations and about six hundred thousand receiving sets. And these lusty infants were violently stepping on the feet of each other's wave lengths.

To find what we ought to do, I called a conference of the radio industry and the broadcasters at the Department of Commerce in February, 1922. It was composed of about 1000 determined and agitated men and women. In looking back over the record of that conference I find that we were not as primitive or ignorant or unimaginative as to the possibilities of radio as those who discover everything over again every ten years might think. It is true we spoke of broadcasting as the wireless telephone; we thought the radio waves traveled through the ether between the molecules of the air; the programs were not very exciting and the stations could sell only a little time. Public men were sought after to make speeches instead of having to beg for time. That was possibly the reason the programs were a little on the dull side. However, we said some things at that first conference over the two-year-old art, which are still good despite all the electronic wisdom that has come into the world since.

In summing up on behalf of that conference in a nation-wide broadcast I find myself saying:

We have witnessed one of the most astounding things that has come into American life. . . . We are on the threshold of a new means of wide-spread communication of intelligence. . . . It has profound importance in public entertainment, education and public welfare. . . . It will yet influence our whole lives.

There were certain principles adopted at that conference which laid the foundations of all our present broadcasting. Summarized they were:

1. That the broadcasting channels should be public property just as are the navigation channels in our waterways.

2. That broadcasting should be conducted by private enterprise and not governmental broadcasting as had already been started in Britain. And I may say, parenthetically, the British have been coming over here ever since to learn the know-how of making good programs which are the consequence of our competitive system.

3. There should be no monopoly in broadcasting.

4. There must be regulation of the traffic to prevent interference.

5. There should be no person-to-person use of wave lengths except by the military and licensed amateurs as there was no room for such service.

6. We divided the then-known wave band into three parts among the broadcasters, the amateurs and the military authorities.

The conference unanimously requested the Secretary of Commerce—that was I—to assign the wave lengths to the stations and they agreed to abide by my decisions.

Curiously enough at this first conference, it was resolved that we ought to have more law, more bureaucratic authority over radio. We were not sure that our voluntary system of regulation would work.

And I may add something of this conference that has been forgotten. That body approved a suggestion of mine that, "It is inconceivable that we should allow so great a possibility for service, for news, for entertainment, for education to be drowned in advertising chatter." But I suppose the gentlemen in particular who compose the little mosquito-toned songs which cluster around every news broadcast were not present when we took that self-denying ordinance.

At one of these conferences I asked the technicians present to invent some kind of a knob on a receiving set by which we listeners could express our feelings to the fellow who was broadcasting. I said that merely turning off the radio in disgust left frustrations and dislikes dangerous to the future of our souls. Now the radio has triumphed with such astounding inventions as radar, I renew a faint hope.

At the second radio conference in 1923, when we were three years old, we found we had 528 broadcasting stations and 1,500,000 receiving sets. And we concluded that we were getting on so well with voluntary regulation and cooperation among stations that we would continue on that line and not look very hard for Congress. We carried on this voluntary regulation for five years, meeting in general conference every year to revise our methods. While it lasted it was a magnificent example of our American capacity to cooperate. But finally a broadcasting station broke away, grabbing someone else's wave length, and we had to press Congress for more law to save the air from chaos. That was a sad day for radio and the beginning of continuous headaches.

Regulating the radio in its early youth had surprises. Once upon a time there was an evangelist in a certain city upon whom it dawned very early that heaven as well as the earth could be reached with a broadcasting station. She bought an outfit and proceeded to broadcast without restraint over all wave lengths. I sent an inspector to argue with the lady that she keep on her own wave length. I can read you approximately the telegram I received from her:

Please order your minions of satan to leave my station alone. You cannot expect the Almighty to abide by your wave length nonsense. When I offer my prayers I must fit into the receiving sets in heaven. You don't know what their wave lengths are and neither do I. Stop this interference with me at once.

About this time a sect, who believed the world was coming to an end in about six months, had sold all their farms and homes and had come to Washington to see me. They wanted to build a broadcasting station; they could buy a sending set; they had the money, all they needed in order to warn the world to make ready for this event was the assignment of a wave length from me. I do not again wish to go through an interview with such a sub-current of real pathos and such a surface of humor. But we had to take the risk of leaving millions of people unwarned of their impending doom. At least we saved their money.

In October, 1927, I called an International Radio Conference. We signed a treaty among some 60 nations, dividing the wave lengths, designating the station symbols and other things. Thereby we cleared up a great deal of international interference. And one of the astonishing things of World War II is that although practically every other treaty has been violated, this one has stuck fairly well.

And today, 25 years after, radio still never ceases to be magic to me. Coming from nowhere into everywhere it brings us not alone news instantly from the spot; it brings the greatest and worst of music; it brings us good and bad speeches; it brings good and less good drama. But it brings them alike to us all— farm house, village, cottages and city cliff-dwellers. It is not only a part of our daily life but it has enriched the lives of all of us. The radio industry and broadcasters, both technically and as a public service, have done a magnificent thing for the American people. All our dreams of 25 years ago have been realized.

On the Exchange of Students with Foreign Countries

Letter to Senator J. W. Fulbright
[February 8, 1946]

New York City

The Honorable J. W. Fulbright
United States Senate
Washington, D. C.

My dear Senator Fulbright:

I have your request of February 1st for my views on S. 1636, the purpose of which is to provide intellectual exchanges between the United States and other countries. I am indeed glad of such a proposal. An actual experience may be helpful to the Committee on this matter.

In 1920, as a disposal of part of the funds from liquidation of supplies, etc. from the Belgian Relief Commission, I established the Belgian-American Educational Foundation, the purpose of which was exactly what you propose. In its twenty-five years, more than 700 individuals (477 Belgians and 225 Americans) were "exchanged" during the period between the World War I and World War II. Several important results have followed. At the outbreak of World War II nearly one-quarter of the teaching and research faculty of the Belgian universities had been graduate students in American universities. One Prime Minister and six Cabinet members have likewise done graduate work in American universities. Numbers of American and Belgian professors and specialists have been exchanged between our American and Belgian universities. I doubt whether there is a country in Europe where the ideals and purposes of the American people are so well understood and so respected as they are in Belgium. And although Belgium is a small country, there is a much greater understanding of it and respect for it in the United States than for some larger and more powerful states.

When Secretary of Commerce in 1923, I endeavored to secure a diversion of the war debts from any country which amounted to less than $100,000,000 to these purposes. That would have provided for such exchanges with some ten countries. We were unable to get it through. Again in the White House, I initiated an organization to carry out such a purpose with the Latin American states, but the depression compelled its postponement.

On a return from Europe in March, 1938, in a public address I made the following statement:

"There is a measure for very modest but long-view action by our Government that could bring great benefits to us and to other nations. It would serve to reduce greatly the area of frictions upon our war debt problems. After the Armistice we established credits for reconstruction and food to Poland, Belgium, Estonia, Latvia, Lithuania, Finland, Czechoslovakia, Hungary, Greece, Roumania, and Jugo-Slavia. Only Finland has staunchly maintained these payments. The others are awaiting the action of the large war debtors. There are likely to be difficulties over these matters for years to come.

"I believe we should consider suggesting to these relief credit countries as distinguished from the war credit countries a readjustment of the debts and—

"That each of them make these payments into a fund in their own country in their own currencies

"That this fund be used for extension of higher education, scientific research and for scholarships in their own universities; also for exchange of post-graduate students, professors, and scientific information between the United States and that country

"That these funds are to be administered jointly by Americans and their nationals.

"There will thus be created a joint interest with us from which we will generate benefits far greater than we will otherwise receive. The cumulative effect over the years of building up a great body of influential men and women in those countries who would understand our country and believe in us would count greatly both in economic relations and in times of international emergency. And we shall have made a contribution to civilization which may be of no quick material value but which will later serve as a great monument to our foresight."

This statement, it seems to me, is entirely applicable to the present situation in the financial settlements necessitated by the war and possible uses to which the proceeds of the sales of United States surplus commodities abroad might be put. That I gladly support your proposals needs no further emphasis.

On Support of National Boys' Club Week

Article for Boys' Clubs of America
[April 16, 1947]

TOGETHER with his sister, the American boy is our most precious national possession.

He presents not only joys and hopes, but also many problems.

Many years ago, thoughtful people, apprehending these problems, established the first Boys' Clubs in some of our New England cities.

SOUGHT TO AID

They sought to stop the gap that idle hands can fill with evil.

These Boys' Clubs in 1906 banded together to form the Boys' Clubs of America, engaged in the business of boys and "what we are going to do about them."

Today there are about 275 clubs throughout the country, embracing over a quarter million boys.

FIND OUTLETS

In these Boys' Clubs, boys find outlets for that explosive energy in play and the land of make-believe.

Their activities stretch all the way from checkers to sandlot baseball, from orchestras to bands.

There are boxing matches, libraries, gymnasiums and swimming pools.

They are led into shops of the arts and the trades to discover their occupational bents.

TAUGHT SPORTSMANSHIP

And above all, they are taught the spirit of sportsmanship and cooperative living.

Here also, boys are given glimpses of the opportunities of a greater America.

The juvenile delinquencies in the areas where these clubs work invariably show a striking decrease.

If you believe I am overstating the case for the Boys' Clubs, inquire of your police, of your magistrates.

Look into what has become of their alumni in the world.

They have produced men of leadership in their communities.

SUCCESSFUL MEN

There are great clergymen, editors, doctors and men in the educational field.

There are men in Government and leaders in business, besides great artists, musicians and, of course, leaders in all types of sports.

But this is not the important thing.

The greatest impact of the Boys' Club is on the average man.

Boys' Clubs have helped to produce thousands of good workers for the factories and businesses of America.

LEARNED TRUE MEANING

All these men have learned the true meaning of America and its opportunities in the Boys' Club—men who have a sense of fair play and respect for the rights of others—men who believe in the American way of life and free enterprise.

Yes, Boys' Clubs of America are building the honest, decent citizen of tomorrow.

I ask that you give a helping hand in this great enterprise.

It is about time we stopped talking about juvenile delinquency and start doing something about juvenile decency.

A Boys' Club is the answer.

Gridiron Dinner

Address, Washington, D. C.
[May 10, 1947]

MR. PRESIDENT, members of the Gridiron Club and your guests: I am deeply moved by your most generous reception.

My first Gridiron dinner was over thirty years ago when I was seated at the far end of the corner table. I had come to Washington to undertake a small mission for President Taft. In these thirty-five years I have been undertaking missions for every Democratic or Republican President—except one.

You are aware that I recently undertook a mission to Europe for President Truman. I am glad in this last skit that you have been able to find some humor in foreign affairs. Apropos of this there was a secret part of that last mission which I will now disclose to you. It seemed to me desirable to investigate whether there was any humor left in European statesmen. It would make our international relations more endurable. Moreover, I hoped that we might at least get for the American taxpayer a few refreshing jokes as repayment for lend-lease and subsequent loans.

Finding little spontaneity anywhere, I tried force only once. A British Food Minister had been moaning at great length over the hardships of their monotonous diet. His grievance was very real, but to introduce a little lightness, I suggested that they could greatly improve matters by reforming that institution of British self-castigation—the eternal boiled potato. I went so far as to suggest their employing a few French or

Belgian chefs to teach them how to cook a potato, at least for official banquets. His response was that we should discuss only matters of importance to the laboring classes.

I had no luck for some time, although some of the statesmen along the Iron Curtain shook my hand smilingly and looked me straight in the pocketbook.

I, however, persisted in my quest through the thickets of innumerable conferences with top officials of many countries. I had no tangible results until I came to the most tragic city of all the world—Vienna. There I found an official who really wanted to help.

To illustrate the problem from which his country was suffering, he described a meeting of the three—Bevin, Byrnes and Molotov. Secretary Byrnes had taken out his plain silver cigarette case, and Bevin, noticing it carried an inscription, read aloud: "To James Byrnes, from his devoted friends in the South Carolina Legislature."

Bevin remarked that he also had received such a gift and produced his plain silver case upon which was inscribed: "To Ernest Bevin, from his devoted friends in the British Labor Party." Under the protocol of appeasement Molotov accepted a cigarette from both of them.

A little later on, Molotov took out his own solid gold and bejeweled case, but, under the same protocol, offered no solace, to his colleagues. However, they observed that the inscription on his case read: "To Prince Esterhazy, from his devoted friends of the Jockey Club of Vienna."

I am not on your operating table tonight. But I can sympathize with Mr. Truman's difficulties in this matter as can no other man. I am fully aware of the skill and earnestness with which you cut up his ideology, his domestic and foreign policies. I can tell him, from long experience, not to look forward to much use of anaesthetics.

The last time I spoke to the Gridiron Club was just after the Republican defeat in 1932. On that occasion your speakers referred to the outgoing Administration in those appreciative tones which politeness and tradition require for the dead. You may need to search your barrel of sermons for that one again. Also at that time, I sought to comfort my colleagues by emphasizing the high importance in the democratic process of their forthcoming position as the opposition party. But to elaborate these themes would be an indelicate implication that I am seeking a recruit to my exclusive union of ex-Presidents.

At that dinner in 1932 I spoke also of the aid and comfort a President received from an opposition Congress. Mr. Truman no doubt has realized during the past six months that they put more emphasis on the advice end of their constitutional relations than upon the consent end. Here again I can sympathize with Mr. Truman more deeply than any other living person. However, he has not yet probed the depths of their capacities in these directions.

Mr. Chairman, our country is most fortunate in that partisanship does not reach such depths of hate and bitterness among responsible men as those which now infect much of this distracted world. In this connection, in closing, may I again use the image which I summoned to you in that address of 15 years ago. I said:

The life stream of our nation is the generations of millions of human particles acting under the impulse of freedom of advancing ideas and religious ideals gathered from a thousand springs. These rills have grown into great streams which have nurtured and fertilized this great land over centuries. Its dikes against dangerous floods have been cemented with the blood of our fathers.

I continued:

What is said in this or that political campaign lasts no longer than the ripples or angry whirls in that stream. But God help the man or group who breaks down those dikes of safety or diverts these channels of progress to selfish ends. These waters will drown them in a tragedy that will be remembered over a thousand years. I said that what counts toward the honor of public officials is that they sustain these freedoms, these channels of national ideals and their dikes of safety. From this labor lies not alone the glory of those officials who attend them, but the future of civilization. Under such officials our children will strengthen these dikes, will create new channels of progress and our land will grow greater and richer in their lives.

Mr. Chairman, I am glad to have this opportunity to say to you that President Truman has given high service to our country in repairing our broken dikes of safety which must guard our national ideals. Moreover, amid the thousand crises which sweep upon us from abroad, he has stood firm with his feet rooted in the American soil. He has brought to the White House new impulses of good will toward men.

Gentlemen, I have received from your dinners over the years much political education. I am grateful to you for the ability and earnestness of your instruction. Some of you may be skeptical of the results. But I have, with time, at least profited by your special prejudice against long speeches. That lesson has been rubbed in because in the past year I have listened to more long speeches in more languages than anyone not in the United Nations. Therefore, it is both a duty and a pleasure to close this address quickly by thanking you for your hospitality and your most kind expressions.

In Celebration of the Bicentennial Anniversary of Princeton University

Address, Princeton, N. J.
[June 16, 1947]

Ladies and Gentlemen:

I GATHER from other speakers that we are assembled here to celebrate the beginning of learning among the Presbyterians. Their first invitation to learning no doubt included the ideology of predestination with a fifty-fifty chance of a hot fire. Being in the neighborhood of the Quakers of Philadelphia, Princeton was naturally weaned away from the predestination part. Sometimes I regret the doubts which are rising about the hot fire end of that ideology. I have at times had great consolation in holding to that part of orthodoxy, because I despaired of an adequate heating place on this earth for some people. However, I will not dwell upon their names at this time.

Anyway, time has mellowed Princeton to the idea that people should be prepared to live as well as to die.

I have listened with great interest to the enumeration of the great contributions this institution has made to American life over the past two hundred years. I had always believed that Princeton was one of the great beacons of national progress. I shall go away believing that it is the only one.

But wanting to make sure that those early Presbyterians had started the nation on the right road in the pursuit of happiness, I inquired if any humor was allowed on the Campus in those

156

early days. My investigation did not develop much except that most of Princeton's present jokes on professors are almost 200 years old.

In all professions, including my own, there is polite contempt for the ignorance and lack of real understanding of all laymen. In my youth my professors expressed it in gentle pity. I therefore agreed to take part tonight with some trepidation at fronting such a mass concentration of collegiate pity potential. However, I will never again have the chance to speak my mind to so many representatives of higher learning from all over the United States. And whatever your inward feelings are, I have you at a disadvantage. I could recall to you the beautiful citations from many of your institutions as to my wisdom and knowledge with which you accompanied honorary degrees. In fact more of these citations than any one of you. With this cuttle-fish preparation, I shall list some of a layman's complaints about professors in general.

I will leave the glories of Princeton to the other speakers with my unreserved endorsement. And I hasten to assure those representatives from abroad who are present that they are not included in my complaints. Their institutions are no doubt perfect.

Someone of our profession recently announced that American colleges had degenerated into service for only the sons of rich men. Not having seen the Washington index numbers for the last hour, I do not know how many rich fathers are left. There are over 2,200,000 youth in institutions of higher learning, and if there are that many rich families in the country after taxes, then the income tax collector has missed over two-thirds of them.

But I recognize that higher education must always be in a perpetual ferment of reform. The sounds emitted, however, give the impression of mixed self-flagellation, sackcloth, ashes, determination that nothing is any good, and that the trustees are to blame. The curious part of this is that despite these no doubt minority convictions that everything in your service is wrong, 2,200,000 students insist on listening to you.

I also read that you, like all other professions—except the lawyers whom you manufacture—are greatly underpaid. I agree that you have not been carried up on our spiral of inflation. Until salvation comes, I offer you a solace. There is an idea promulgated by one wing of your faculties which implies that the full professors' salaries should be averaged down with the instructors'. I assure you that we right-wingers will support you against compulsory application of this equalitarian idea.

May I mention also an occasional attitude of a certain wing of our faculties who hold that the elders and forebears of these two million youngsters have done a wholly bad job in this land of ours and that it must all be upset. Perhaps it could have been done better. I am sure that if I ran the place it would be better. However, the worm's eye view has its values in discovering bugs, but the bird's eye view sees the glories of the landscape.

After all, in this 200 years since the founding of Princeton, a God-fearing people under the blessing of the right-wing system of freedoms have built up quite a plant and equipment on this continent. It teems with millions of comfortable farms and homes, cattle and hogs. It is equipped with railroads, power plants, factories, highways, automobiles and death warnings. It is studded with magnificent cities and traffic jams. The terrible reactionaries have filled the land with legislatures, town councils, a free press, orchestras, bands, radios, jukeboxes and other noises. It has a full complement of stadiums, ball players and college yells. Furthermore, they have sprinkled the country with churches, laboratories, built ten thousand schools and a thousand institutions of higher learning. And somehow, these right-wing taxpayers are squeezing out the resources which maintain a million devoted teachers, a hundred thousand able professors, and the keep of these two million youngsters in colleges and universities. Possibly, another ideology could do better in the next two hundred years. But I suggest we had better continue to suffer the evils of right-wing freedoms than to die of nostalgia.

I will not dwell on worm's eye views longer. A bird's eye view shows that your profession is today doing the most amazing thing in all the history of human culture. You are providing training and the inspiration of ideals to more youth than in all the rest of the world put together. Yet we are only 6 per cent of the world's population. And as a reference to my own state of California is necessary on all public occasions, I may tell you that we have more such students in higher education than in the whole United Kingdom. You have taken the burden of the G.I. flood in your stride and without complaint.

It comes my way to visit many colleges. I am confident that their two million American youth under your guidance and inspiration are the best and most promising body of future leadership this country or the world has yet seen. That they have flocked to your classrooms and laboratories is proof that they believe in you. Out of your labors there is rising a greater host of efficient, morally and patriotically inspired men and women, with a better understanding of their public responsibilities, than has any generation and any nation yet possessed. You are contributing not only to the American people but to the whole world. You are performing an exacting task requiring not only knowledge but patience, tact and vision. Yours is indeed a glorious mission, magnificently performed. You are entitled to retain your pity of all laymen.

Gentlemen, I will close by relating to you an incident which occurred on this campus 200 years ago. It may be an apochryphal story, but it is at least hoary with age. About this time of night a member of the new Princeton faculty rushed into the office of the sheriff of Mercer County. Excitedly he announced that he had killed a man, that he had committed murder. The sheriff told him to be calm and to tell him all about it. The professor explained that they were having a banquet on oatmeal mush to initiate this new college on its 200-year mission; there were eight speakers, just as there are tonight. And he said that when the eighth speaker had drooled a long while, "I could not stand it any longer, I fetched the college blunderbuss and shot him dead." The sheriff remarked: "You have come to the wrong place. You should go to the Scrivener's office— he pays the bounties for varmints."

With these dangers surrounding me, I close with one further remark:

This University has in 200 years poured a magnificent stream of ideals and leaders into our country. The American people will gladly celebrate its birthday again 200 years hence.

PART V

WORLD FAMINE, 1946-1947

On President Truman's Appeal to Save Food

Press Statement, New York City
[February 8, 1946]

PRESIDENT TRUMAN'S appeal to save food to meet the famine in many countries should be supported by the whole American people. The President's statement of the need is backed up by innumerable investigations and reports going back as far as General Eisenhower's strong statement of last August.

The food shortage in the world affects the supplies available for import by Britain, France, Belgium, Holland and Norway as well as Central and Eastern Europe, India and China.

UNRRA is devoting itself largely to helping Eastern Europe and while the problem is not one of charity for Western Europe, whose supplies can be financed, yet it is no less urgent that food must be made available.

And there lies within these problems not alone of food adapted to adults. There should be organization of special food to undernourished children and mothers over the whole of Europe, including Germany. The infant mortality is very high everywhere on the Continent and unless special supplies are available it will be still higher. In some areas it is now over 50%. Peace and progress will not be restored if those who survive are to be infected by a generation of men and women stunted in body and distorted in mind. After the last war, through the women in each European country, we systematically organized such special feeding of undernourished children and at times had more than 10 million of them receiving such support.

I am convinced that it is entirely possible for us to meet this need of increased food exports by voluntary action to eliminate waste and unnecessary consumption and to do it without compulsory rationing. We have now had experience with both systems. In the first World War we placed food consumption on a moral and Christian appeal and voluntary organization of the housewives, eating places and the food trades. We have now, in this war, had experience with compulsory rationing, and an examination will show that consumption per capita was no greater and probably less under the voluntary system. In either case with a proper understanding of the gravity of the situation a greater surplus of food can be created to save human lives. In any event, there is a stern job ahead of us.

On World Famine

*Statement before the Famine Emergency Committee
Meeting, Washington, D. C.*
[*March 11, 1946*]

THE world faces the gigantic emergency of famine among
five hundred million people due to war exhaustion of
agriculture and drought.

A great human cry has come to us to save them over a terrible four months until the next harvest. The Western Hemisphere alone has the aid to give, and a heavy part of the burden
falls upon the United States.

These people can survive if we provide a minimum of bread
and fats to them. Of breadstuffs, wheat can best be transported
and used in the famine countries. Therefore, we are asking our
citizens to make a voluntary sacrifice of 40 per cent of their
consumption of wheat products and 20 per cent of food fats
and oils during this next 120 days.

For public eating places, we ask that they use no more than
an average of two pounds of flour per customer per week. This
means about two pounds of bread and one-half pound of other
wheat products. We ask that the service of food fats be reduced
by 20 per cent.

For householders, we simply ask that you reduce your purchases of wheat products by 40 per cent and fats by 20 per cent.

We have adequate food beyond what we must ship to meet
the needs of the starving. Even if we send them every possible
pound of wheat and fats, the quantity of food remaining in

our country still will be greater than prewar. We are asking that all who can grow victory gardens and thus help to assure continued abundance of food.

In order to avert hunger, we cannot fail to meet this call. If we fail we shall see a world of disorders which will paralyze every effort at recovery and peace. We shall see the death of millions of fellow human beings. Guns speak the first word of victory, but only food can speak the last word.

On World Famine

Broadcast over the National Broadcasting Company
[March 14, 1946]

THE stark facts of the world famine problem are these:
The inevitable aftermath of six years of war in Europe
and Asia is terrible famine. It is inevitable because men
are taken from the farms, animals and machinery are destroyed,
the crops are less and less. Today we are faced with areas in
twenty nations where over 500 million people are in danger
of starvation during the next 120 days before the harvest of
next July. The amount of breadstuffs now visible to supply
these people from the surplus countries is about 450,000,000
bushels, but that is about 400,000,000 bushels short of enough
to maintain their present meagre rations until the next harvest
comes. And we also have a great gap in supplies of fats.

The major burden of bridging this gap is by consuming less
and making available more food from the Western Hemisphere
and the heaviest part of the burden falls upon the American
people if hundreds of millions of lives are to be saved from
disease or death.

I fear it is now so late that there are many thousands who
cannot be saved. But we must relax no effort to minimize the
loss.

These stark facts point our path. The war's end closed a
horrible era of the killing of millions of men, women, and children. Today we must transform the world from this era of
killing to an era of saving of lives. The dawn of a new era

can be made to glow with new faith and new hope to all the world if we are willing to make the sacrifice now.

We talk about starving people—but the word "people" is too indefinite. People are, in majority, youth and children. From them the future of civilization must be built. If they are to die or to be stunted in body and distorted in mind all hope of peace and progress is lost.

This is also an issue of religious faith and morals which affects not only our country but our individual selves. Saving of human life is a moral and spiritual duty. If your neighbors and their children were hungry, you would instantly invite them to a seat at your table. These starving women and children are in foreign countries, yet they are hungry human beings —and they are also your neighbors. Could you not imagine one of these helpless women or children as an invisible guest at your table? By following the voluntary rules for saving food you give life to that starving person just as surely as if he sat at your table.

To whatever extent we succeed in this task, we shall have given that much health, courage and faith to a despondent and discouraged world.

We must realize the calamity that has befallen man. I have no desire to relate the horrors of starvation. I can only appeal to your pity and your mercy. I know that the heart of the American people always responds with kindliness to suffering. Will you not take to your table an invisible guest?

On World Famine

Broadcast over the American Broadcasting Company
[*March 16, 1946*]

TWO weeks ago I was asked by President Truman and Secretary of Agriculture Anderson to advise upon what measures and what sort of organization should be set up to cope with the famine which now stretches over 500 million in foreign lands. I advised upon the essential organization and the methods adapted to this emergency. My recommendations were fully stated in the press on February 26. I do not need to repeat that outline.

I am glad to say these recommendations have all been adopted with one exception; that relates to the transfer of powers to Secretary Anderson which would make him a real food administrator capable of stopping the excessive amounts of human food now being consumed by livestock.

I wish to dispel at once one misunderstanding. I have no administrative authority or responsibility. I am acting in an advisory capacity.

The Emergency Food Administration is in good hands. The new organization is under the able direction of Secretary Anderson, Mr. Chester Davis, and the Famine Emergency Committee. They are making rapid progress. Secretary Anderson has selected Mr. Walter Straub as central director in Washington and he has appointed a food administrator in each state and county from Department officials. A program of voluntary rationing has been approved for householders, public eating places and the trades. Committees in the trades have been set up to see that it works.

The emergency will extend over four months until the next harvest in July. There should be a breathing spell after that.

The voluntary rules for conservation have been reduced to great simplicity and have been confined to only wheat products and fats. With sufficient of those we can stop starvation and we have faith in the voluntary action of the American people. Housewives are asked to make three loaves of wheat bread do the work of five and that their purchases of fats be reduced 20%. Public eating places have been asked to limit their purchases of wheat flour or its equivalent to two pounds a week for the average number of their customers and to reduce their consumption of fats 20%. That is not starvation for the American people because it can be made up by other abundant foods and saving waste. This amount of denial would alone save the health or lives of at least 35 million additional women and children.

There are some matters which I hope our people understand.

1. I fear it is now too late to save all the starving people. Our purpose is to save the last one possible.

2. The number of lives that we can save depends upon the extent to which the American people will comply with the Famine Emergency Committee's rules and their appeal.

3. It also depends upon the extent of measures by the Washington Administration to reduce livestock consumption of bread grains and to increase the available fats.

4. It further depends upon the extent to which Latin-American states will cooperate by reducing their consumption and waste of breadstuffs and fats to the end that they also send us the last pound and that they import the very least amount.

5. Even with success in these measures, we have insufficient food for all the millions of women and children and every atom of increase means life and hope somewhere.

I could discuss at length the repeated warnings and recommendations that I have made during the past five years—that effective organization and preparation of world supplies should be made against this inevitable after-war famine. But this is a time for cooperation and not controversy. Our duty is to serve starving people.

Now that the work of the Emergency Food Administration has been started, President Truman has asked me to go on a mission to the countries where there is danger of famine. I leave tomorrow morning by plane. I am accompanied by a number of men who were associated with me in relief and rehabilitation during and after the first world war. Our purpose is to study means and methods of making the available food supplies in the world, save the maximum number of lives and present the situation as clearly as we can to President Truman and to the American people together with such advice as we can give.

And I should like, in leaving my country, to repeat to this different audience part of what I have said elsewhere.

This is an issue of religious faith and morals which affects our country as a whole and each individual. Saving of human life is a moral and spiritual duty. If your neighbors and their children were hungry, you would instantly invite them to a seat at your table. These starving women and children are in foreign countries, yet they are hungry human beings—and they are also your neighbors. Could you not imagine one of these helpless women or children an an invisible guest at your table.

I can only appeal to your pity and your mercy. I know that the heart of the American people will respond with kindliness and generosity. Will you not take to your table an invisible guest.

On World Famine Crisis

*Reply to the French Minister of Foreign Affairs
at Luncheon in Paris*

[*March 21, 1946*]

Mr. Minister:

I AM greatly honored by your generous references to my many years of cooperation with the people of France. These rooms awake many recollections of friendly association with a long list of your able predecessors. And you, Mr. Minister, are also carrying forward the great tradition and contribution to world peace which has given this office a century of distinction.

I return to France to find grievous contrasts with other visits over the past forty years. I am greatly saddened by the continuing evidences of the deep injury and suffering of the French people. Even the streets proclaim the stilling lack of the vivaciousness and gaiety of other days. The people are lethargic and silent. It is profound expression not only of the shortage of food, but the effect of six long years of war, of German occupation and strain.

You have referred to my associations with France during the first World War. I was young in years at that time, but today I find myself, like the old family doctor, called from retirement to consult again in a most grave illness of the world. I have indeed been called in late in the crisis.

The spectre of starvation rises among 500 million people in many nations. It haunts our every thought. But there is one satisfaction, if we can find satisfaction in it. We know that the wolf at the door will go away after 120 days. We will then be released from his siege and the bondage of the fears he brings. If we can carry on during that short time to the harvest, the wolf will be gone, I hope forever.

And by our joint efforts we will carry through this last supreme effort, for this crisis is a moral and spiritual crisis, in which the world must serve to save human life. That is a command from the depths of our religious faith.

Mr. Minister, we are in that last stage of seven years of an era of appalling killing of men, women and children, and their barbaric reduction to starvation. It has been the most terrible era of all human history. But today the Four Horsemen are exhausted. A new era dawns. And in that era France will rise from her sufferings to that high place in civilization to which she has contributed so much over so many centuries.

On the Food Story of Italy

ROME

[*March 25, 1946*]

THE food story of Italy is that of decreased production from war and drought, exhaustion of stocks before harvest four months hence, and increasing difficulties of distribution. The government cereal ration, which was about 10 ounces per person per diem, has been reduced to about 7 ounces. The stocks of cereals on hand and supplies en route will hold this reduced ration about 30 days, and it is urgent that further supplies be loaded at once. Otherwise the cereal ration will need to be further reduced. The fat ration is 6 ounces and the sugar ration is about 4 ounces per month per person. Immediate shipments are necessary if even these rations are to be continued.

Supplementary to the above, supplies of meat are given by the government to hard workers, and milk to children and persons in institutions. A large part of the farm population takes care of itself, although requiring bread ration in some parts.

These three officially rationed commodities at the present levels comprise about 700 calories per diem, which, together with supplemental feeding of groups and institutions, some available vegetables and the black market, indicate an average total of 1,500 to 1,600 calories a day for the city populations. This compares with 2,550 calories Italian consumption prior to the war and is less than one-half the normal American consumption. Malnutrition, disease and mortality show increases, but the population generally could pull through on the present calories for the next four months. However, that cannot be provided without continued imports. These conclusions were the result of careful inquiry of several competent American experts working over the past few months.

In the black market, butter is $1.50 per pound; olive oil is $1.10, and meat $1 per pound. Those with money can go to the restaurants where such food is served, and live luxuriously, but Italians with average skilled wages of about $40 per month, and of clerical wages of about $50 per month, could not buy four meals a month for their families at black market restaurants.

Italy has hopes that the Argentine and Brazil may realize her plight and join the United States and Canada in the burden of their urgent supplies.

If the present Government rations are lowered as the result of failure of imports, it will be a disaster to white-collar and working classes. Starvation does not start until supplies cease coming. The problem here, as everywhere, is to prevent starvation during the next 120 days until the harvest. That fate will fall on the lower income groups and children in the cities soon after arrivals of overseas food stop.

On the Food Situation in France

Broadcast over Blue Network Radio from Paris
[March 27, 1946]

I HAVE been impressed by the vast difference in France, and especially in Italy, between the impressions gathered by casual visitors from the United States, who dine in black market restaurants and live in luxurious hotels, and the misery which the trained investigator finds when he leaves the tourist thoroughfares.

We have made surveys of the food situation in these two countries during the past week. We had organized the collection of detailed information in advance of our visit through our American agricultural agents in these countries, through the specialists of the United States Army, and our other American Government agencies. To this we have had the advantage of the information in the hands of the heads of the relief organizations conducted by Americans, British and Swiss. We have checked this information with departments of the French and Italian Governments, and our staff has inspected typical localities. It was thus possible to arrive at the truth, and to do it very rapidly.

Food conditions cannot be expressed except by the use of statistics. While measurement of food in calories is not everything, yet it gives a comparative idea. We Americans consume an average, taking in everybody ranging from infants to heavy physical workers, of over 3,200 calories per day per person. The French city populations have less than 1,900 calories, and the Italians have less than 1,600 calories, possibly under 1,500 calories per person per day. That is about half our American consumption. The food shortage falls worst upon the white-collar and worker groups in the cities, and more still on their children. By and large the agricultural population and the villagers have more and can get through to the next harvest. There is already a large increase in disease, and consequent mortality, particularly in children. The increase already amounts to three times prewar.

Although these city groups will suffer, yet they will mostly pull through the next 120 days until the harvest if the present meagre food supply can be kept up. That is the rub. If overseas supplies were to stop for a month to any one of these nations, there would be wholesale loss of life.

In these nations, the job is one of prevention—it has not reached the starvation stage and will not do so if supplies can be kept up. The only way this can be done is by reduction of consumption of food and thus larger surpluses from the Western Hemisphere. The number of people who can be preserved is now a factor of how much our people are willing to reduce their food consumption and eliminate waste. And the major job falls upon the United States.

The program of the Famine Emergency Committee would provide additional margins between the rations falling below the starvation level for a number just about equal to our United States population, or 130,000,000.

The American people should not be misled by reports of American travelers who judge the food supply of tens of millions of people by the kind of a meal that can be bought in a black market restaurant. Such meals cost from $2 to $5 per person. Even white-collar and skilled workmen in Italy and France earn less than $60 a month. Their entire pay for a month would support a family of five for only one or two days from such sources, and many of them are unemployed and without income. If our people are misled by such reports into slackening their efforts, it will be interpreted into the loss of from thousands to millions of human lives.

Italy and France are now surviving on the wheat and fats

Americans are sending them. I have not found even the hardest-hearted tourist, well fed with a black market meal, who suggests that this contribution from the United States be stopped.

I am leaving for Czechoslovakia and Poland tomorrow and I will in due time report on those two countries.

On Food Conditions in Czechoslovakia

PRAGUE

[*March 28, 1946*]

O UR report on Czechoslovakia can be stated very briefly, although brevity and statistics do not express the human picture of these people.

Their food is vigorously rationed and in different quantities, from children to heavy workers. The average content of the ration is probably less than 2,000 calories per day, for city populations. The farmers take care of themselves. There is practically no black market. The ration is badly deficient in fats, which average only about 20 ounces per month per person. The Czechoslovak ration is already one-third below normal and cannot be fully maintained until the next harvest without some further overseas breadstuffs and fats. Czechoslovakia has the additional background that the country has been short of food ever since the German occupation which began over seven years ago. Without UNRRA, the Czechoslovaks could not have carried on thus far. But with some additional supplies during the next few months until the harvest—which comes in August—there will be no starvation.

The food shortage has its worst expression in the children. They need additions to lift the ration above the danger level, where it now is. A special reserve of milk is provided for the 3,200,000 children under fourteen years of age, but at least one and one-half million of them are badly undernourished and need more protein and fats. The growth of tuberculosis, anemia and rickets among children is appalling. The whole child question urgently requires vigorous reorganization to provide an extra meal a day for the subnormal cases, in the same way we did it after the last war.

The American Red Cross, the American Relief for Czechoslovakia and the American Catholic Welfare Association are endeavoring to extend special feeding of children. But with all their efforts, no more than a third of the need is covered, for lack of supplies.

The Czechoslovak people are working hard at recovery. They are getting under control the serious inflation left by the Germans. Coal production is already back to normal. If climatic conditions continue to be favorable, their own food production will be much greater next year. Other industries are being repaired and put into production.

Remarks at Dinner of President Bierut

Mr. President:

M Y COLLEAGUES and I deeply appreciate not only the generous words which you have addressed to us but also the splendid hospitality which we have received from you and from the Polish people on every hand.

You have referred to the bonds which bind our two nations. There is, however, not alone the historical association of great men to which you have referred. Today, one-fifth of the Polish race live within the United States. And a stronger bond even than this is the sympathy of the American people for suffering, and their admiration for the gallantry of the Polish people.

We Americans had to fight but once for our independence. That war was fraught with hardship and heroism, which is a treasured tradition of the American people. But the Polish people have had to fight over and over again during a thousand years to attain their independence. If history teaches anything, it is that from the unquenchable vitality of the Polish race, Poland will rise again from her ashes.

Mr. President, you have referred to some of the great governmental, political and social problems which confront the Polish people. There may be differences in the thinking of the American people from that of the Polish Government on some subjects, but no matter how important these problems may be, the purpose of my Mission is solely the problem of food. Indeed, all differences shrink into immateriality in the face of the common hunger and the spectre of famine which overhangs the world. In this America has but one object and that is to save human life.

We have spent the day in close consultation with Polish officials and have heard reports from the Americans we have sent to Poland in advance of our visit, and other American experts here. There is no great difference as to the situation and the needs. And I would call your attention, Mr. President, to the fact that five of my colleagues on this journey were associated in the relief of Poland in 1919, so that we are not unfamiliar with the problem itself.

Mr. President, I can echo the sentiment you have expressed as to the imperative need of lasting peace in the world. After a great second World War, the nations are trying again to organize cooperation in the prevention of war. America is joining with full spirit in this organization. It is true we are separated from the old world, not only by huge distances, but by three hundred years of development of a new civilization. Yet twice in a lifetime we in America have been called upon to intervene with our military strength to secure the liberation of Europe, at huge sacrifices to ourselves. Twice in a lifetime we have been called upon to rescue the world from famine as a result of war. We know we cannot have peace in the presence of the spectre of famine. And we know we can only have peace by cooperation to prevent war.

And now may I propose a toast to the head of the Provisional Government of Poland, and to the gallantry, hopes and courage of the Polish people.

On the Food Situation in Poland

WARSAW

[March 30, 1946]

THIS is the worst situation we have seen so far in every respect. It is lightened only by the hope and gallantry of the Polish people. They are digging themselves out of the greatest physical, political, intellectual and moral destruction ever known. But my Mission has no part in political, economic or social matters. It is solely concerned with food.

Armies have four times swept over Poland, living on the country, and she had five years of German occupation. The population of new Poland, about twenty-four million, will be about eleven million less than old Poland, of which probably 5,000,000 were killed. A Polish woman remarked to me today, "We are weary of dying."

There has been enormous destruction of housing, amounting to 90 per cent in Warsaw alone. Most of the people in the destroyed areas are living in hovels without adequate clothing, furniture, or heat.

Compared to pre-war, the horses remaining are stated to be only 45 per cent; cattle, 33 per cent; sheep, 36 per cent; swine, 17 per cent; and they are mostly underfed. But of even more importance has been the intellectual destruction and physical weakening of the human beings.

The food situation has become sudden and heartbreaking due to miscalculations. The breadstuffs and potatoes in stock and enroute from overseas will theoretically last only until May 7th on a reduced ration. The bread ration is a theoretical average of seven ounces per day per person, and two cities, Crakow and Lodz, have already been without bread for three weeks at a time. The fat ration, when you can get it, is 16 ounces per month per person. The average caloric intake, including hospital inmates, is perhaps 1,500 (mostly starches), but inability to create effective distribution makes any estimate unreliable. Examination by American experts shows over 2,500,000 children are estimated to be terribly sub-normal from under-nourishment. Dairy products are practically unknown to the great majority of city children. Samplings indicate an infant mortality of 20 per cent per annum, with a huge increase of tuberculosis and other under-feeding diseases among all children and adolescents. There are 1,100,000 orphans and half-orphans. Five million children should have more food and more appropriate food at once. Children cannot wait for their reconstruction until some other time; their future is being made now. Unlike after the first World War, there has been no over-all organization to care for and rebuild the children. There are gallant efforts by Polish women in local areas, conducted under unbelievable difficulty. They are receiving some assistance from the American Red Cross and the American Catholic Welfare.

Added to all the other problems is the migration of some millions of Poles westward from the territory annexed by Russia, and the expulsion of Germans west from the territory annexed by Poland. Both migrations add to the already disorganized food situation.

It is a forbidding picture, but, with food until the next harvest, Poland can rise again from her ashes.

On Food Administration in Finland

HELSINKI

[April 1, 1946]

THE food administration in Finland is so efficient that our report can be made brief.

Her major supplies in sight to maintain the Government ration will be exhausted at the end of June. Finland is so far to the North that the harvest does not come in until the end of September. Part of this gap from June to September can be provided from the new harvest in countries farther South, but there is still a gap that must be filled at once from somewhere. The Government ration is very tight, and it must be supplemented from the free market, where prices are very high.

There are three groups in great distress. There is a deficient food supply in the lower-income groups of the cities. The second are 400,000 people in the areas devastated by the Germans and by battle. The third group is the 400,000 refugees from the areas transferred to Russia. Thus, there are, in addition to the lower-income group of the cities, 800,000 people in especial distress out of a total population of 3,800,000. Further provision of food outside the Government ration is urgently needed for these groups. The farm population look after themselves.

The situation among children is that priority in milk supplies are given to infants under two years of age. But there are in all groups about 500,000 children above this age, and adolescents who are badly undernourished. The usual diseases from undernourishment are serious among the children of these groups. The American Quakers, the Lutherans, the Red Cross, and UNRRA, are giving service to the children and adults in these distressed areas and the refugees. But it is insufficient. They need greater financial support and supplies. All this is besides provision to carry the major Government ration over the gap. Finland has a fine determination to help itself. The Finnish people are working to their utmost capacity.

The removal of the 400,000 people from the area transferred to Russia amounts to about twelve per cent of the whole population being re-settled among the remaining 3,400,000, of whom 400,000 in the devastated areas of Finland are in distress. This is a burden on a people already short of housing from destruction, and upon farms already small. It is a situation comparable to moving all of the people in the three Pacific Coast States onto the people East of the Rockies.

If the Finns are to be re-established to their place in the world, they must be helped, and quickly.

Emergency Conference on European Cereal Supplies

Address, London, England
[April 5, 1946]

I T IS an honor to be asked to address this Conference. The very character of the Conference is based on the knowledge that the few months until the next harvest are the most critical food period in all modern history. With the coming harvest, world food problems are by no means ended, but with favorable weather conditions, the situation after the harvest will be much easier. We shall have a breathing spell. The hungry wolf now at the door of the world should then go away. The next few months are the crux of the problem.

You may be interested in some impressions I have received as to the countries we have visited and others from which we have more information than is to be derived from documentary reports. In this mission, I have been accompanied by Dr. Fitz-Gerald, of the United States Department of Agriculture, and Messrs. Gibson, Tuck, Pate, and Galpin, officials of the relief in 1919.

The apprehensions which I entertained before beginning this journey have not decreased. They have increased. Hunger sits at the table thrice daily in hundreds of millions of homes. And the spectre of possible starvation haunts equally the halls of government and squalid hovels in the ruins of war.

The world uses the words "starvation" and "famine" very loosely. Some travelers glibly report there is no widespread death-dealing famine on the Continent of Europe. In modern civilization, whole nations do not lie down and die. The casual observers do not realize that famine would have already struck great groups and classes were it not for past overseas supplies, and that it is inevitable unless we land, for the next months, every ton of overseas food that we can summon. And nothing is more preposterous than the opinions of travelers on the Continent who live on black market food at prices out of reach of ninety-nine per cent of the people.

And let me say at once that paper reports do not convey the information or give the basis for conclusions that come from personal investigation on the spot. Only by personal contact with officials, and especially by intimate discussions with the leaders of the many different relief agencies who are working intimately among the people, can information be checked and cross-checked. Only by judgment upon this information on the spot by men experienced in food problems does the picture become clear.

I may say at once that I always distrust statistics in discussing problems of hunger. They convey little of the weight of human suffering that lies behind them. But there is no other way of painting the picture in its definite, and often grim, perspective.

The situation varies among all of the nations on the Continent. And it varies among groups within each country. There is some pressure on nearly every one of these twenty-two nations of 300,000,000 people from the Russian frontier to the English Channel. There are only four or five small nations, aggregating possibly 40,000,000 people, which can be said to have assured supplies until the next harvest.

We may particularize the problem still further. The bitter experience of centuries of war has instilled a squirrel-like instinct in the peasants of Europe to store for the protection of their own families. Thus, possibly one-third can take care of themselves—they are the "self-suppliers" of statistics. There are some exceptions to this rule in areas stricken with most unusual drought.

The major impact of shortages thus falls upon the city and industrial areas in the sixteen or seventeen nations in which there are over 170,000,000 people. The prevalence in many countries of black markets permits a small class, mostly by sacrifice of their savings, to provide supplementary food at prices prohibitive to the great mass of people. Some industrial groups, such as miners and other heavy workers, are receiving priorities in food in a desperate endeavor to maintain essential services. Thus, again the dangerous area narrows a few millions more.

However, the mainstay of the great city masses today is the government ration. The medial government ration in only a few of these nations exceeds 1,250 calories per day, and in over half the estimated city masses it does not exceed 1,000 calories. These masses, by various devices and some free commodities, secure some supplements. Indications are that the supplements range from 200 to 500 calories. When you define the words "starvation" and "famine," it might be well to set some caloric standards, considering that about 2,300 calories of balanced medial ration is regarded as the minimum for health. On any definition, millions are today at the danger level.

But even that is not the whole story. The stocks in hand and supplies en route with which to maintain the meagre government rations will not last, in many countries, beyond the end of May, and in some of them only to the end of April.

Nor is even this the whole story. The predominant diet of these city masses is very short of protein and fats. Adults can stand this for long stretches of time, but the effect upon children is disastrous. The first expression of famine is to be found among the children. Infant mortality in some cities exceeds 20 per cent a year. This is an indication of slow famine.

It would not be an immoderate estimate that from the Russian frontier to the Channel there are today twenty millions of children who are not only badly undernourished, but steadily developing tuberculosis, rickets, anemia, and other diseases of subnormal feeding. There may be a much larger number.

If Europe is to have a future, something must be done about

these children. Unless they are better fed, many will die and others will grow up with stunted bodies and distorted minds. They will furnish more malevolents in the world.

It is true that efforts are being made to aid the children. Some Governments are giving food to school children. There are priorities in dairy products for children in some nations, but even so, milk supplies in many cities are so meagre as to serve only to slow up the starvation of children. Some Governments are conducting feeding stations for under-school age. What I saw of it, and my information from all sources including voluntary charitable organizations, shows that all these efforts are pitifully limited because of the lack of proper supplies.

The American, British, Swiss and Swedish religious relief organizations, and Red Cross societies, are doing splendid work, but the efforts are limited. These agencies probably do not provide adequate food for more than 500,000 children altogether. They have only touched the fringes of the problem.

It is a matter of profound regret that the experience of the last World War was not followed and an effective organization set up to give one extra meal of 400 or 500 calories a day to all undernourished children and certain classes of mothers. Experience shows that the normal recuperative powers of children is such that, if not too far gone, a few months of food of the right kind could recover much of the losses of years of privation. There is abundant proof of this in the handling of ten to fifteen million subnormal children in this way in 1919 and 1920. Strong bodies and clear minds were created in the vast majority of those served.

The rehabilitation of children cannot wait. It cannot be postponed until some other day. They are not like a bridge or a factory. They lose ground every day that is lost. Already almost a year has been lost. The world cannot hate children, even of the enemy. Our children must live in the same world with them. Nor is this a question of vast quantities of food; such an extra meal a day would not involve the import of more than four thousand tons a month for every one million children.

It is not too late to expand this work at once, and it is imperative to prepare for its continuance over the next twelve months.

One of the major problems before you is the supplies for the basic governmental rations on the Continent. Their demands for the months until harvest aggregate possibly 5,000,000 tons of cereals. And fats are needed. Some of this burden of cereals is being carried by generous action of Russia. The supplies from the Western Hemisphere must also be divided with the United Kingdom and the Far East, where there is also desperate need.

The present visible supplies may be augmented by the conservation measures in the United States. They could be augmented if South America can be aided in their efforts to cooperate. But after all this effort, there is still a gap in full supplies. This can mean but one thing for importing nations: every nation must expect to tighten its belt. Every measure of self-help must be exhausted. The American people, under President Truman's leadership, have responded generously to the call for drastic reduction in their consumption of breadstuffs and fats. We shall scrape the bottom of the barrel.

I am impressed with the fact that there is not, nor has there been, a sufficiently effective over-all organization of world food since hostilities ceased. We do have the excellent work of the Combined Food Board in Washington, but they influence only a part of the surplus-producing countries. UNRRA, which is perhaps thought to serve such an over-all purpose, covers less than thirty per cent of the people from the Channel to the Russian border who are short of food. Whether nations buy their food or get it on charity, or from armies, they are drawing on the common stock and they are competing with each other for supplies.

Had such a central organization been really functioning in the world last September, with a realistic appraisal of European production, the crisis would have been realized then, instead of five months later. Larger supplies could have been had if both surplus and importing countries had taken more extensive steps earlier to conserve food. Some of the present suffering and physical degeneration would have been lessened. The outstanding need for the future is more effective coordination.

It is inconceivable that European agriculture will have made full recovery, even in the ground crops, with the harvest of 1946. The recovery of live stock will be slower than ground crops, and while the meat and fat situation should improve with good harvests, it will take two or three years, at least, for their recovery. The first voice of victory is the guns. But the first voice of peace is food. The world has organized to maintain peace. Surely it can organize to maintain life.

Gentlemen, the responsibility of saving human life rests heavily upon the world. We have emerged from a terrible era of killing of men, women and children. The world must look forward with hope, and the dawn of that hope can be made glorious by an era of saving of health and life.

On the World Food Crisis

Broadcast Over Mutual Broadcasting Company from Cairo, Egypt

[*April 19, 1946*]

THIS is our report and our recommendations upon the food crisis.

We have now surveyed the problem in seventeen nations, to determine the minimum amounts required to sustain life. We have indirectly established the position of four others. It has been possible to arrive quickly at sufficiently accurate conclusions through the advance work of my colleagues, the officials of our Government and of the various nations visited and those of the various relief organizations. Particularly do I mention the most able service of Dr. FitzGerald, of our own Department of Agriculture.

We have already reported upon many nations. The dimensions of the European part of the world food crisis as a whole can be quickly summed up. There are about 300 million people on the Continent of Europe from the Russian frontier to the English Channel. A few small countries on the Continent, comprising about 40 million people, have enough food to last until the next harvest. Of the other nations, about one-third of the remainder are farmers who are able largely to feed themselves. Thus, there are over 170 million people, mostly in towns and cities, of whom perhaps less than 10 per cent can support themselves from black markets and country relatives. The final remainder, of 150 million, mostly the lower-income groups, must have overseas supplies during the next four months if widespread famine is to be prevented.

Hunger has placed three words every hour of the day on the tongues of these 150 millions of people. The first is "bread." Bread has a reality as the symbol of life as never before in history. To reduce the bread ration is a symbol of calamity. It is now the symbol of the life of nations. The second word is "fats," for which there is an insatiable craving and physical need. The third word is "calories." That is the common denominator. Calories are only a partial yardstick of food, but that word has become everywhere the grim measure of the steps along the road from plenty to hunger and to starvation. Europe has become a vast involuntary experimental laboratory as to different levels of calories which the population are to have in their rations.

Do not forget that the caloric level of America is an average of about 3,200 per person per day. Britain has about 2,800. Experts say an average level of 2,200 calories is the minimum at which public health and progress can be maintained in a nation. There are thirteen countries where the city populations have an average intake of less than 1,900 calories. Of these, six countries are at or below the 1,500 caloric level. There are millions of people below 1,000 calories. Somewhere down these various levels starvation begins. And its immediate expression is the disease rate in children and in death rates of the infants and the old people.

In making our estimates of food which must be imported to the Continental countries from overseas, we have used the grim and dangerous base of about 1,500 calories, with less for young children and more for heavy workers. In this figure of 1,500 calories, we have included the domestic as well as the imported supplies and the unrationed food. At this level, we believe most of the adults could come through the short period of four months until the next harvest. They will, no doubt, be weakened morally and physically, and very susceptible to disease. It is a sad job to make such a base, for under it many of the children and the aged will fall by the wayside.

To provide this minimum to the next harvest, there must be loaded on ships for the Continent during each of the four months from the first of April to the end of July a total of at least 5,300,000 tons of cereals, 300,000 tons of fats, and an additional 100,000 tons of special food is urgently needed to restore subnormal children.

A few days ago I started a rough estimate that there are 20 million subnormal or diseased children on the Continent. My able and experienced colleague, Maurice Pate, who has gone to the bottom of this sole problem throughout Europe, insists that my estimate was too low. He points out that there are probably 11 millions of orphans and half-orphans alone. He also points out that the mortality among children under two is already over 25 per cent per annum in many cities. The reconstruction of the children is more precious than factories or bridges. They will determine the good or evil future of Europe.

The food supplied by UNRRA to the nations they serve has been an untold blessing. For various reasons, they do not cover much over 25 per cent of the total food problems of the Continent. They have recently received wholly inadequate supplies.

But Europe is not the only claimant on the world's food. Of cereals alone, the British want 1,500,000 tons shipped to them in these four months. And South Africa is demanding supplies. There are Latin-American countries which import large amounts of breadstuffs. Although we have not yet examined the situation in Asia, we know a very large amount of cereals are needed there.

After the most drastic scaling down, as closely as we can give a tentative estimate now, the total requirements of cereals alone for Europe and Asia during the next four months is a minimum of about 11 million tons. And, in addition, as much fats as can be secured.

As against this need, the grim fact is that in normal commercial supplies there is not much over 6 million tons available. The problem before us, if we would preserve millions of lives, is to make up this gap of 5 million tons of cereals. I believe this could be done by self-denial and cooperation of the people of the better-supplied nations in the world. There are seven substantial sources where these supplies can possibly come from. They are Canada, the United States, Britain, the Argentine, Russia, Australia and Siam.

To narrow this 5 million ton gap between supply and the minimum need to save life, I have six suggestions. I shall state them bluntly. With some experience in these matters, I say this is the only way by which millions of lives can be saved at this late date. At once let me say that these proposals are only my personal views. It is my duty to exhaust every possibility of saving these people. If there is criticism of the proposals, it should be directed to me alone. My suggestions are:

First: Our Government has asked our people to voluntarily reduce their consumption of wheat products by 40 per cent and fats by 20 per cent. My proposal is that our Government do as they did during the war and acquire enough of our wheat and its products to assure an export to the famine areas of an average of 1,100,000 tons per month during the months of April, May, June and July. This will effectively back up those consumers who are supporting the starving. It will make the conservation campaign effective beyond any doubt. We need similar action as to fats. In making these sacrifices of bread and fats, the American people have a right to expect other nations also to cooperate to the full.

Second: By the American program above, the American consumption of wheat products will be reduced to an equivalent of about 200 grams per person per day in European terms. European nations need more wheat bread than we do because they have less substitutes or supplemental food. I propose that all nations in Europe who now exceed a cereal ration equal to 300 grams of bread per person per day, should reduce it to 300 grams. This would, I know, be a burden to such countries as Britain, Holland, Denmark and Yugoslavia.

Third: I suggest to the British that as they are carrying about a million tons of breadstuffs in their pipeline and stocks, instead of one-half this amount before the war, they could release half a million tons to the starving.

Fourth: My next suggestion is to the Latin-American States. The largest part of the Argentine exports are going to Chile, Brazil and other neighboring countries. Other Latin-American States, such as Cuba and Mexico, are drawing large amounts of wheat and flour from the United States and Canada. If the United States, Canada and the Argentine would reduce these exports by 40 per cent during the next four months, and if these Latin-American states would cooperate by accepting this reduction, it would furnish most valuable assistance. Their sacrifice would be no greater than we are asking from the United States. It would be a translation into action of the eloquent appeal of His Holiness, Pope Pius XII, a few days ago.

Fifth: My next proposal is in respect to Russia. At the request of the Soviet Government, I organized and directed the relief of the great Russian famine of 1922-1923. America made a gift of over 3 million tons of food and overcame that famine. The Soviet Government expressed its warm appreciation to myself and my colleagues. I learned at that time of the sacrifice which millions of Russians made for their more helpless neighbors. I know full well the suffering of her people during this war. I am advised, however, that their food situation has somewhat improved since the war. She has been able to make available a generous supply of about 75,000 tons of grain per month to France. If her contribution to the general pool could be raised to 300,000 tons per month for each of the four months of the crisis, it would be a great human service.

By these methods, over 90 per cent of the gap between supply and minimum need of the famine areas would be met.

Sixth: I suggest that priority in supplies be given to the smaller liberated nations. They have suffered most. Their domestic resources are more limited than others. They comprise only 15 per cent of the whole European problem.

If these proposals were adopted, the United States would be furnishing to the famine areas about 44 per cent of the total; Canada about 20 per cent; the United Kingdom about 10 per cent; Australia about 10 per cent; the Argentine, through co-operation of other States, say 6 per cent; and Russia 12 per cent.

The burden will be very heavy upon the United States and we cannot do more. Europe and other countries must look to the other sources for the balance.

The current world crisis is unique among all crises in history. This crisis has a definite terminal date. That date is the arrival of the next harvest. It is, therefore, a short pull.

If every source of supplies will do its utmost, we can pull the world through this most dangerous crisis. The savings of these human lives is far more than an economic necessity to the recovery of the world. It is more than the only path to order, to stability and to peace. Such action marks the return of the lamp of compassion to the world. And that is a part of the moral and spiritual reconstruction of the world.

On the World Food Situation

Broadcast from Bombay, India
[April 24, 1946]

To the great radio audience:

I AM glad to have the opportunity of broadcasting to India and particularly to Australia. I shall give some summary of the world food situation, with emphasis upon the problems of India. And in so doing, I recall many happy years spent in Australia and in abiding admiration for her people and her institutions which I received from those happy times.

This acute phase of the world crisis in food will continue until the August-September harvest in the Northern Hemisphere. There are nations of about 500,000,000 people without enough food to manage until these harvests come in. Under instructions from President Truman, I and my colleagues have now covered over twenty countries in this survey. Subject to some possible revision on completion of our work, we now estimate that about 11,000,000 tons of cereals for human consumption are needed to barely maintain life over these four months. The apparent available commercial supplies within this period are only 6,000,000 tons. There will be an immense loss of life if this gap of 5,000,000 tons cannot be bridged. And the problem is not only to cover this cereal gap but also to provide fats and special food needed for subnormal children. Of these alone, there are probably 40,000,000 in Europe at this moment, to say nothing of Asia.

I have made some suggestions whereby with the cooperation of the United Kingdom, the United States, Canada, Australia,

Argentina, Siam and Russia, this gap of 5,000,000 tons of cereals can be mostly closed.

The enormity of the Indian problem can be shortly expressed. The total population of the provinces of India and Ceylon normally dependent upon imports, plus those provinces affected by the great drought, is about 240,000,000. Even after deducting certain localities which are self-supporting, other localities less affected, and the farmers who supply themselves, the number in jeopardy of life runs into tens of millions. Unless there can be a large and constant flow of overseas food, the loss of life will mount to numbers too horrible to contemplate. Due to able, careful administration, and drastic rationing, there is no stark starvation of the famine type in India yet. This is a job of prevention. Every ton of food received will lessen the loss of life from the gigantic danger which impends. It is a striking fact that whatever other differences there may be in India, there is complete unity in an endeavor to solve the famine problem.

The Indian Government officials estimate that they must have arrivals from overseas of wheat, rice or millet amounting to 315,000 tons in June, of which only about 100,000 tons are now en route. They estimate a minimum need of 441,000 tons in July and 522,000 tons in each of August and September. And there must, in addition, be supplies to Ceylon, Malaya, and some other deficient Indian Ocean areas.

It is difficult indeed to define the stages of more food shortage, of insufficient supplies to maintain health, of famine or starvation. Hunger has forced three words into every language every hour of the day. The first is "bread." Bread has a reality as the symbol of life as never before in history. The ration is now the symbol of order and hope of peace. To reduce the bread ration is a symbol of calamity. The second word is "fats," for which there is an insatiable craving and physical need. The third word is "calories." That is the common denominator. Calories are only a partial yardstick of food, but that word has become everywhere the grim measure of the steps along the road from plenty to hunger and to starvation. The world has become a vast involuntary experimental laboratory as to different levels of calories which the population are to have in their rations.

Australia has over 3,000 calories per person per day. Experts say an average level of 2,200 calories is the minimum at which public health and progress can be maintained in a nation. With the meagre supplies asked for by India, it is estimated that the stricken people will be receiving less than 1,200 calories daily per person, and that includes the ration of about twelve ounces of cereals per day per person. No one can say it is too much. Under such a regime, the adults can pull through a period of four months, but many of the children and the aged will drop by the way side through increased disease which is always the result of lowered vitality. However, the overseas supply necessary to maintain even this level of food is not yet in sight.

I have no right to address the Australian people on what further measures they could take to aid in this situation. But the critical jeopardy of millions of lives should be my justification.

I may recount that in the United States we have, by direct appeal and by Governmental action, undertaken to reduce our own wheat products consumption below five ounces per day per person. Our people, like Australians, eat a much smaller proportion of bread and have more substitute foods than most nations. In the famine areas of India the cereals ration of twelve ounces per day will constitute at least 80 per cent of their whole food intake. Most of the people in the southern famine areas of India live on rice. There is not a sufficient supply of rice. Wheat must be substituted. They eat it by boiling it, just as they do rice. Most of them cannot prepare wheat flour products; they do not know how, and they have no equipment to bake bread. They must have wheat grain; and the flour millers of the world should stand aside temporarily and allow shipment of the wheat grain itself.

There is another urgent help needed, from Australia. Supplies for the June and July requirements of India from North

America are too far away to arrive in these months. It would be an immense help if delivery of Australian supplies could be advanced to cover these critical months.

There is one meagre consolation in this tragic situation. The current world food crisis differs from political and military crises. This food crisis has a definite terminal date. That date is the arrival of the next harvest in the Northern Hemisphere. It is, therefore, a short, hard pull.

If every supplying country will do its utmost, and if we can have full cooperation everywhere, we can pull the world through these most dangerous months. The saving of these human lives is far more than an economic necessity to the recovery of the world. It is more than the only path to order, to stability, and to peace. Such action marks the relighting of the lamp of compassion on the earth. And that is a part of the normal and spiritual reconstruction of the world.

On Food Difficulties in India

BANGALORE
[April 26, 1946]

INDIAN Provinces containing about 230,000,000 people are involved in food difficulties. The enormity of the food problem can be expressed in numbers. This is the only way its dimensions can be demonstrated, but figures are a poor vehicle with which to convey the extent of the danger and the human misery involved.

The causes of her food difficulties come from three directions:

First, India normally imports considerable food supplies, especially from Burma. This source has been largely curtailed for this year.

Second, South India has suffered from a disastrous drought; and

Third, the standard of living of the great mass of Indian people has always been low and a marginal group has always been on the borderline of what we in America would regard as starvation.

After making all of the statistical deductions by way of certain local parts of the Provinces which are self-supporting, other localities less affected, the farmers who supply themselves, the remaining people in jeopardy of life runs into tens of millions unless they obtain additional food from outside the short areas. There has been drastic rationing of large sections in the deficit areas in order to lengthen the domestic supplies. Before the recent reduction in the ration, the calory content of the authorized ration, plus some supplements, probably amounted to less than 1,800 calories, mostly cereals. Now the ration has been reduced to about 1,400 calories daily per person, including such supplements as the mass of people can find. The intelligent use of rationing has prevented stark starvation of the widespread famine type familiar in India up to this time. However, we have today motored through parched districts in Mysore where even this ration has begun to break down. About two-thirds of the cereal ration is less nutritious ground nuts and cattle food.

If this were all of the story, the situation might be looked at as a great sea of misery awakening the world's sympathy, but not one of unparalleled potential tragedy. That tragedy lies in the fact that large districts cannot, without outside supplies, maintain even the present reduced ration for more than 30 to 90 days. Many districts are on the edge of the precipice. It is impossible to hazard what the death rate might be if there were no imports into the deficit areas. It would be too terrible to contemplate. Every ton of food imported into these areas will lessen the loss of life.

In order to carry the ration, including supplements, through on the present meagre basis of about 1,400 calories, the Indian Government officials estimate that they must have arrivals in the deficit areas of rice, wheat and millet of 346,000 tons in May, 315,000 tons in June, of 441,000 tons in July, of which only about 300,000 tons appear now to be actually enroute from overseas. Some of these supplies will not arrive until July. The government officials estimate a minimum need of 522,000 tons in each of August and September. They will need supplies beyond that date, but after that time the world supplies should be easier.

There has been great delay in the dispatches of ships, and there are areas which should have had major supplies long before now. We are informed that there is a surplus in Siam from the last harvest of somewhere between one million and a million and a half tons of rice. There have been interminable arguments ever since last October over acquiring it. A comparatively small amount has so far been shipped. This, however, is no time for recrimination, but rather to make recommendations to meet the situation. The first of these remedies lies in Siam. Siam is nearby; the rice could be quickly brought to the famine districts. If the Siamese rice could now be brought into play for the various nations in this quarter of the world, it would go a long way to solve the immediate problem.

Another source of possible immediate aid would be for Australia to expedite her program of shipments of wheat grain to India, and to begin at once deliveries on quantities which hitherto had been reserved for later in the year. It takes three weeks to bring food from Australia, whereas it will take the better part of six weeks to bring it from North America. Certainly it cannot arrive in time from North America, even if all the needs of India were available from that source, which they are not.

The Indian problem is a part of the whole world problem. We estimated that the world's need of cereals on April 1st to maintain the then rations was about 11,000,000 tons, while the total supply commercially available was only about 6,000,000 tons. From this gap of 5,000,000 tons, the potential danger in Europe parallels that in Asia. The American people, with extraordinary effort and with all their impulses to serve starving humanity, cannot make up but a portion of the gap of 5,000,000 tons. I made some suggestions at Cairo of equal effort from other nations to bridge the gap. In this emergency of the immediate weeks, the deficient areas in India must canvass every possible additional source, not only Australia and Siam, but by borrowing from Indian surplus areas for repayment later on; such sources as Burma, Iraq, and Java; and borrowing cereals from Egypt against the new crop. There needs to be more coordination of effort over the whole Indian Ocean area. When all this has been done, a large part of the solution must come from the Western Hemisphere.

The situation of these stricken people must appeal to every humane person in the world. It is not insoluble. But cooperation and devotion from every quarter is essential. The American people will stretch every resource to help.

On the Food Problem in
the Philippines

MANILA
[April 29, 1946]

IT IS a relief to find a nation whose food problem is not difficult to solve. The Philippine people could apparently get through until supplies are available from the 1946 harvest in the United States with some 50,000 to 60,000 tons of foodstuffs. The shortage of supplies in the world is that of the 1945 harvest.

The great need is rice, as the household equipment of the great countryside is not adapted to the use of wheat. The only possible rice supplies are those in Siam and Cochin-China. There is surplus rice in these countries. They need transport to get their rice to seaboard. We are about to negotiate the sale of trucks and other surplus war material to the Siamese and Indo-China Governments. It would seem to be a proper procedure for this equipment to be exchanged for rice for the Philippines. If this could be done, plus some comparatively modest amounts of wheatflour from the United States, the Philippine problem would be solved.

It is urgent that Filipinos be encouraged to cultivate all the catch crops which they can to help carry them over, even after supplies are available from the 1946 North American harvest.

On the Food Needs of China

SHANGHAI

[*May 3, 1946*]

THE food need of China is enormous. They have had
eight years' war destruction and agricultural degeneration, to which both drought and flood have now been
added. There are no adequate data upon which to accurately
compute the tonnage needs. In any event, they are greater than
the transportation facilities into the interior. These will be
fully taxed to distribute 200,000 tons of food a month during
the critical months from May to September.

With the absence of all adequate statistical services, due to
long disorganization, it is impossible to compute the numbers
of people in a critical condition, but no doubt they run into millions, as several Provinces are involved.

Both Chinese and foreign authorities report that some death
from starvation is in progress in interior Provinces and still
more from lowered resistance to epidemics. The death of
whole villages over wide areas has not yet taken place, but will
no doubt occur within a few weeks unless supplies have reached
the deficit spots.

Magnificent effort is being made, against great odds, by the
Chinese officials, the UNRRA staff, the American Naval and
Military authorities, our Government officials, and the various
religious and other relief organizations.

On the Japanese Food Supply

TOKYO

[*May 6, 1946*]

JAPAN must have some food imports. Without them, all Japan will be on a ration little better than that which the Germans gave to the Buchenwald and Belsen concentration camps. It is an impossible concept that the American flag fly over such a situation. Aside from any Christian spirit, food imports are required if the American boys here are not to be endangered by disorders and not involved in the sweep of epidemics that are inevitable from starvation. Moreover, unless there are food imports, the people will not have the stamina to work upon reconstruction or in the fields for the next crop.

The amounts required for Japan will not prejudice the supplies to China, India, the Philippines, or Korea—provided there is full cooperation in supply and distribution over the entire world during the crisis between now and the next harvest.

The whole situation would be greatly helped if Russia would release to China and Korea a part of the foodstuffs they have secured in Manchuria.

On the Effects of the Railroad Strike on World Famine

SAN FRANCISCO
[May 10, 1946]

THE world is faced with the greatest potential famine in all human history.

There is only from thirty to sixty days' supply of food in the famine area of twenty-seven different nations. They have five months to go until the next harvest.

The potentiality of the famine is so imminent that if this coal strike continues, hundreds of thousands will die in the famine areas from delayed food shipments.

If the railroad strike takes place, it will mean death to millions.

If the shipping strike takes place, it will be a holocaust.

Many of the men working in these industries are descended from countries where famine is on the doorstep.

I of course am unable to make a report on the situation abroad until I have seen President Truman. I shall deliver an address from Chicago next Friday evening, May 17th, in which I shall fully report on the whole world famine situation to the American people.

World Famine

Report to The President
[May 13, 1946]

Washington, D. C.

The President
The White House
Washington, D. C.

Dear Mr. President:

We have completed your instructions to survey the principal nations affected by food shortages which have resulted, or may result in widespread famine; to evaluate the minimum needs of those areas until the next harvest; and to discover such additional food resources as possible. In accordance with your instructions, we have also presented the American point of view on the food problem to these nations and the interest and understanding of our people in their plight. Finally, we have constantly advised American officials and the American public as to the situation as we found it.

We have traveled some 35,000 miles, visited twenty-two countries which have a deficiency of food, and informed ourselves of the situation in several others. The only country of large reported deficiency we did not visit was the Union of South Africa. We visited five self-sufficient or surplus countries and informed ourselves of the situation in other consequential surplus nations.

The dominant need of the world in this crisis is cereals, particularly wheat and rice. There is great need of fats and special food for children, but as cereals can furnish 85 per cent of an emergency diet, we considered cereal requirements were the first concern, and the best indicator. If a foundation of bread can be assured, and as much fats and children's food as possible, mass starvation can be prevented.

At the time of our departure, the Combined Food Board's estimate of the available cereal supplies from surplus countries showed a deficit as compared with stated requirements of 11,-000,000 tons, or 43 per cent.

REQUIREMENTS

We attach hereto (Table I) a country-by-country, month-by-month minimum program of required cereal imports to the deficit and famine areas from May 1st to September 30th.

These programs represent a considerable reduction from the hitherto stated requirements of the various nations. The amounts have in most cases been agreed upon by their governments. In the case of China, we regret to say our program is less than minimum need but is all, or more, than can be transported inland to the famine areas.

The totals are:

Europe	8,390,000	tons
Latin America	1,000,000	tons
South Africa and New Zealand	198,000	tons
Middle East	100,000	tons
Indian Ocean area	2,886,000	tons
Pacific Ocean area	1,910,000	tons
Total	14,484,000	tons

Of course, every country would be better off if more could be furnished.

SUPPLIES

We have found some increases in supplies possible during the crisis through development of certain new sources of supply; through additional loans of cereals from early-crop countries which may not themselves have annual surpluses; through substitution of other cereals for wheat and rice; and as a result of conservation up to this time.

Our estimate (Table II) of Probable Supplies as of May 1st to September 30th are:

From

United States	4,220,000	tons
Canada	2,300,000	tons
Australia	992,000	tons
United Kingdom	200,000	tons
Argentine	2,375,000	tons
Brazil	200,000	tons
Other Western Hemisphere States	40,000	tons
Burma	75,000	tons
Siam	195,000	tons
Russia to France	300,000	tons
Total	10,897,000	tons

Therefore the gap in supplies between May 1st and September 30th can be reduced to about 3,600,000 tons, as against an 11,000,000 tons gap in the earlier appraisals.

In addition to the above supplies there is a "possible" about 1,500,000 tons more, as indicated in Table III.

We are confident that if until the end of August, there can be further vigorous conservation in surplus countries, mainly wheats and fats, and more energetic cooperation between nations, the remaining deficit can be largely overcome. The cooperation of Russia and the Latin-American states would greatly aid in meeting the problem. If mass starvation is to be prevented it will require constant effort.

It is of interest to note that the quantities which are provided by UNRRA as charity comprise about 20 per cent of the world's cereal needs, whereas nations representing 80 per cent are being financed by the importing countries themselves. But the need in these latter is no less urgent.

You will recognize that these statements are estimates. They, however, comprise a reasonable basis upon which to formulate policies.

We wish to express our especial appreciation of the unfailing aid and courtesy of the Secretaries of Agriculture, State and War, and the American officials abroad. We are also deeply indebted to Generals George and Saville of the Air Transport Command, their efficient crews, and for their provisions for our comfort and safety.

Yours faithfully,

> HERBERT HOOVER.
> D. A. FITZGERALD.
> HUGH GIBSON.
> W. HALLAM TUCK.
> PERRIN C. GALPIN.
> MAURICE PATE.

Table I

CEREAL REQUIREMENTS *(including Rice)*

EUROPE

* Visited by the Mission

MINIMUM ARRIVALS REQUIRED DURING CRISIS PERIOD

(Loadings at seaboard about 30 days earlier)

Based on not to exceed 300 grams cereals per person per day

Country	Population millions	May	June	July	Aug.	Sept.	Total
			(thousands of tons)				
*France	39.1	350	350	350	350	350	1,750
*No. Africa	12.0	100	—	—	—	—	100
*Italy	41.5	225	225	225	100	—	775
*Switzerland	4.2	—	—	30	30	30	90
*Czechoslovakia	13.5	60	60	60	60	50	290
*Poland	23.5	85	85	85	85	—	340
*Finland	3.8	—	—	25	40	40	105
*Norway	3.0	—	—	—	30	30	60
*United Kingdom [1]	47.5	400	400	400	400	400	2,000
*Belgium	8.0	60	60	60	60	60	300
*Holland	9.0	—	—	—	—	80	80
*Germany:							
Am. Zone	18.0	50	50	50	65	60	275
Br. Zone	23.3	180	180	180	180	180	900
Fr. Zone	6.0	30	45	45	45	30	195
Russ. Zone							
				Data unknown			
*Austria	7.0	30	55	55	55	30	225
Spain	26.0	60	60	60	60	—	240
Portugal	8.0	30	30	30	30	—	120
Albania	1.0	5	5	5	5	—	20
*Yugoslavia	16.0	50	50	50	50	50	250
*Greece	7.5	55	55	55	55	55	275
EUROPEAN TOTALS	317.9	1,770	1,710	1,765	1,700	1,445	8,390

[1] Including indigenous supplies.

LATIN AMERICA

Country or province	Population millions	May	June	July	Aug.	Sept.	Total
Latin America		200	200	200	200	200	1,000

NEW ZEALAND AND SOUTH AFRICA

		May	June	July	Aug.	Sept.	Total
New Zealand		—	9	9	0	0	18
South Africa		40	40	40	30	30	180
		40	49	49	30	30	198

NEAR EAST

		May	June	July	Aug.	Sept.	Total
Near East		20	20	20	20	20	100

INDIAN OCEAN

(Loadings from Eastern Hemisphere 1 month and Western Hemisphere 2 months earlier)

Country or province	Population millions	May	June	July	Aug.	Sept.	Total
*India (Provinces affected)							
Bombay	22.0	—	55	85	95	95	330
Mysore	7.6	14	25	25	25	25	114
Madras	51.4	210	170	170	170	170	890
Tranv.	6.5	18	10	10	10	10	58
Cochin	1.5	8	7	7	7	7	36
Deccan	2.9	43	19	19	19	19	119
Behar	37.9	19	14	20	20	20	93
Un. Provinces	57.6	24	—	—	60	60	144
Bengal	61.3	—	—	90	106	106	302
Other		50	50	50	50	50	250
Ceylon	7.0	60	60	60	60	60	300
Malaya and Straits Settlements	3.6	50	50	50	50	50	250
TOTAL		496	460	586	672	672	2,886

PACIFIC OCEAN

*Philippines	14.0	12	12	12	12	12	60
*China [1]	220.0	120	150	200	200	200	870
*Japan	75.0	50	250	270	200	100	870
*Korea [2]	14.0	15	30	45	10	10	110
		197	442	527	422	322	1,910

GRAND TOTAL   2,723 2,881 3,147 3,044 2,689 14,484

SURPLUS OR SELF-SUFFICIENT COUNTRIES

Country	Population millions	May	June	July	Aug.	Sept.	Total
Sweden	6.2	—	—	—	—	—	—
Denmark	3.8	—	—	—	—	—	—
Hungary	9.1	—	—	—	—	—	—
Roumania	12.1	—	—	—	—	—	—
Bulgaria	6.5	—	—	—	—	—	—
Egypt	17.3	—	—	—	—	—	—
Iraq	4.0	—	—	—	—	—	—
Siam	14.0	—	—	—	—	—	—
TOTAL	73.0	—	—	—	—	—	—

[1] Utmost capacity of inland transportation.
[2] American zone.

TABLE II
POSSIBLE WORLD CEREAL SUPPLIES FROM SURPLUS AREAS

May 1st to September 30th
(000 tons)

	Second Quarter Loadings (April, May, June)			Loadings in July and August			Total
	Wheat	Coarse grains	Rice	Wheat	Coarse grains	Rice	
U. S. A.	2,200	500	20	1,400	100	—	4,220
Canada	1,650	150	—	400	100	—	2,300
Australia	700	—	17	275	—	—	992
United Kingdom	200	—	—	—	—	—	200
Argentine	500	800	—	275	800	—	2,375
Brazil	—	50	60	—	50	40	200
Other Western Hemisphere States	—	—	40	—	—	—	40
Burma	—	—	40	—	—	35	75
Siam	—	—	75	—	—	120	195
Russia to France	150	—	—	150	—	—	300
	5,400	1,500	252	2,500	1,050	195	10,897

GRAND TOTAL
Wheat   7,900
Coarse grains   2,550
Rice   447
          10,897

TABLE III
FURTHER SUPPLIES POSSIBLE

	Second Quarter Loadings (April, May, June)			Loadings in July and August			Total	Remarks
	Wheat	Coarse grains	Rice	Wheat	Coarse grains	Rice		
Indo-China	—	—	50	—	—	—	50	
Iraq	—	125	—	—	100	—	225	
India	—	—	—	—	200	—	200	Surplus Provinces
Punjab and Sind	100	—	—	100	—	—	200	Could be borrowed
Egypt	30	—	10	50	—	25	115	Could be borrowed
United Kingdom	300	—	—	—	—	—	300	Released Stocks
Russia to France	75	—	—	—	—	—	75	
Siam	—	—	—	—	—	200	200	
	505	125	60	150	300	225	1,365	
Iraq (dates)							140	
							1,505	

TABLE IV
PROVISIONAL BALANCE SHEET OF WORLD REQUIREMENTS AND SUPPLIES
(000 tons)

MINIMUM CEREAL REQUIREMENTS

Europe	8,390	
Latin America	1,000	
Southern British Empire	198	
Middle East	100	
Indian Ocean	2,886	
Pacific Ocean	1,910	
		14,484

CEREAL SUPPLIES PROBABLE

April-May-June Loadings	7,202	
July-August Loadings	3,695	
		10,897

DEFICIT PROBABLE 3,587 tons or 24 percent

Further possible cereal supplies 1,505

TABLE V

COMPARISON OF THE COMBINED FOOD BOARD BALANCE SHEET OF MARCH 1, 1946 (retrospective to January 1, 1946) AND HOOVER MISSION BALANCE SHEET AS OF MAY 1, 1946

(000 tons)

	Stated Requirements	Estimated Supplies	Deficit	Deficit %
Combined Food Board				
Jan. 1—Sept. 1	25,900	14,900	11,000	42.5%
Shipments to May 1	7,000	7,000		
Original Balance as at May 1	18,900	7,900	11,000	58%
As Revised by Hoover Mission:				
May 1—Sept. 1	14,484	10,900	3,587	24%
	—4,000	+3,000	—7,413	

Thus, the Requirements were revised downward by 4,000,000 tons and the Supplies revised upward, through new sources developed, effect of conservation, drafts on earlier crops in some countries, etc., 3,000,000 tons.

The estimated gap as of May 1st . . . . 3,600,000 tons

World Famine Situation

Address under auspices Famine Emergency Committee
Sherman Hotel, Chicago
[*May 17, 1946*]

THIS is my report to the American people upon the world famine situation. Three weeks ago I broadcasted from Cairo our report upon the situation in Europe. Since then we have examined the food problems in Egypt, Iraq, India, Siam, the Philippines, China, Korea and Japan, thus compassing most of Asia.

I can therefore now consolidate our findings in twenty-five countries which we visited and upon several more upon which we have received competent information.

At the request of President Truman I have acted as a sort of Food Ambassador to determine needs; to discover possible further sources of supplies; and to coordinate the world's effort to master this danger to the lives of millions. Beyond this, it has been my duty to represent the solicitude of the American people and their desire to aid.

Along the 35,000 miles we have traveled, I have seen with my own eyes the grimmest spectre of famine in all the history of the world.

Of the Four Horsemen of the Apocalypse, the one named War has gone—at least for a while. But Famine, Pestilence and Death are still charging over the earth. And the modern world has added four more to this evil brigade. Their names are Destruction, Drought, Fear and Revolution. This crisis is not alone due to war destruction of agriculture. On the top of that calamity has been piled drought in the Mediterranean, drought in India, drought in China and partial drought in South Africa and the Argentine. Never have so many evil Horsemen come all at one time.

Hunger hangs over the homes of more than 800,000,000 people—over one-third of the people of the earth. Hunger is a silent visitor who comes like a shadow. He sits beside every anxious mother three times each day. He brings not alone suffering and sorrow, but fear and terror. He carries disorder and the paralysis of government, and even its downfall. He is more destructive than armies, not only in human life but in morals. All of the values of right living melt before his invasions, and every gain of civilization crumbles. But we can save these people from the worst, if we will.

In our Mission through Europe, I have had the devoted co-operation of my six colleagues, all of them with long experience in famines. We secured independent investigations in advance of coming; we consulted at length with the heads of state and with the food and agricultural experts of each government; we checked and cross-checked all information with American officials in those countries; we have checked it again with the Relief organizations of many nationalities who are working closely with the stricken peoples. And above all, my colleagues and I have gone into the byways to see for ourselves. I am confident our conclusions are close to reality.

On this journey I have seen much which I could criticize as to the management of the famine relief. I criticized such matters to many officials in the world frankly. I could criticize them bitterly. But, after every boiling of inward indignation at men and at nations, I come back again and again to the fact that millions are in grave danger of starvation. To explode into public criticism in this crisis would only weaken the amount of support and diminish the food they will receive. Criticism can wait for history. I only want to record that all has not been perfect in the world that I have witnessed. It all adds emphasis to the fact that today the vital need is unity and cooperation *now*, so that we may master this crisis.

In appraising the world situation, I could give you reams of figures of rations, of calories, of tons of this and that, for every country and each district. I could give you their stocks of foods on hand, in transit, and the further need of each famine area. I could give it by the month, or for the crisis. I could give the time required for ship transport with details of port, railroad and truck capacities for distribution. This sort of detailed information would convey little to you, but it is full of meaning in the lives of men, women and children to my colleagues and myself. For in these figures lurks the certainty of hunger to hundreds of millions, and even the spectre of mass starvation before this crisis is passed. Rather than such details, time requires that I give you a global picture, in the hope that it will convey to you the gravity of the situation, and the need for our utmost further effort.

I have said before that calories are the yardstick of hunger, of starvation, of famine, and finally death. And I may remind you that an average of 2,200 calories per person per day is the minimum in a nation for healthy human beings. And do remember that we Americans, the British, the Canadians, the Australians, the Swedes, the Argentinians, and most of the Western Hemisphere are consuming over 2,900 calories per day right now. If these 800,000,000 people should receive no more relief, and if we assume that their own remaining resources could be evenly distributed, which they could not, the measure of their hunger with the caloric yardstick is about as follows:

About 100,000,000 people would be reduced to the 2,000 calory level.

About 100,000,000 more people would be reduced to an 1,800 calory level.

About 150,000,000 more would be reduced to an 1,500 calory level.

About 150,000,000 more would be reduced to an 1,200 calory level; and

About 300,000,000 more would be reduced to a 900 calory level, or below—and that is slow death.

As we descend this scale, we move step by step from the stage of hunger to the stage of disease and epidemics, to the stage of public disorder, to the stage of starvation of all but the strongest, and finally, at less than 900 calories we come to mass starvation. The Nazis at Buchenwald and Belsen gave almost that amount to their prisoners. But long before a population is reduced to these lower levels, government would break down.

All this sounds like an engineering formula. It is; but it is a formula which means life and hope to nations. At the best we can do, it means gnawing hunger to millions, but it is not mass starvation.

We must prevent the descent to these lower levels. Reconstruction and peace in the world would go up in the flames of chaos if we fail.

The transcendent question is the available overseas supplies with which to fulfill this formula. And I shall discuss breadstuffs only, for they are the symbols of life and hope. The problem of fats is no less urgent, but I will not burden your memories with more figures than necessary. And in breadstuffs I include all human food cereals that are available.

We have two sources of breadstuffs supply for this crisis— the residues of the 1945 harvest in the surplus countries, and the earlier part of the coming harvests of 1946. The harvest of some countries comes in June, others as late as October, and some supplies from the new harvest can be available to the countries of late harvests. If the present harvest prospects continue favorable, relief will come to the world within a few months. By September new supplies should be available and the immediate crisis will ease.

In March last, the Combined Food Board in Washington made an estimate of the amount of food needed by all the deficit nations for the first six months of 1946, and of supplies available from the food-surplus nations. These estimates of need were based upon the requirements as stated by the nations who must have overseas supplies. Adding in estimates of the need between June and the fall harvest, the total requirements of cereals were listed at, roughly, 26,000,000 tons. For the same period supplies were estimated at 15,000,000 tons. Thus, there was an unbridgeable gap of 11,000,000 tons, or nearly 43 per cent. And that would be a calory level below human endurance. That gap of 11,000,000 tons spells death to millions.

During these past months shipments have been moving, and mass starvation has so far been prevented. Our Mission examined the stocks now in the hands of each country and the amounts of their own production that could be expected. We measured the needs of each nation on a drastic caloric basis such as would pull them through, would prevent mass starvation, would maintain order and economic life. We kept the 1,500-1,800 calory bedrock figure always in mind. Most of the nations we visited joined earnestly with us in working out the very minimum they could do with, as they all realize the desperation of other nations.

The net of these drastic revisions was to reduce the total world requirements of breadstuffs by about 4,000,000 tons. By developing some new sources, by substitution of other cereals, by shifting between early and late harvests, by our sacrifices in America and by spreading sacrifice into other surplus areas, we estimate supplies for the hungry will be increased by a minimum of about 3,000,000 tons. Thus, the gap has been decreased from 11,000,000 tons to 3,600,000 tons. But the gap is still there—and it is a tragic gap.

I can illustrate how tragic that gap still is. It equals the whole amount necessary to save 40,000,000 people. We would, of course, not concentrate the shortage on one nation but if we spread it over all, the results are about the same. There are Americans who believe it right, and a duty, to feed women and children even of a surrendered enemy. No one is the enemy of children. There are others who believe that the only hope of a peaceful world is to save the enemy peoples from starvation and thus start building them into peaceful, cooperative peoples. There are others who, remembering the immeasurable crimes the enemy has committed against all mankind, believe in "an eye for an eye," a "tooth for a tooth." To these, let me say that to keep five hundred thousand American boys in garrison among starving women and children is unthinkable. It is impossible because, being Americans, they will share their own rations with hungry children; it is impossible because hunger brings the total destruction of all morals; it is impossible because of the danger to American boys of sweeping infectious diseases, which rise from famine. It is unthinkable because we do not want our boys machine-gunning famished rioters. It is unthinkable because we do not want the American flag flying over nation-wide Buchenwalds.

And what of the children in Europe?

This 1,500 calory bottom level is dreadfully hard on children. It is hard because a larger portion of the average ration must go to heavy workers if essential services be kept going. While this diet, which is as much as 85 per cent bread and the balance a little fat, sugar and vegetables, will pull adults through, it is not adapted to children. Several nations give them priority in what little dairy supplies there are; extra food is given in some schools; and the charitable agencies are doing the best they can. But in all, they are touching only the fringe of the problem. The proof is an annual infant mortality rate as high as 200 per 1000 among children under one year in many cities. The further proof is that there are somewhere from 20 to 30 million physically subnormal children on the Continent. After the war in 1919-1920, we gave a good extra meal a day, of 500 or 600 calories of restorative food, to 10,-000,000 children. I deplore that this special aid for children has had no counterpart through a wide-spread organization set-up after this war. Civilization marches forward upon the feet of healthy children. It is not too late to stop this most costly retreat and its debacle of endless evil.

Much the same could be said of tens of millions of children in Asia. There many millions of these children have been falling far short of full life since long before this famine. And they are harder to reach and help because of age-old rooted customs.

Our Mission has stimulated some action for children, both in Europe and Asia. I have already proposed not alone a systematic handling of this problem of sub-normal children, but a drastic reorganization of the world's food administration for the next harvest year. It is a primary job for the United Nations Organization if peace and good will are to be re-established on earth.

UNRRA, with its earnest staff, attends to about 20 per cent of the world's food needs. Their supply is by charity, of which the vast majority comes from America. But great as this work is, 80 per cent of the problem is not charity—it is the furnishing of supplies which people can buy, yet they are just as hungry as the destitute.

Before closing, I should pay tribute to my colleagues on this journey, and to the great army of men and women in every nation over the world who are working unceasingly to save these millions of lives. The volunteer organizations of the religious bodies, of the Red Cross of many nations, are in the field, unceasingly doing their best—but they can remedy only a fraction of the suffering.

There are some hopes of further decreasing this gap of 3,600,000 tons.

First: Still more intensive conservation of breadstuffs and fats in North America. Before I went on this journey, we asked the American people to reduce their consumption of wheat products to two pounds per week per person and to cut their purchases of fats by 20 per cent. Hundreds of thousands of families have responded by cutting out wheat products all together. Public eating places in many cities have cooperated. I regret to say there are too many who have not cooperated with some hungry human being. I earnestly hope that every American will remember that an invisible guest sits with him at every meal.

Second: We have need that every farmer bring every grain of cereal to market.

We are seeking for still further cooperation in other nations. The Latin-American states have responded to our appeals and to those of Pope Pius XII for cooperation. At President Truman's request, I shall visit these governments to consult with them on measures of coordination of our efforts.

If we can succeed in persuading every man and woman, every nation to do their utmost, we shall master this famine. And we shall save the lives of hundreds of millions from the greatest jeopardy in all the history of mankind. We shall have saved infinite suffering.

I was asked by the President to undertake this work in a purely advisory capacity and with the further journey to the Latin-American states, my service ends. The responsibilities of administration of the programs I have outlined lie with our officials. I bespeak for them the full support of all Americans in their efforts to meet this terrible world crisis.

In conclusion, do I need to reinforce this report with more urging to do your utmost? I may repeat again what I said three weeks ago from Cairo: "If every source of supplies will do its utmost, we can pull the world through this most dangerous crisis. The saving of these human lives is far more than an economic necessity to the recovery of the world. It is more than the only path to order, to stability and to peace. Such action marks the return of the lamp of compassion to the earth. And that is a part of the moral and spiritual reconstruction of the world."

A New World Food Organization Needed

Address before the Food and Agricultural Organization of the United Nations

WASHINGTON, D. C.

[May 20, 1946]

I HAVE been asked to present to you my views upon world food organization for the next harvest year. There should be drastic reorganization. A new set-up should take over on September first next, when this immediate world crisis shall have passed. We can hope for some breathing spell from the tensity of the present situation at that time. What the final authority of such an organization should be and what methods it shall use cannot be determined until we see more clearly the food outlook for the next harvest year. We will know what the situation is for the Northern Hemisphere by September 1st. But the broad lines of such organization can be determined at once.

Up to date the climatic conditions for the next harvest appear fairly favorable. If these conditions continue favorable it should be a more plentiful year than the harvest year through which we are now passing. We have to remember that the present crisis was not all due to the war degeneration of agriculture. It was partially due to the destruction and looting of food, and it was also due to the unprecedented combination of droughts in the Mediterranean, India, China and a partial drought in the Argentine and South Africa.

It would be fortunate, however, if those states of Europe, torn by major military operations, should in the coming harvest produce a 75 per cent ground crop. I need not recite the effect of shortage of fertilizers, farm machinery and man power which will affect the coming harvest. These deficiencies will, except for some unusual climatic blessing, seriously affect the production. In animal products it will be a still slower recovery than cereals because of the war destruction of herds in many countries and a probable continued shortage of feed. But even with a 75 per cent ground crop and the absence of droughts, it will be a tight year in world totals of cereals and fats.

For all these reasons it is necessary now to begin some more effective world organization to take the place of present improvisations. I am not here going to criticize the world food policies of the past year. But they must have vigorous reorganization if we would avoid another crisis like that which we are now in. As I have said, how elaborate that organization must be will depend of course upon the volume of resources from the coming harvest.

But in any case, certain major suggestions are warranted for immediate consideration:

1. That a new organization be created now under the auspices of the United Nations Security Council, or better still under your committee. For convenience, I will refer to this organization as the United Nations Food Administration.

2. That a single food administrator be appointed with a small advisory committee. That the advisory committee should in majority represent the surplus food producing nations as they will have to furnish the supplies.

3. That under the United Nations Food Administration certain regional organizations be set up, say one for Europe, including North Africa, one for the Far East, one for South America, and one for the Indian Ocean area, which should include Australia, New Zealand and South Africa.

4. That this agency serve only during the period of food scarcity and agricultural reconstruction from the war.

5. That this agency should absorb from September 1st, the

food and agricultural activities of UNRRA, which covers only 20 per cent of the present world problems. Director General LaGuardia favors such a course. The new administration should incorporate also the combined food board, and all other international agencies connected with food and agricultural reconstruction.

6. That it be the purpose of the United Nations Food Administration to return to normal commerce the food, fertilizer and farm supply business of the world with all speed possible. Commerce will secure more economical distribution; it will serve with far more assurance and efficiency to farmers, merchants and consumers than governments. Moreover, the world must quit charity as a basis of widespread food distribution. I cannot too strongly emphasize that charitable distribution is hugely wasteful and inefficient. Charity should be organized separately. Nations should from September 1st forward finance their own food purchases by other means than charity.

7. That the United Nations Food Administration should have by agreement among the supply nations the direction of the destination of some marginal quantity of food so that it can fill in any neglected chinks of commerce. What that percentage may be can be estimated when we know the amount of the world's food resources.

8. That this agency should be empowered to advise nations on measures of conservation, on voluntary relief activities, on stimulation of the production of fertilizers, farm machinery and other materials of agricultural reconstruction.

9. Special feeding and medical care of physically subnormal children should be organized systematically and should be the sole charitable contribution of governments. That is the most needed reconstruction effort in the world. It does not call for large figures.

The primary purpose of the United Nations is to give security and peace to the world. Effective distribution of food during scarcity and the reconstruction of agriculture, and above all, the reconstruction of human beings is essential to order and peace of the world. The first voice of war is the guns—but the final voice in making peace is food.

On Effect of the Railroad Strike on Relief to Famine Areas

Press Statement, Washington, D. C.
[May 25, 1946]

THE power over food or no food to half of the people in the United States and hundreds of millions in famine areas has now been taken over by half a dozen men who have never been elected to that power by the American people. I hope they realize that our own cities and all famine areas have less than a month's food reserves. While American cities have some reserves, most famine areas have none. Every delayed ship costs the lives of some human beings.

The Mission to Determine Needs of the Famine Areas

MEXICO, D. F.

[May 28, 1946]

TO CLARIFY my mission, I may say that during the past two months I have visited some twenty-five different nations at the request of President Truman. The purpose of the mission has been to determine the needs of the famine areas in the world and the volume of supplies available from surplus food countries; to secure coordination and cooperation in overcoming this, the worst famine in all history.

I am not an official of UNRRA. That institution mostly looks after the nations which are unable to pay for their supplies. These constitute about 20 per cent of the world famine needs. The other 80 per cent pay for their food, but they have need of it just as much as the UNRRA countries. My mission is concerned with the whole world situation, of which UNRRA is of course an important part, and I am deeply interested in that organization, as well as the other famine areas, securing the supplies they need.

There are about 800,000,000 people affected by the famine, or about one-third of the whole population of the world. The famine is now in its most acute stage, and this stage will last until about September, when the harvests in the Northern Hemisphere will arrive. After that there will be a breathing spell, although a shortage will continue in many countries.

There is a large deficit in the supplies as yet available for the famine areas, and unless we can by extra effort overcome this deficit, the death of hundreds of thousands of people is inevitable. It is our hope, however, that by devising further expedients and stimulating further supplies, it may be possible still further to reduce this gap. And a great part of the burden of providing these supplies falls upon the Western Hemisphere.

Our success in securing supplies will be measured largely by the degree of collaboration to be found among the countries in a position to help. Mexico is on a balanced food basis between exports and imports of food. She exports large amounts of meat in the form of cattle and some pulses, and requires the import of some margins of cereals, fats and sugars. The shortage in these commodities is particularly acute, but there should be no difficulty in the exchange of conservatively-established needs.

I have been particularly pleased to have the opportunity of discussing the world aspects of the situation with President Avila Camacho and the various Ministers of the Mexican Government. I have been gratified to find among them such a high conception of the international aspects of the problem and the need for world-wide collaboration. Mexican leadership and Mexican moral support are of infinite value in the task with which I am concerned.

On World Famine

BOGOTA, COLOMBIA
[May 31, 1946]

URING the past two months, I have visited some twenty-five different nations at the request of President Truman. The purpose of the mission has been to determine the needs of the famine areas in the world and the volume of supplies available from surplus food countries; to secure coordination and cooperation in overcoming this, the worst famine in all history.

There are about 800,000,000 people affected by the famine, or about one-third of the whole population of the world. The famine is now in its most acute stage, and this stage will last until about September, when the harvests in the Northern Hemisphere will arrive. After that there will be a breathing spell, although a shortage will continue in many countries.

Of these 800,000,000, about 300,000,000 will be reduced to complete mass starvation if we fail in our overseas supplies to them during the next four months.

There is a large deficit in the supplies as yet available for the famine areas, and unless we can by extra effort overcome this deficit, the death of hundreds of thousands of people is inevitable. It is our hope, however, that by devising further expedients and stimulating further supplies, it may be possible still further to reduce this gap. And a great part of the burden of providing these supplies falls upon the Western Hemisphere.

Our success in securing supplies will be measured largely by the degree of collaboration to be found among the countries in a position to help. Colombia is on a balanced food basis between exports and imports of food. She exports large amounts of meat in the form of cattle and large amounts of coffee, and requires the import of some margins of cereals, fats and sugars. The shortage in these commodities is particularly acute.

The people in the United States have reduced their consumption of breadstuffs nearly fifty per cent and their consumption of fats twenty-five per cent, in order to share with these starving millions.

I have been particularly pleased to have the opportunity of discussing the world aspects of the situation with the President of Colombia and the various officials of the Colombian Government. I have been gratified to find among them such a high conception of the international aspects of the problem and the need for world-wide collaboration. Colombian leadership and Colombian moral support are of infinite value in the task with which I am concerned.

On the Food Mission

QUITO, ECUADOR

[June 1, 1946]

M Y MISSION to Ecuador is only to learn the food requirements and resources of the country, and to inform the people of Ecuador of the famine crisis now raging in the world.

Any decision as to the purchase of the 32,000 tons of rice now offered by Ecuador must be made by Director-General LaGuardia, of UNRRA, or some Government. I have no authority in these matters.

I am indeed grateful for the sympathetic reception that I have received and the full information given to me by the officials here.

On the World Famine Crisis

Address at Luncheon given by the President of Peru
at Lima
[June 2, 1946]

Mr. President and gentlemen of Peru:

I AM deeply affected by the warmth and cordiality of your welcome and the welcome I have received from the people of Peru for a second time. I have thought that perhaps before proposing your good health and the prosperity of the Peruvian people, I might try to paint to you some picture of the problem with which the world is confronted during the next four months until the harvests in the Northern Hemisphere, when there will be more supplies.

And in trying to paint that picture, I am constantly forced back to the use of figures, although figures fail to convey the suffering which these quantities involve.

This world crisis appeared last March. At that time, President Truman did me the honor to ask for my collaboration in the great crisis that faced mankind. As my first duty, I have journeyed over the world to evaluate the minimum needs of the great famine areas and to discover such additional food resources as possible. I have also endeavored to coordinate and bring about as great a solidarity as possible of the nations to meet this crisis. I was more than glad to undertake this effort, in order to contribute what experience I had gained as the head of the organization which fought the great famine after the first World War. But more than all that, especially did I desire that in this tremendous crisis of human life, there should be a demonstration to my countrymen that, no matter what our other differences in views might be in our opposite political parties, there could be no division of effort in the problem which revolved around the saving of human life, and of civilization itself.

I will not recite to you the names of the twenty-six countries which I have now visited in the space of a little more than sixty days and in traveling over 40,000 miles. In each of these major countries of Europe and Asia, I have been received with the utmost consideration. We have had the cooperation of most of the officials in these nations in the face of need for a common front against the great peril which confronts the world. In coming to South America, I am endeavoring to complete this, the first task of the battle against famine.

Of the Four Horsemen of the Apocalypse, the one named War has gone—at least for a while. But Famine, Pestilence and Death are still charging over the earth. And the modern world has added four more to this evil brigade. Their names are Destruction, Drought, Fear, and Revolution. This crisis is not alone due to war destruction of agriculture. On top of that calamity has been piled the plundering by armies of the last harvests. And to this immensity of misery has been added drought—drought in the Mediterranean, drought in India, drought in China, and partial drought in South Africa and the Argentine. Never before have so many evil Horsemen come all at one time.

Hunger today hangs over the homes of more than 800,000,-000 people—over one-third of the people of the world. Hunger is more than privation to some individual. He is a silent visitor who comes like a shadow. He sits beside every anxious mother three times each day. He brings not alone suffering and sorrow, but fear and terror in cities and whole nations. He carries disorder and the paralysis of government, and even its downfall. He is more destructive than armies, not only in human life but in morals. All of the values of right living melt before his invasions, and every gain of civilization crumbles.

With my own eyes I witnessed the sufferings of the millions of people in many nations. I have witnessed human beings striving to live on a ration of only two cupfuls of grain for each of them once a day.

Thus, hunger sits at the table thrice daily in these hundreds of millions of homes. And the spectre of possible starvation haunts equally the halls of government and squalid hovels in the ruins of war. It haunts governments because the failure of food supplies spells the breakdown of the whole political and social order—of civilization itself.

Mr. President, we use loosely the terms of "famine", "starvation", and "hunger". Today, we are not alone faced with hunger, but we are faced with the problem of mass starvation. And by that term I mean whole villages—whole cities—and even whole nations—might be condemned to death did we not make our every effort. So far, we have prevented mass starvation.

And hunger has placed three words every hour of the day on the tongues of these 150 millions of people. The first is "bread." Bread has a reality as the symbol of life as never before in history. To reduce the great ration is a symbol of calamity. It is now the symbol of the life of nations. The second word is "fats", for which there is an insatiable craving and physical need. The third word is "calories". That is the common denominator. Calories are only a partial yardstick of food, but that word has become everywhere the grim measure of the steps along the road from plenty to hunger and to starvation.

And may I remind you that an average of 2,200 calories per person per day is the minimum in a nation for healthy human beings. If these 800,000,000 people should receive no more relief, and if we assume that their own remaining resources could be evenly distributed, which they could not, the measure of their hunger with the caloric yardstick is about as follows:

About 100,000,000 people would be reduced to the 2,000 calory level.

About 100,000,000 more people would be reduced to an 1,800 calory level.

About 150,000,000 more would be reduced to a 1,500 calory level.

About 150,000,000 more would be reduced to a 1,200 calory level; and

About 300,000,000 more would be reduced to a 900 calory level, or below—and that is slow death.

As we descend this scale, we move step by step from the stage of hunger to the stage of disease and epidemics, to the stage of public disorder, to the stage of starvation of all but the strongest, and finally, at less than 900 calories we come to mass starvation. The Nazis at Buchenwald and Belsen gave almost that amount to their prisoners. But long before a population is reduced to these lower levels, government would break down.

In March last, the Combined Food Board in Washington made an estimate of the amount of food needed by all the deficit nations for the first six months of 1946, and of supplies available from the food-surplus nations. These estimates of need were based upon the requirements as stated by the nations who must have overseas supplies. Thus, there was an unbridgeable gap of 11,000,000 tons of breadstuffs, or nearly 43 per cent. And that would be a calory level below human endurance. That gap of 11,000,000 tons spells death to millions. And, besides, we were short 2,000,000 tons of fats.

Our Mission examined the stocks now in the hands of each country and the amounts of their own production that could be expected. We measured the needs of each nation on a drastic caloric basis such as would pull them through, would prevent mass starvation, would maintain order and economic life.

The net results of these drastic reductions in some nations and newly-developed supplies was to reduce this gap to about 3,600,000 tons.

But the gap is still there—and it is a tragic gap.

I can illustrate how tragic that gap still is. It equals the whole amount necessary to save 40,000,000 people. We would, of course, not concentrate the shortages on one nation but if we spread it over all, the results are about the same.

There is a phase of this problem which causes infinite anxiety in the minds of all those who understand it. The world has developed an art in the rationing of peoples. Where it is necessary to reduce the food consumption of people by thirty or forty per cent, it can only be done if the government of that country takes possession of all the supplies from the farms, from the merchants, and from overseas imports. In that case, governments, as is the case in all those in Europe and many in Asia, establish distribution points where the people may come with their ration cards. These measures of direct governmental action are necessary because otherwise supplies would escape into the black markets and be absorbed by the well-to-do. That would be disaster to the poor. But this has brought a great danger to those nations, because if the supplies flowing into the hands of the government were to cease for half a month, it would mean that in the face of inevitable mob violence there would be complete collapse of political, social and moral order. And there is scarcely a government in Europe, or indeed many in Asia, where the supplies in the hands of the governments at the present moment exceed thirty days. Therefore, if there should be a failure in our stream of overseas food, we shall have chaos in great areas. As I have said before, since the crisis developed, we have so far been able to prevent that calamity of mass starvation. And we shall cross this dreadful sea if we can hold the helm straight for another four months.

The burden of supplies to these gigantic famine areas in Europe and Asia falls almost wholly upon the Western Hemisphere and upon Australia. We in North America are making every effort to comply with the demands of conscience and of our Christian faith. We have greatly restricted the food supplies of our people, and we are doing perhaps more than that—we are taking these supplies, at the hands of the government, and exporting them to the famine areas irrespective of what the deprivation of our own people may be.

You, Mr. President, have referred to the measures taken by the Government of Peru to cooperate in this problem. Soon after the crisis developed, you had taken measures to restrict imports of breadstuffs and fats, which are the essential munitions in this battle. In so doing, you and the people of Peru are enabling us to increase the supplies to the famine areas. That is saving thousands of human lives. You have expanded the exports of foodstuffs which you can spare from your own production.

And, Mr. President, may I appeal to the people of Peru, as I have appealed to people of many nations, to support their government in these measures.

I realize fully that these restrictions of your imports cannot go beyond certain limits, for the people of Peru must also have bread to maintain life and health. We, therefore, carry the needed supplies for Peru, although restricted, in all our programs of division of the world supplies.

Mr. President, we are faced with two problems.

The acute crisis that we are now in, as I have said, will last until the harvests of the Northern Hemisphere.

And we have before us further problems after this immediate crisis has passed, for while we may confidently hope that there will not, during the next year, be the plundering of armies or the coincidence of great droughts, with their load of famine, yet the depletion of soils, scarcity of fertilizers, of farm machinery, and the huge destruction of food animals over the world will continue.

Mr. President, you have referred to the second problem— that is, the period after this immediate crisis. The world must reconstruct and expand its agriculture. And as one who directed the world food supplies after the first World War and now has been called again to this crisis, may I be bold enough to make a suggestion to the people of Peru.

The period of war in the world may not be at an end. In any event, one thing stands out, and that is that the nations who have made themselves self-supporting in food are the nations whose continuance of public order, of political and social life, and even of civilization, are assured. While we all realize the great values of combining agricultural and industrial life, yet the ability of a country to provide its own food supplies in emergencies is, to my mind, a transcendent obligation of statesmanship.

Gentlemen, the responsibility of saving human life rests heavily upon the world. We have emerged from a terrible era of killing of men, women and children. The world must look forward with hope, and the dawn of that hope can be made glorious by an era of saving of life and the vigor of civilization.

If we can succeed in persuading every man and woman, every nation, to do their utmost, we shall master this famine. And we shall save the lives of hundreds of millions from the greatest jeopardy in all the history of mankind. We shall have saved infinite suffering and degeneration to civilization—we shall have made peace possible in the world.

And may I repeat a statement which I have made elsewhere: "The saving of these human lives is far more than an economic necessity to the recovery of the world. It is more than the only path to order, to stability and to peace. Such action marks the return of the lamp of compassion to the world. And that is a part of the moral and spiritual reconstruction of the world."

On the World Food Crisis

*Address at Luncheon given by American Ambassador
to Chile at Santiago*
[*June 5, 1946*]

Mr. President and gentlemen of Chile:

I AM deeply affected by the warmth and cordiality of your
welcome and the welcome I have received from the people
of Chile for a second time. I have thought that perhaps
before proposing a toast to the prosperity of the Chilean people,
I might try to paint to you some picture of the problem with
which the world is confronted during the food crisis which has
been raging for the past three months and will continue for the
next four months until the harvests in the Northern Hemisphere, when there will be more supplies.

And in trying to paint that picture, I am constantly forced to
the use of figures, although figures fail to convey the suffering
which these numbers involve.

This world crisis appeared last March. At that time, President Truman did me the honor to ask for my collaboration in
the great crisis that faced mankind. As my first duty, I have
journeyed over the world to evaluate the minimum needs of
the great famine areas and to discover such additional food resources as possible. I have endeavored to make clear to the
world the gravity of the problem. I have also endeavored to
coordinate and bring about as great a solidarity as possible of
the nations to meet this crisis. I was more than glad to undertake this effort, in order to contribute what experience I had

gained as the head of the organization which fought the great famine after the first World War. But more than all that, especially did I desire that in this tremendous crisis of human life, there should be a demonstration to my countrymen that, no matter what our other differences in views might be in our opposite political parties, there could be no division of effort in the battle to save human life, and civilization itself.

At this point, I should like to make it clear that I am not an official of UNRRA, although I am very much interested in the success of that organization. UNRRA serves nations unable to pay for their food, but many nations who have the means, or can secure the means, to pay for their food, are equally hungry and equally in danger. UNRRA covers only about twenty per cent of the world problem with which we are confronted, and it is my mission to deal with the whole one hundred per cent.

I will not recite to you the names of the twenty-seven countries which I have now visited in the space of a little more than sixty days and in traveling over 40,000 miles. In each of these major countries of Europe and Asia, I have been received with the utmost consideration. We have had the cooperation of most of the officials in these nations in the face of need for a common front against the great peril which confronts the world. In coming to South America, I am endeavoring to complete this, the first task of the battle against famine.

Of the Four Horsemen of the Apocalypse, the one named War has gone—at least for a while. But Famine, Pestilence and Death are still charging over the earth. And the modern world has added more horsemen to this evil brigade. Their names are Destruction, Drought, Fear and Revolution. This crisis is not alone due to war destruction of agriculture. On top of that calamity has been piled the plundering by armies of the last harvests. And to this immensity of misery has been added drought—drought in the Mediterranean, drought in India, drought in China, and partial drought in South Africa and the Argentine. Never before have so many evil Horsemen came all at one time.

Hunger today hangs over the homes of more than 800,000,-

000 people—over one-third of the people of the world. Hunger is more than privation to some individual. He is a silent visitor who comes like a shadow. He sits beside every anxious mother three times each day. He brings not alone suffering and sorrow, but fear and terror in cities and whole nations. He carries disorder and the paralysis of government, and even its downfall. He is more destructive than armies, not only in human life but in morals. All of the values of right living melt before his invasions, and every gain of civilization crumbles.

The people of Chile are deprived of many things they need as the result of the war. They have a right to complaint. But there is no starvation in Chile. And when the people complain, perhaps they will remember the far greater sufferings of the millions of people in many nations. I have witnessed human beings striving to live on a ration of only two cupfuls of grain for each of them once a day.

Hunger sits not only at the table thrice daily in these hundreds of millions of homes. The spectre of possible starvation haunts equally the halls of government and squalid hovels in the ruins of war. It haunts governments because the failure of food supplies spells the breakdown of the whole political and social order—of civilization itself.

Mr. Ambassador, we use loosely the terms of "famine", "starvation", and "hunger". Today, we are not alone faced with hunger, but we are faced with the problem of mass starvation. And by that term I mean whole villages—whole cities—and even whole nations—might be condemned to death did we not make our every effort. So far during the past three months, we have prevented mass starvation.

And hunger has placed three words every hour of the day on the tongues of these 150 millions of people. The first is "bread". Bread has always been the symbol of life but it looms now as never before in history. It is now the symbol of the life of nations. To reduce the bread ration is a symbol of calamity. The second word is "fats", for which there is an insatiable craving and physical need. The third word is "calories". That is the common denominator. Calories are only a partial yardstick of food, but that word has become everywhere the grim measure of the steps along the road from plenty to hunger and to starvation.

And may I remind you that an average of 2,200 calories per person per day is the minimum in a nation for healthy human beings. The people of Chile apparently enjoy an average of over 2,500 calories. If these 800,000,000 people should receive no more relief, and if we assume that their own remaining resources could be evenly distributed, which they could not, the measure of their hunger with the caloric yardstick is about as follows:

About 100,000,000 people would be reduced to the 2,000 calory level.

About 100,000,000 more people would be reduced to an 1,800 calory level.

About 150,000,000 more would be reduced to a 1,500 calory level.

About 150,000,000 more would be reduced to a 1,200 calory level; and

About 300,000,000 more would be reduced to a 900 calory level, or below—and that is slow death.

As we descend this scale, we move step by step from the stage of hunger to the stage of disease and epidemics, to the stage of public disorder, to the stage of starvation of all but the strongest, and, finally at the 1,200 and 900 calory levels we have come to mass starvation. The Nazis at Buchenwald and Belsen gave about 900 calories to their prisoners. But long before a population is reduced to these lower levels, government would break down.

In March last, the Combined Food Board in Washington made an estimate of the amount of food needed by all the deficit nations for the first six months of 1946, and of supplies available from the food-surplus nations. These estimates of need were based upon the requirements as stated by the nations who must have overseas supplies. Thus, there seemed an unbridgeable gap of 11,000,000 tons of breadstuffs, or nearly 43 per cent. And there was likewise a deficiency in fats. That would mean a calory level below human endurance and that gap spells death to millions.

Our Mission examined the stocks now in the hands of each country and the amounts of their own production that could be expected. We measured the needs of each nation on a drastic caloric basis—about 1,500 to 1,800 calories—such as would pull them through, would prevent mass starvation, would maintain order and economic life. To provide this margin is our battle.

The net results of drastic reductions in some nations and newly-developed supplies was to reduce this gap in supplies to about 3,600,000 tons. But the gap is still there—and it is a tragic gap.

I can illustrate how tragic that gap still is. It equals the whole amount necessary to save 40,000,000 people in India. We would, of course, not concentrate on the shortage of one nation, but if we spread it over all, the results are about the same.

There is a phase of this problem which causes infinite anxiety in the minds of all those who understand it. The world has developed an art in the rationing of peoples. Where it is necessary to reduce the food consumption of people by thirty or forty per cent, it can only be done if the government of that country takes possession of all the supplies from the farms, from the merchants, and from overseas imports. In that case, governments, as is the case in all those in Europe and many in Asia, establish distribution points where the people may come with their ration cards. These measures of direct governmental action are necessary because otherwise supplies would escape into the black markets and be absorbed by those more able to purchase. That would be disaster for the poor. But this method has brought a new danger to those nations, because if the supplies flowing into the hands of the government were to cease for half a month, it would mean that in the face of inevitable mob violence there would be complete collapse of political, social and moral order. And there is scarcely a government in Europe, or indeed many in Asia, where the supplies in the hands of the governments at the present moment exceed thirty days. Therefore, if there should be a failure in our stream of overseas food, we shall have chaos in great areas. As I have said before, since the crisis developed, we have so far been able to prevent that calamity of mass starvation. And we shall cross this dreadful sea if we can hold the helm straight for another four months.

The burden of supplies to these gigantic famine areas in Europe and Asia falls almost wholly upon the Western Hemisphere and upon Australia. We in North America are making every effort to comply with the demands of conscience and of our Christian faith. We have greatly restricted the food supplies of our people, and we are doing perhaps more than that— we are taking these supplies, at the hands of the government, and exporting them to the famine areas irrespective of what the deprivation of our own people may be.

The Government and the people of Chile have, by definite action in the support of UNRRA, and otherwise, shown their sympathetic and devoted interest in this problem. Chile, as we all know, enjoys a great immunity in these times, because she is, on balance, self-supporting. She does import minor amounts of one or two food commodities. She has some small margins to export. For these reasons, she is not among the great supplying nations. Nevertheless, her sympathy and moral support of her representatives all over the world in the measures necessary to meet the problem have been most helpful. And I congratulate the people of Chile upon the industry and statesmanship which has made her immune from this calamity.

We are faced with two problems.

The acute crisis that we are now in, as I have said, will last until the harvests of the Northern Hemisphere.

And we have before us further problems after this immediate crisis has passed, for while we may confidently hope that there will not, during the next year, be the plundering of armies or the coincidence of great droughts, with their load of famine, yet the depletion of soils, the destruction of fertilizer production, farm machinery and the huge destruction of food animals over the world will continue.

After this immediate crisis, the world must reconstruct and expand its agriculture. And as one who directed the world food supplies after the first World War and now has been called again to this crisis, may I be bold enough to make a suggestion to the people of Chile.

The period of war in the world may not be at an end. In any event, one thing stands out, and that is that the nations who have made themselves self-supporting in food are the nations whose continuance of public order, of political and social life, and even of civilization, are assured. While we all realize the great values of combining agricultural and industrial life, yet the ability of a country to provide its own food supplies in emergencies is, to my mind, a transcendent obligation of statesmanship.

Gentlemen, the responsibility of saving human life rests heavily upon the world. We have emerged from a terrible era of killing of men, women and children. The world must look forward with hope, and the dawn of that hope can be made glorious by an era of saving of life and the vigor of civilization.

If we can succeed in persuading every man and woman, every nation, to do their utmost, we shall master this famine. And we shall save the lives of hundreds of millions from the greatest jeopardy in all the history of mankind. We shall have saved infinite suffering and degeneration to civilization,—we shall have made peace possible in the world.

And may I repeat a statement which I have made elsewhere: "The saving of these human lives is far more than an economic necessity to the recovery of the world. It is more than the only path to order, to stability, and to peace. Such action marks the return of the lamp of compassion to the world. And that is a part of the moral and spiritual reconstruction of the world."

On the World Food Crisis

BUENOS AIRES, ARGENTINA

[*June 10, 1946*]

P RESIDENT PERON and the newly-installed Argentine authorities have shown the utmost cooperation with my mission, recognizing the great food crisis in the world. They are arranging for an increased volume of exports of cereals and fats from the Argentine to the nations which must have imports. The Argentine exported about 600,000 tons of foodstuffs in May, and the President is taking vigorous steps to increase this rate of shipments in June, July and August, which are the critical months in this world crisis. With the arrival of Northern Hemisphere crops in September, the situation will be greatly eased.

The limiting factor in Argentine food shipments is the railway, truck and port facilities, which are naturally run down by the war years. There is no question as to enough supplies in the Argentine for such a program, as the surplus above domestic needs in cereals, meats and fats is larger than can in any event be transported. However, I am sure the measures being taken will greatly increase the volume during the critical months.

There are only four major nations from which overseas supplies of relief can come to the 800,000,000 people who are short of food during those months. Those are the Argentine, the United States, Canada, and Australia. These four nations comprise about 90 per cent of the possible supplies. A preliminary estimate shows that the shipments from the surplus countries needed in these three months is about 9,500,000 tons.

There is still a gap in the visible supplies, and the Argentine increase will be invaluable in closing this gap.

The Argentine people have shown a fine generosity in the situation, for they have made free gifts of about 400,000 tons of food to various organizations and nations. Beyond this, and even more important, they are selling their large exports to many nations on credit. To increase the volume of food to those who wish to pay for it eventually is, at this time, of equal importance for they comprise 80 per cent of the nations in need.

It is a great service that President Peron is undertaking for all the hungry people in the world.

On Communist Press Practices

RIO DE JANEIRO, BRAZIL
[June 15, 1946]

IN BRAZIL, as well as the thirty-seven countries which we have visited, wherever there is a Communist press (and that is in most of them), that press has universally attacked this effort to provide food for the hungry working people of the world, mostly on the ground that the food is to be used for political purposes. In Latin America it takes also the form that we are trying to take food from the people.

This unity of opposition is interesting, because the Communist press is aware that the Christian world is today denying itself of food in order that the working people in France, Belgium, Italy, and twenty other countries, may be saved from starvation. And among these people, there are millions of Communists who have received their full share and whose lives have been alike saved. It is still more interesting because of the fact that, after the first World War, at the request of the Soviet Government I organized the relief of the great famine among the working people in South Russia, and received most fullsome documents of thanks and appreciation, signed by the highest officials of the Russian Government.

As we are feeding Communists in all countries, there obviously has been no use of food for political purposes, or no intent to make such use.

There can be only one explanation; that is, that the universal party line of the Communist Party in every country is to try to break down the provision of food for hungry people, and thus produce chaos where they can fish in troubled waters. If this is not the case, it would appear that this is the time for Moscow to establish a new party line in the Communist press of the world.

On the Latin-American
Food Situation

Press Statement, Washington, D. C.
[June 19, 1946]

W E HAVE had a generous welcome and excellent cooperation from Latin America. These countries fall
into two groups, from a food point of view: those that
export food, and those that import food. A few, of course,
import certain foods and export others. Our concern has been
exclusively with the world crisis until the harvest in the Northern Hemisphere in September.

On April 19th, I broadcast to Latin America an appeal that
the exporting countries expand and accelerate their exports as
much as possible, and that the importing countries drastically
reduce their imports during the world crisis. This request was
greatly aided by His Holiness, Pope Pius XII, who addressed
an urgent appeal to these nations. And the full information
issued by the press has kept the leaders of these countries informed upon the world crisis.

The governments without exception requested that I explain the world situation to their people as an aid to them
in measures they were taking to reduce imports and increase
exports.

Colombia, Venezuela, Chile, Peru, and Uruguay have all
reduced their cereal and fats imports to a minimum. Some of
them generously offered to do without these imports during
the critical months. Mexico, Ecuador, Chile, Peru, and Uru-

guay are increasing their exports of beans, rice, meats, fats, or sugar, as the case may be.

Brazil is normally the largest Latin-American importer of wheat—about 100,000 tons per month. She has reduced her imports during these critical months by over 40 per cent and made available much larger than normal exports of corn, rice and beans. Thus, she is making a double contribution.

The Argentine is one of the world's most important food exporting countries. She suffered a partial crop failure, and her surplus this year, while considerable, is less than normal. Nevertheless, the Argentine during these months will supply 90 per cent of Latin-American food exports. Although President Peron was inaugurated only two days before our arrival, he took time for an exhaustive discussion of the world famine situation. He went thoroughly into the contribution the Argentine could make, and the measures for making it effective. I have now received telegraphic word that President Peron has signaled his cooperation by a decree creating strong emergency measures to speed up exports to the utmost during the crisis.

During March, April and May, the Argentine has exported an average of about 450,000 tons of cereals a month. Under these new emergency measures, I am in hopes the average during the next three months will rise to seven or seven hundred and fifty thousand tons a month, although our estimates are for a less amount. Argentina has undertaken to provide for the major needs of most of the importing South American countries during the critical months, thus greatly relieving the drain upon Canada and the United States.

As a result of these arrangements, we are now able to revise substantially our previous appraisals of the situation in these nations. All estimates are necessarily approximate, but they have been compiled upon a month-to-month basis after investigation by our staff and discussion with the governments concerned. It will be noted that the figures given below for requirements are one month later than those of shipments, about this time being required for delivery.

The estimates which we gave in a report on the world situation to President Truman on May 13th included an estimate that the importing Latin-American states would require a minimum of about 800,000 tons of cereals for the four months from June 1st until September 30th, or about 200,000 tons per month during the remaining acute stage of the world food crisis. We are now able to reduce this requirement for these four months to about 420,000 tons, or an average of about 105,000 tons a month. The importing countries in Central and South America could effectively use more than this quantity, but they will willingly get along if further supplies are not available.

In the same report to President Truman, we estimated total possible exports of cereals and beans from these countries during the four months from May 1st to August 31st at about 2,150,000 tons. We now estimate the total possible shipments of cereals and beans during these four months at about 2,600,-000 tons, with a possible increase beyond this from the Argentine of 300,000 tons.

The five months' balance sheet in our previous estimate showed net exports from Latin America, taken as a whole—that is, deducting total imports from total exports—of about 320,000 tons of cereals a month during the critical period.

Taking into account the decrease in requirements and the increase in supplies, our new four months' balance sheet shows a net export possible from Latin America of about 520,000 tons a month of cereals and beans, or a net total of about 2,120,000 tons during the four months, with still further possible increases. In other words, the cooperation of the Latin-American countries renders available about 800,000 tons more cereals and beans than we had previously estimated. There are still further possibilities from the Argentine. The changes in the situation of fats and oils are in the same favorable directions.

These nations are making a real contribution to closing the gap in supplies to the hungry world.

Report on the World Famine

*Address broadcast over the Canadian Broadcasting
Company from Ottawa
[June 28, 1946]*

Mr. Prime Minister:

I HAVE been honored by your invitation to make from Canada the final report upon my food mission to 38 nations I am glad for this privilege. It gives to me the opportunity to pay tribute to the magnificent service Canada has given to the world. To Canada flows the gratitude of hundreds of millions of human beings who have been saved from starvation through the efforts of this great Commonwealth of the North.

Upon four nations—Canada, the United States, the Argentine and Australia—has fallen 90 per cent of the overseas burden of relief to this, the greatest famine in all human history. Over 10,000,000 tons of food have been shipped to the 800,-000,000 people short of food since this famine became acute. Canada has provided over one-fifth of this supply. Without this gigantic flow of overseas food, hundreds of millions would have died and other hundreds of millions would have survived only as permanent physical wrecks. And when we use this impersonal word "people," let us not forget that most of them are women and children. Far beyond our humanitarian responsibilities lay the necessity to save the political and social structure of the world from sinking into a chaos in which recovery and the making of peace would be impossible.

We can see the future more clearly if for a moment we look

back over our months of effort to drive the wolf from the door of the world.

CAUSES OF THIS CRISIS

This crisis, of course, had its roots in the degeneration of agriculture and manpower in the war-torn areas. But to this was added the plunder by armies of several million tons of food out of the last harvests in Germany, Eastern Europe and Manchuria. The crisis was further aggravated by the large feeding of bread grains to animals in the earlier months of the harvest year. But on top of all these disasters has been the unparallelled coincidence of five great droughts—in the Western Mediterranean, India, China, South Africa, and a partial failure in crops in the Argentine.

The full realization of the impending calamity came early in March.

TWO SEPARATE PROBLEMS

At once it was evident that there were two quite different problems.

The first was the months of acute crisis until the arrival of the Northern Hemisphere harvests which come in from July to September and thus renew the depleted world larder.

The second is the problem of better organization over the year following the present harvest. My immediate concern was naturally limited to the crisis months. It is essential that this dual nature of the problem be borne in mind, otherwise the issues become confused and the cure chaotic.

In pursuance of President Truman's wishes, I have traveled some 50,000 miles visiting all of the important famine and food-deficit areas in the world and all of the major food-surplus areas excepting South Africa and Australia. I have discussed crops, animals, calories, rations, stocks, ships, railroads, supplies and hunger with the Presidents, the Prime Ministers, the food officials of each of these nations.

Without any special authority my function has been mostly advisory—or perhaps persuasive would be a better word. Certainly I am deeply indebted for the most extraordinary welcome and cooperation accorded to me and my associates.

THE APPARENT GAP IN FOOD SUPPLIES LAST MARCH

When the potential dangers were realized four months ago, the Combined Food Board estimated that there was an 11,000,-000 ton gap in the necessary amounts of cereals to meet the minimum demands of hungry nations—and a similar appalling shortage in fats and other foods. With this gap facing us it did not seem possible to prevent mass starvation. I felt compelled to say publicly at that time, "Our task is now to minimize the loss of life."

THE GAP IN FOOD SUPPLIES REDUCED

On my return from Europe and Asia a month ago, my colleagues and I felt assured that as of May 1st the gap in the bare subsistence supply of cereals had been reduced from 11,-000,000 tons to about 3,600,000 tons, with a corresponding reduction in the gaps of fats and other essentials. This reduction was due to the development of new sources of supplies; to substitutions; to the success of our appeal for self-denial in the surplus food countries. The reduction of the gap was due especially to the willing acceptance in the food deficit countries of drastic curtailment of their requested import programs. It meant for some of them drastic regimes of bare subsistence.

Our determination has been to hold the lowest of them up to a level of 1500 to 1700 calories per person per day. If we could hold these levels it would at least prevent mass starvation. But even this drastic program was endangered by that tragic gap of 3,600,000 tons. If it could not be overcome, we were defeated.

THE GAP IN SUPPLIES HAS BEEN MET

But something like the widow's cruise is happening. In this two months since those estimates the world has developed even further additions to world supplies. The Latin-American states have greatly reduced their import requirements during the crisis months. Especially the Argentine is greatly expanding its contribution of supplies. The other Latin-American states are giving aid. The British Government has reduced its pipe line supplies. Larger diversions have been made in India from the surplus provinces to the famine areas. The conservation measures in Canada and the United States are contributing even more largely to our potential exports. The United States harvest has arrived earlier than usual.

From all these gains I am happy to announce to you that it now seems assured that the tragic gap of about 3,600,000 tons in minimum supplies with which we were haunted two months ago can now be closed. I am humbly grateful to be the one to make this announcement.

But it cannot be emphasized too strongly that this ultimate victory over mass starvation is based upon three assumptions:

First, that the drastic food regimes in the food-deficit countries will be continued during the crisis months until the danger is absolutely over.

Second, that the people in the food-surplus countries continue their sacrifice in the consumption of wheat and fats during the remaining few months of the crisis.

Third, that supplies be shipped overseas in an uninterrupted stream over this period.

The precariousness of the situation is not over. Scarcely any of the major food-deficit areas have stocks of as much as 30 days overseas food even on the basis of their much reduced living. If we fail in shipments, mass starvation will be instantly upon us.

DANGER OF MASS STARVATION PASSED EXCEPT IN CHINA

It is at least reassuring that if we have continued cooperative action of the various nations, mass starvation will be prevented, with one exception. That exception is China, where transportation to the interior and inadequate organization has rendered relief only partially successful.

In other famine areas there will be suffering. We truly need more supplies than just enough to prevent mass starvation. Many of the old people and the weaker children will fall by the wayside, nevertheless the great majority of the endangered will be saved. Beyond this saving of human life, the political and social stability of nations, upon which alone peace can be builded, will be preserved.

WHERE CREDIT IS DUE

For success in preventing mass starvation credit must first go to the Combined Food Board in which Canada plays so important a part. That Board has had the stern task of dividing the world's food between nations upon the agreed programs. UNRRA deserves praise in the limited field it covers—that is the 20 per cent of the people who cannot finance their food imports. And no tribute can be great enough to the magnificent cooperation of the responsible officials in the forty nations which have joined in a gigantic effort to save life.

THE PROBLEM OF THE NEXT HARVEST YEAR

My present concern is with the immediate crisis months. But naturally my colleagues and I on this mission have been deeply interested in the food prospects of each nation after the coming harvest. Moreover, hope in the outlook for the next year affects the courage and morale of hungry people to endure for the next few months. More especially is this so as famine has its worst moments just before the new harvest, for then the reserves are gone.

THE PROSPECTS BETTER THAN THE PAST YEAR

I may say at once that I do not take the extreme pessimistic view of the world supplies after the coming harvests that has been expressed in several quarters. We can at least hope there will be no plundering by armies during the next year. We have reason to believe that there will not be five coincident great droughts again in one year. In three of these drought areas the harvest prospects are very much improved. For instance, it is already estimated that France and North Africa will require 2,500,000 tons less of food imports than during the past year. With continued favorable weather, we in North America seem destined to have abundant harvests again.

It must not, however, be thought that all trouble is over. The war-devastated areas will not have fully recovered their ground crops nor have restored their flocks and herds during the next year. And famine will linger in China and India until November when the rice crops come. The food situation of the world in the next year will not be easy, but next year in my view will not be one of such dreadful crisis and drastic regimes as the one which we are now in.

WORLD ORGANIZATION

To prepare for the next harvest year the United Nations are now setting up the International Emergency Food Council. It will consolidate various world agencies into more effective organization. The selection of one of my colleagues upon this mission—Dr. Dennis FitzGerald—as Secretary General is a complete assurance of efficient action.

But there is a further step beyond the present United Nations proposals which the world sorely needs.

THE HOST OF SUBNORMAL CHILDREN

This 1500 to 1700 calory bottom level in many areas is dreadfully hard on children. While it will see adults through, the kind of food is not the most suitable for children. Disease and mortality among the little ones are ever the sensitive barometers of starvation and poverty. Several nations have done the best they could by giving the children priority in their meagre dairy products; some extra food is given in some schools; and the scattered charitable agencies are doing the best they can in limited areas. But in all, they are only touching the fringe of the problem. Millions of mothers are today watching their children wilt before their eyes. The proof of this is an annual mortality rate in many cities as high as 200 per 1000 among children under one year of age. The further proof is that there are somewhere from 20 to 30 million physically subnormal children on the continent of Europe. There are other millions in Asia.

After the first world war, we gave a good extra meal a day of restorative food, to 10,000,000 undernourished children. I deplore that this special aid for children has had no counterpart through a widespread organization set-up after this war. And I repeat that civilization marches forward upon the feet of healthy children. We cannot have recovery of civilization in nations with a legacy of stunted bodies or distorted and embittered minds.

TO REDEEM THE CHILDREN

I would like to suggest that the redemption of these children be organized at once by the newly-created International Emergency Food Council and that all nations be called upon to contribute to its cost. The job could be done with three or four hundred million dollars—a charge beyond any organized private charity but not a great sum from the world as a whole.

Mr. Prime Minister, I have held this statement to sober words. I have not tried to describe the grim visage of famine in action. I have not attempted to express the emotion which every decent human being feels in the presence of the scenes of hunger and of sickly children I have witnessed. Nor have I tried to express the sympathy and pride which swells in one's heart for those hundreds of thousands of heroic men and women in the world who are struggling to save these millions of human lives. They labor for their countrymen in villages, in cities and in the halls of government. They know that hunger is a destroyer far worse than war. Great as its toll of life may be yet its destruction of morals, of social and political institutions are infinite.

May I repeat here a statement I have made to men of government in each of these 38 nations?

"The world has ended a bloody and horrible era of killing of even women and children. The jeopardy to mankind by famine gives to us an opportunity to change the energies of the world from killing to saving life. These months can bring the glow of a new faith and a new hope for the dawn of a new era to mankind.

"To succeed is far more than a necessity to economic reconstruction of the world. It is far more than the path to order and peace.

"It marks the return of the lamp of compassion to the earth. And that is part of the moral and spiritual reconstruction of the world."

Address at a Banquet in Honor of His Excellency, the Prime Minister of Greece

NEW YORK CITY
[*December 16, 1946*]

Prime Minister Constantine Tsaldaris and Our Guests:

SIX months ago I visited Greece on behalf of our Government and the American people in the interest of her starving people. What we were able to give in that world crisis last year was little enough—and while many other countries have emerged from that desperate world famine, the difficulties of Greece are not over. The severity of her plight in the winter ahead tugs again at our heart strings.

I need not repeat that the difficulties of Greece today are a result of the six years of war she has fought for her independence and for the freedom of her people. Her women, children and staunch men were butchered, her homes burned, her farms laid waste, her industries destroyed, and her people are sick and hungry.

International relief through UNRRA will cease in fifteen days. The Greek Relief Committee, of which I happen to be Chairman, is appealing to the American people for voluntary aid to tide her over a period of great hardship. To aid in this task, I believe our Government should contribute some of our surplus food. But even beyond food are the essential services to the multitude of orphans to the hordes of sick and destitute which can be provided only through the efforts of this Committee.

Mr. Prime Minister, there is no nation to whom America is more indebted than to the Greeks. From Greece came the foundations of Western civilization.

Your Excellency will find here in America that we begin to learn of Greece in our childhood from the text books in our elementary schools. You will find that we study her history, her ancient language and her literature in our high schools and colleges. You will find our language teeming with Greek words. Her heroes and their heroic deeds are symbols in our daily expressions.

But beyond these, we inherit from her the basic philosophic ideas of freedom which so influenced the founders of our Republic. Even our public buildings everywhere are the reflections of her mighty architects.

Her heroic defense against the hordes of Persia swept back the Asiatic tide which would have submerged the beginnings of Western civilization. Thus its spread over Europe and ultimately to America was assured.

Today, after 25 centuries, Greece still remains an outpost of Western civilization. She has fought Nazi domination and is still struggling against Asiatic tides in their new form—Asiatic communism. She still stands as a bastion of freedom for men. Her heroes and her heroic deeds of these last years equal those of her ancestors. We owe much to those founders of freedom, but we have an equal debt to those who, today, are continuing the struggle.

Your Excellency, you are in our midst seeking political justice for Greece. You are seeking the moral support of the United Nations that she shall not be overwhelmed by these invasions from outside her borders. Every American hopes our Government will be at your side.

German Agriculture and
Food Requirements

Report to The President
[February 26, 1947]

The President
The White House
Washington, D. C.

Dear Mr. President:

I have now completed the Economic Mission to Germany
and Austria, which I undertook at your request.

I enclose herewith a memorandum on the economic conditions affecting food supplies for the newly combined American
and British Zones, together with estimates of supplies and costs
involved in deficiency appropriations for the last half of the
fiscal year 1946-1947 and appropriations for the fiscal year
1947-1948. I shall submit detailed annexes to this memorandum as soon as they are completed.

I shall report separately on Austria, and at a later date I
shall have some further report on other economic and health
problems in these areas.

In this examination of food questions in the combined zones,
I have had the invaluable service of Dr. Dennis A. FitzGerald
in food questions and that of Dr. William H. Sebrell, Jr. in nutritional and health questions, together with the able assistance
in other economic questions of Mr. Hugh Gibson, Mr. Louis
Lochner, Mr. Frank Mason, and Dr. Gustav Stolper. I have
received the full cooperation of Generals McNarney, Clay and

Draper, Colonel Hester, and their able staff, as well as General Robertson, Sir Cecil Weir and Mr. T. F. Griffin, and their able staff on the British side.

My thanks are also due to the devoted service of Mr. Tracy S. Voorhees, Special Assistant to the Secretary of War, and to the Air Transport Command for their cooperation and skill.

*   *   *   *   *

INTRODUCTION

At the time of her surrender, Germany had exhausted all of her reserves and most of her stocks of consumer goods and raw materials. We now know that, driven back into her own borders, she would have blown up in chaos within a short time without further military action.

Promptly after the surrender, her liquid resources from which she could have been provided with supplies were seized and divided as reparations. The population thus became largely dependent for its life upon the armies of occupation.

It is hardly necessary to repeat that parts of Germany were annexed to Poland and Russia and that the shrunken territory was divided into four military occupation zones between the Russians, French, British and Americans. The American and British Zones have now been administratively combined, each nation bearing one-half the expense, and this report relates to that area only.

CHANGES IN POPULATION AND MANPOWER

The changes which have taken place in population profoundly affect all economic problems. The population of the combined zones in 1939 was about 34,200,000. The Germans expelled from the Russian and Polish annexations together with those from Czechoslovakia, Hungary, and Austria, have raised the population in the American and British Zones to about 41,700,-000. It is estimated that an additional 1,000,000 will come

into this area by December 1947. There are also about 400,-
000 British and American military and civil personnel. Thus,
the two zones will have to accommodate about 43,000,000 people, bringing the population approximately 9,000,000 above
that in 1939.

The skilled manpower and the ratio of working males in the
population have been greatly affected by the war. For the
whole of Germany, it is estimated that 5,700,000 were killed
or permanently injured. It is also estimated that over 3,000,-
000 prisoners of war are held in work camps in Russia; 750,000
in France; 400,000 in Britain; and 40,000 in Belgium. The
detention of large numbers of skilled Sudeten German workmen in Czechoslovakia bears on this problem.

As applied to the American and British Zones, this represents a present subtraction of over 6,000,000 of the most vital
and most skilled workers in the population. Likewise, the 90,-
000 Nazis held in concentration camps and the 1,900,000 others
under sanctions by which they can only engage in manual labor
naturally comprise a considerable part of the former technical
and administrative skill of the country, and the restrictions
upon them, however necessary, add to administrative and industrial problems.

One consequence of these distortions is that in the age groups
between 20 and 40 there are 6 men to 10 women, and in the
age group between 40 and 60, about 7 men to 10 women. Thus,
there are in these groups between 6 and 7 million more women
than men. The results upon productive power are bad enough,
but the consequences to morals are appalling.

HOUSING

The housing situation in the two zones is the worst that modern civilization has ever seen. About 25 per cent of the urban
housing was destroyed by the war. Therefore, 25 per cent of
the urban population must find roofs from among the remaining
75 per cent, in addition to all the destitute "expellees" and
other groups brought in. There has been little repair of dam-

aged houses, due to lack of materials and transportion. The result of all this is that multitudes are living in rubble and basements. The average space among tens of millions is equivalent to between three and four people to a 12′ x 12′ room. Nor is the overcrowding confined to urban areas, for the "expellees" have been settled into every farm house. One consequence is the rapid spread of tuberculosis and other potentially communicable diseases.

COAL

The shortage of coal is, next to food, the most serious immediate bottleneck to both living and the revival of exports to pay for food. The Ruhr, which is now almost the sole coal supply of the Anglo-American Zones, is, due to lack of skilled men and physical vitality in labor, producing only 230,000 tons per day, as against a former 450,000 tons per day. Of the present production, a considerable amount must be exported to surrounding nations which are also suffering. The shortage leaves the two zones without sufficient coal for transport, household and other dominant services, with little upon which to start exports in the industry.

The coal famine all over Western Europe and the unprecedented severity of the winter have produced everywhere the most acute suffering. As an example in Germany, no household coal has been issued in Hamburg since October. Other German cities have been but little better off.

AGRICULTURAL PRODUCTION

It must be borne in mind that about 25 per cent of the German pre-war food production came from the areas taken over by Russia and Poland. Moreover, the Russian Military Zone in Germany was a large part of the bread basket of Germany. Some millions of tons formerly flowed into the American and British Zones from these areas. These sources now contribute nothing.

The British and American armies and civilians are entirely

fed from home. The large Russian army is fed upon their zone.

Due to a lack of fertilizers, good seed, farm implements and skilled labor, the 1946 agricultural production in the American and British Zones was about 65 per cent of pre-war. A generalized appraisal indicates that in the American Zone the harvest of 1946 yielded a supply, beyond the needs of the farmers (self-suppliers), equal to about 1,100 calories per day for the "non-self suppliers." The similar supply in the British Zone was about 900 calories per day average to the "non-self suppliers." These amounts contrast with 3,000 calories of the pre-war normal German consumption.

With the efforts being made to improve agricultural production, there is an expected small increase from the harvest of 1947, especially in potatoes (if better seed is provided in time). The steps which I recommend, however, should show greater production from the 1948 harvest.

FOOD DISTRIBUTION

This terrible winter, with frozen canals and impeded railway traffic, has rendered it impossible to maintain even the present low basis of rationing in many localities. The coal shortage and the consequent lack of heat, even for cooking, has added a multitude of hardships. The conclusions in this report as to the food situation are, however, not based upon the effect of this temporary dislocation, but upon the basic conditions, to which the winter has added many difficulties.

From the food point of view, the population of the combined zones has been divided as below, based upon the German census undertaken last autumn. The table must not be regarded as precise for the different groups, as the Berlin sector was not distributed on the same basis as others. It is, however, accurate enough for food computation purposes.

"Self-Suppliers," i.e. farmers and their
families 7,640,000
"Non-self suppliers," i.e. urban population:
Prospective and nursing mothers 660,000
Children 0-6 years of age 3,070,000
Children 6-15 years of age 4,495,000
Adolescents, 15-20 years of age 2,100,000
"Normal Consumers," 20 years up 17,910,000
Moderate hard workers 2,500,000
Heavy workers 1,910,000
Extra heavy workers 720,000
Displaced persons 680,000 34,045,000
_____
Total population, two zones 41,685,000

The base ration is 1,550 calories per person per day to the
"normal consumer" group, with priorities and supplements, as
the situation requires or permits, for other groups. For instance,
milk and fats are given in priority to nursing mothers and children up to six years of age; more food, including more meat,
is given in supplement to hard workers, etc.

This base ration for the "normal consumer" compares with
the minimum temporary maintenance food intake recommended
for "normal consumers" by eminent nutritionists, as follows:

	Present German	Recommended Minimum	Percent Deficiency
Carbohydrates	283 grams	335 grams	16%
Fats	24 grams	45 grams	47%
Protein	25 grams	65 grams	20%
Calories	1,550	2,000	24%

Thus with the deficiency in quantity and in fats, protein and
other nutrients, the 1,550 ration is wholly incapable of supporting health of the groups, which do not have supplements.

NUTRITIONAL CONDITION OF THE POPULATION

The nutritional condition of the above different groups, irrespective of the immediate consequences of the hard winter, are:

(A) The 7,640,000 self-suppliers are, naturally, in good condition.

(B) The supplements and priorities in special foods given to 3,730,000 prospective and nursing mothers, and children under six years of age, appear to be enough to keep them in good condition.

(C) Over half of the 6,595,000 children and adolescents, especially in the lower-income groups, are in a deplorable condition. Their situation is better in limited localities where school feeding has been undertaken but outside these limits stunted growth and delayed development is widespread. In some areas famine edema (actual starvation) is appearing in the children. A study of groups of boys between the ages 9 and 16 years showed 5.5 lbs. under minimum standard weights, with girls 5.1 lbs. below such standard. Other groups studied showed even worse conditions.

(D) A considerable part of the "normal consumer" group of 17,910,000 is likewise in deplorable condition.

This group comprises the light physical workers and is in large majority women and many are aged. Some portion of this group are able to supplement the 1,550 calorie ration by purchase of some supplies from the black market, from the free markets in the vegetable seasons, and from package remittances. Some part of this group are too poor to purchase even the 1,550 calorie ration.

In any event, a large part of the group shows a steady loss of weight, vitality and ability to work. A study in the British Zone shows urban adult males over 19 pounds and females nearly 5 pounds under proper weight. A study in the American Zone showed from 5 to 20 pounds under proper weight. Famine edema is showing in thousands of cases, stated to be 10,000 in Hamburg alone. The increased death roll among the aged is appalling. In persons over 70, in three months last autumn the increase was 40 per cent.

(E) While the workers' rations, due to supplements, are perhaps high enough in themselves, yet the universal tendency is for the worker to share his supplement with his wife and children, and therefore it does not have its full effect in supplying energy for the worker himself.

(F) The 680,000 displaced persons are about one-third in the British Zone and two-thirds in the United States Zone. In the British Zone they receive the German ration only. In the United States Zone they receive supplements which amount to 700 calories per day, so there can be no doubt as to their adequate supply in that area. In fact, the American ration is above the "normal ration" of the other nations on the Continent, except the former neutrals.

These nutritional conclusions are based upon surveys made by Dr. William H. Sebrell, Jr., of the United States Public Health Service, who was a member of my Mission. At my request, he also visited Italy, France, Belgium, Holland and Britain, to study the comparative nutritional situations of these countries with that of Germany. He reports that the nutritional condition in those countries is nearly pre-war normal, while the special German groups that I have mentioned are not only far below the other nations but disastrously so.

A NEW PROGRAM

The Anglo-American bi-zonal agreement of last autumn calls for an increase of rations by 250 calories per day at some undetermined date. Such an increase is highly desirable. However, the world shortage in cereals, evidenced by the early reduction of bread rations in several other nations, renders such an increase impossible until after the harvest of 1947. Such a program also implies increased import supplies which, in terms of grain, would add 1,260,000 tons and $136,000,000 annually to costs, above the already huge burden upon the taxpayers of our two nations.

As the present base of 1,550 calories for "normal consumers" is not enough to maintain health in many children or health and working energy in many adults, I propose a different program. This new approach is to repair the weakest spots in the nutritional situation. I believe that this method will accomplish the major purpose of the proposed general increase in ration as nearly as can be accomplished within the limits of available supplies and finances for the remainder of the fiscal year 1946-1947.

In many ways, I believe it is a better program, and if this method proves a successful remedy during the next few months, it may modify the necessity of so large an increase in imports in the fiscal year 1947-1948 as has been proposed under the bizonal agreement.

There are two groups to which this repair of weakness should be given quickly:

First are the children over six years of age and the adolescents. The number of this group who are undernourished is estimated to be about 3,500,000 or more than 50 per cent. To cover this group and assure that the food reaches the child, the British in their zone, aided by the Swedish and other charities, are giving a small ration in certain schools. There is no systematic school feeding in the American Zone. A system of soup kitchens to provide a hot meal of appropriate body-building foods (meats, fats, milk, etc.) of at least 350 calories daily is imperative for the children in the worst areas of the combined zones, if a future Germany of wholesome character is to be created.

In order to start this system at once, I recommend using the Army surplus 10-in-1 rations, now enroute, and certain excess stocks not adapted to Army feeding and now in control of the American Occupation Forces. These resources can form the major base of this system for a considerable period. This is the more possible as it is proposed to slaughter during 1947 over 5,000,000 head of cattle, hogs and sheep in order to lessen the animal consumption of ground crops, and a portion of these meats and fats can be applied to this program. These various supplies, together with some minor cereal allotments, should carry the program for six months.

The second group demanding immediate relief is the "normal consumer" group of about 17,910,000 persons, now receiving 1,550 calories per day. I strongly recommend several lines of action. (a) A certain portion of them should be advanced to the group of moderate heavy workers and receive the supplement applicable to that category. (b) An emergency supply of cereals should be allotted to the German welfare organizations with which to provide a supplement to families in need and the soup kitchens. (c) I recommend that the aged in the "normal consumers" group, and others where medically certified, be issued tickets upon the soup kitchens for the meal of 350 calories per day during the school week, to be consumed either at these kitchens or taken home. These supplemental measures will substantially improve, and will at least carry over, the most needy part of this group.

By aid to the children and adolescents, some pressure will be removed from the "normal consumer" group, who naturally tend to cut their own food to help their children.

In support of the above program for children and "normal rations," I have included in the recommended deficiency appropriation an emergency supply of 65,000 tons of cereals. These measures as I have said, are in substituiton for the great increase otherwise necessary to import for the proposed program of a lift in the whole ration system by 250 calories.

In addition to these measures, I have included in the sums given below which I recommended to be appropriated for the balance of this fiscal year 1946-1947 an amount necessary for the shipment of 400,000 tons of surplus potatoes from the United States. The object is two-fold.

Due to spoilage during this unprecedented winter, and other causes, there are not enough potatoes by 250,000 tons to cover that portion of the minimum 1,550 calorie ration until the next harvest. Certainly we cannot allow the ration to fall below its already dangerous levels.

Of even more importance, most of the potato seed of our

zones normally comes from the Polish-annexed area and the Russian Zone and is not available. If we can forward 200,000 to 250,000 tons of good potato seed, with some already in hand, we should be able to assure a yield from the 1947 harvest of 5,000,000 tons, and thereby effect some savings in overseas food imports for the fiscal year 1947-1948.

NECESSARY IMPORTS AND FINANCE

The supply and finance of food and collateral relief imports and the development of exports with which ultimately to pay for these imports, has been organized upon the basis of dividing foreign trade into two categories:

Category "A" covers imports of food, fertilizers, and petroleum products for the civil population. This category is to be paid for by appropriations, and thus one-half by the taxpayers each of the United States and the United Kingdom. It has not been determined whether seeds fall in this group. In my opinion they should, and I have included them in my estimates of supply and cost which appear below.

Category "B" is under the Joint Export-Import Agency, which regulates the importation of raw materials and the export of coal, some other raw materials and manufactured products. The organization started with a certain working capital and all exports of coal and other commodities are credited to this fund until the exports exceed the raw material imports, when the surplus will be applied to the cost of Category "A." It is hoped that the export surplus will begin to contribute to Category "A" in the last half of 1948 and cover virtually all the cost in the calendar year 1950.

Therefore, the cost of Category "A" for the balance of the 1947 fiscal year, in which a deficiency appropriation is involved, and the whole of the 1948 fiscal year, will fall upon the taxpayers of America and Britain.

COST AND SUPPLIES OF CATEGORY "A" IMPORTS FOR THE LAST
HALF OF FISCAL YEAR 1946-1947

The program of supplies and costs to cover Category "A" for the six months from January 1st to July 1st, 1947 will appear large compared to the program given later for the whole fiscal year 1947-1948. The reasons are that imports were unduly low during the last six months of 1946 and the drain on indigenous food unduly large. Also, it is necessary to include the cost of purchases and shipments prior to July 1st so as to provide in June for arrivals in Germany during the period July 1st to August 15th, for which appropriations for the 1947-48 fiscal year cannot be available until after July 1st. This works to lessen the burden on the fiscal year following that date. I have, as said, included the allotment of 65,000 tons of cereals to support the "normal ration" group, and the potato imports.

The following is the estimated cost for both zones, for the six months January 1st to July 1st, 1947, in which are included the supplies already shipped for this period:

Cereals (wheat equivalent) 2,505,000 tons	$288,000,000
Other foods, 720,000 tons	54,000,000
Fertilizers	17,500,000
Seeds	12,500,000
Petroleum products (civil population)	12,000,000
Total	$384,000,000

The United States contribution of one-half of this is $192,000,-000.

What portion of these expenditures are already covered by appropriations, and what portion must need be covered by deficiency appropriations, is not known to me.

SUPPLIES AND COSTS FOR FISCAL YEAR 1947-1948

In considering the supplies and cost of Category "A" for the fiscal year 1947-1948, the supplemental supports I have proposed to strengthen the children, adolescents and "normal ration" group, should undoubtedly carry through these groups until October, especially with the Spring and Summer produce. Therefore, it will not, in any event, be necessary to increase the general ration by the 250 calories provided in the bi-zonal agreement until that date. It is my hope that the revised methods by which the weak places in the system are strengthened may partially or wholly avoid this necessity after that date. I have, however, provided in the estimates an item of $62,300,000 for such an increase after October. I have also included in these estimates an enlarged fertilizer and seed program. It is my belief that these latter measures will greatly lighten the burden on our taxpayers in the fiscal year 1948-1949.

The following is my estimate of the supplies and costs needed for the fiscal year 1947-1948 covering Category "A":

Cereals (in terms of wheat) for 1,550 calorie level, 2,785,000 tons	$278,500,000
Cereals for 'normal consumers" emergency supplemental feeding, 192,000 tons	19,200,000
Child feeding program (includes special foods), 130,000 tons	35,000,000
Other foods, 450,000 tons	75,000,000
Fertilizers (available)	45,000,000
Seeds	27,000,000
Petroleum products for civil population	25,000,000
	$504,706,000
Cost of ration increase to 1,800 calories on or about October, 1947	62,300,000
Total	$567,000,000

Of this the United States share of 50 per cent amounts to $283,500,000.

Due to these changes in method, the above program is different from that submitted by the War Department for the fiscal year 1947-48, but the total cost is no greater.

It is my conviction that these appropriations for Category

"A" for both the 1946-1947 and the 1947-1948 fiscal years should have first consideration, even in priority to appropriations for military purposes. The occupation forces cannot be reduced without these assurances of minimum food supply. From the point of view only of maintaining order, the need for these forces is not great, if we can meet the food needs. Their size will depend upon other considerations.

FURTHER SAVINGS TO THE TAXPAYERS THAT CAN BE MADE

There are ways by which these costs could be reduced, although they are not certain enough to be deducted in advance against appropriations which must now be determined.

1. If these changes in rationing program render the general calorie lift unnecessary, there would be a saving of $62,000,-000.

2. If through the 1947 deficiency appropriation the seeds are provided in time, there should be substantial additions to the German potato harvest, in relief of 1947-1948 expenditures. If the fertilizer and seed recommendations for the fiscal year 1947-1948 are accepted, there should be savings by increased indigenous production in the year 1948-1949.

3. There would be savings if prices proved lower and if climatic conditions for the indigenous crops turned out exceptionally favorable.

4. The Potsdam Declaration results in Germany having no consequential overseas shipping. If we could effect some temporary operation by German crews of, say, seventy-five Liberty ships, now laid up, to transport food and raw materials, all of the expense could be paid by the Germans in marks, except for fuel, and thus save a very large amount of dollars otherwise coming from the American and British taxpayers. This would probably amount to $40,000,000 per annum.

5. A further saving of possibly several million dollars could be made for the taxpayers if the large American Army return equipment, now being transported at high ocean rates, were sent home on the return voyages of these Liberty ships.

6. There are food surpluses in the control of other nations than ourselves and the British. They comprise possible increased catches of fish in Norway, Sweden and Denmark, which otherwise are little likely to find a market, and some surpluses possible from the South American States. It would seem to me that some supplies could well be furnished by these nations, being repaid as indicated below, *pari passu* with the British and ourselves.

7. The Germans lost a considerable part of their deep sea fishing fleet. If more such boats could be found and leased from American surplus small shipping, the fish supply could be greatly increased. The fishing grounds in the Baltic and North Seas are being limited against German fishing. As there are ample supplies of fish in these seas, it seems a pity that with this food available, British and American taxpayers are called upon to furnish food in substitution for fish the Germans could catch for themselves.

Fish is particularly needed, as the present diet is sadly lacking in protein content.

8. A still further saving to British and American taxpayers is possible if maximum expedition could be made of exports of German manufacture. The Joint Export-Import Agency is doing its best, but such exports are hampered by the lack of coal for manufacture, by Trading-with-the-Enemy Acts, and restrictions on free communication, together with limitations on dealings between buyers and sellers. The restoration of trade is inevitable, and every day's delay in removing these barriers is simply adding to the burden of our taxpayers for relief that could otherwise be paid for in goods. No one can say that in her utterly shattered state, Germany is a present economic menace to the world.

Should there be such good fortune as to realize all these possibilities, we could not only increase the food supply to health levels but also lessen the joint costs by $150,000,000 during the fiscal year 1947-1948. However, as I have said, I am convinced that the larger sum should be provided for.

GERMAN REPAYMENT FOR THESE OUTLAYS

The great sums hitherto spent on relief of the German civilian population from outside Germany's borders, together with those in the future, should not be an irrecoverable expenditure to our two Governments.

I have, therefore, urged upon the American and British authorities that it be announced as a policy, and stipulated in all peace arrangements, that these expenditures for the relief of the civil population, (Category "A") past and future, should be made a first charge upon the economy of Germany and repaid from any future net exports from Germany before any payments to other nations of any kind.

At my instance, all Allied nations in the first World War agreed that German civilian relief expenditures at that time should be repaid from any liquid assets and ranked ahead of any reparation claims. They were so repaid. The grounds which I advanced at that time are no less valid today. By these relief expenditures, we are rebuilding the economy of the German people so that other payments can be made by them. These costs should be a sort of "Receiver's Certificate." If this policy be pursued, these appropriations for relief asked from the Congress, and the Parliament, can become a recoverable expenditure and not a charity loaded onto our taxpayers. It would seem that a tax upon exports, of some per cent, to be paid in dollars after July 1, 1949 might be an effective implementation of such a provision.

ORGANIZATION

I have made certain recommendations to the joint Military Governments of the two zones as to organization matters, which I believe will improve administration, now that bi-zonal operation, under larger German responsibility, has been undertaken.

CONCLUSION

It may come as a great shock to American taxpayers that, having won the war over Germany, we are now faced for some years with large expenditures for relief for these people. Indeed, it is something new in human history for the conqueror to undertake.

Whatever the policies might have been that would have avoided this expense, we now are faced with it. And we are faced with it until the export industries of Germany can be sufficiently revived to pay for their food. The first necessity for such a revival is sufficient food upon which to maintain vitality to work.

Entirely aside from any humanitarian feelings for this mass of people, if we want peace; if we want to preserve the safety and health of our Army of Occupation; if we want to save the expense of even larger military forces to preserve order; if we want to reduce the size and expense of our Army of Occupation—I can see no other course but to meet the burdens I have here outlined.

Our determination is to establish such a regime in Germany as will prevent forever again the rise of militarism and aggression within these people. But those who believe in vengeance and the punishment of a great mass of Germans not concerned in the Nazi conspiracy can now have no misgivings, for all of them—in food, warmth and shelter—have been sunk to the lowest level known in a hundred years of Western history.

If Western Civilization is to survive in Europe, it must also survive in Germany. And it must be built into a cooperative member of that civilization. That indeed is the hope of any lasting peace.

After all, our flag flies over these people. That flag means something besides military power.

On Relief Assistance to Countries Devastated by War

Statement before Committee on Foreign Affairs, House of Representatives

[February 28, 1947]

MR. CHAIRMAN, I rather hurriedly prepared a very short statement on the problem before this committee. I have been rather busy for the last 48 hours and could not give as much attention to it as I would like. I would be glad to amplify it in any way the committee may request.

To this proposed appropriation of $350,000,000 must be added large sums for areas under the American flag in Germany and Japan and Korea. In addition, two other important funds are in the offing to which our Government is expected to contribute. Those are the United Nations Refugee Organization, to look after displaced persons in Europe, and the United Nations child-feeding program. I suggest to the committee that, although other congressional committees may be dealing with these other relief programs, you should, at least, have all the proposals before you, so that you may consider the demands for relief upon the United States for the balance of this fiscal year and during the next fiscal year.

I have made no personal inquiry into the relief programs except those of Germany and Austria and the children's fund. I have brought the committee a copy of my report on German agriculture and food requirements and should be able to furnish such information on Austria in a few days.

In view of the world shortage of food and the great strains that are already upon the American taxpayer, I have thought it necessary to recommend that we hold the German and Austrian programs to the very minimum under which public health and ability to work can be sustained.

I would like to suggest to this committee that relief funds to the countries which are proposed under this appropriation, in view of the very same considerations, should be put on no higher levels than those we have proposed for Germany and Austria.

I have especially favored aid to the United Nations project for the special feeding of subnormal children. This fund to which you will be asked to contribute, however, would take some part of the relief burden of the countries that it is proposed to serve under this $350,000,000 appropriation, and also, as I have set up child feeding in Germany and Austria, that should in turn take some of the load off of the proposed United Nations children's fund.

Now the total of all these claims upon the generosity of the United States comes to a very large sum. I might interject—somewhere from $1,200,000,000 to $1,500,000,000 to cover the period up to the end of this next fiscal year.

We must not forget that these sums are supplemental to the five or six millions that we have already spent on civilian relief since the war from our own American sources.

Charitable relief by the Government is today a double tax on the American people. It is not only a direct burden upon the taxpayer, but these unremunerative and unbalanced exports keep up prices and keep up the cost of living. In their misery, these peoples abroad believe that our possibilities of giving are unlimited. They do not realize that our taxes, Federal and local, are now, 2 years after the war, still taking about 35 per cent of the whole national income, so that it is in the interests not only of ourselves but of the whole world that we stop, look, and listen in connection with these appropriations.

Now America, even with all of our burdens, never has ceased, and I hope never will cease, to do its utmost to prevent starvation in any country, but I am completely convinced that from now on we must limit our charitable giving to the sustaining of human lives alone.

We should bring governmental relief to an end as soon as possible. We should encourage it by encouraging the assumption of this burden by well-equipped organizations. Moreover, I believe we should begin to secure repayment of these sums. We have the full right to demand efficiency and economy in the use of public funds for relief, and we have further right to see that they contribute to that productivity and peace which alone will relieve us of these burdens.

Therefore, I would like to make a series of suggestions to the committee of some policies and methods that should be placed either administratively or legally into this proposed appropriation. These suggestions are not in criticism of the proposed legislation but in the hope they will be helpful in accomplishing the real end which America desires.

The first of these is, I suggest that no relief other than food, medicine, seed, and fertilizers should be furnished under these appropriations. There may be some cases of limited clothing supplies, especially for children.

Second, I believe that relief from our contributions to these funds should be limited to United States products and to the transportation of them. We should not use American dollars for purchase elsewhere. I may say that supplies from other quarters could be contributed by other governments who have surpluses.

Thirdly, none of this fund should be used for countries which are able to pay in cash or to secure credit or supplies through other channels.

Fourthly, a further careful estimate of the needs and costs of this relief in each of these countries should be made after full consideration and examination on the ground by specialists appointed by the United States Department of Agriculture, the

United States Public Health Service, and the International Emergency Food Council.

These estimates, except for Austria, in my view, should first include the period from the end of UNRRA until the 1947 harvest.

At that time the whole relief problem should be taken up afresh in the light of the situation that then exists.

I will elaborate that point a little later so as to make it a little more clear as to the next fiscal year.

In view of the world supplies and the needs of the taxpayer, any further relief program beyond that period to the next harvest, I believe, should be calculated on no higher basis than that we have proposed for Germany and Austria, where with experience and the readjustment of programs, we are certain we will be able to maintain public health and ability to work.

Fifth, this distribution should be continually under the supervision of, and satisfactory to, specialists from the agencies I have already named.

The problem of inspection of the distribution of food is a matter for experts.

Sixth, no obligations or promise should be entered into with any country for any specific amount of relief. The distribution should be put on a month-to-month program, terminable at any time.

There are many reasons for such an action that are implied in the emergency nature of the situation.

Moreover, difficult policy questions arise in connection with relief to peoples whose governments are said by our Government not to have kept their promises or agreements with the United States.

Another such difficult question is that of the governments of small countries, which are maintaining military forces far beyond any necessity for police purposes. And as criteria of their necessities there is an easy calculation; and that calculation is to have an army or military force not more than one-half of 1 per cent of the population.

Any mobilization beyond that point keeps men from producing food or producing the things that could be exported to pay for food, and therefore becomes a direct drain on the American taxpayer.

We have no desire to fail to do our full part in alleviating the starvation of women and children, and civilian men, merely because of the actions of their officials, but at some point American patience and American humane action are likely to be exhausted.

Seventh, no food from relief or from domestic production in these countries should be used for political pressure, and there should be no racial or other discriminations.

Eighth, no relief should be given where either commodities or cash are going out of that country for reparations or the purchase of arms. Such commodities or such cash could be used to pay for food.

Ninth, in my view any nation receiving relief should now begin to obligate itself to pay for the cost of it. That obligation should either be to the United States and the other donors to this same fund, or preferably to a fund to be established by the United Nations for future famine relief.

The nations receiving reparations from relief countries should be asked at once to defer reparations until these relief costs are repaid. Justice of this proposal lies in the fact that this relief obviously serves to preserve the manpower productivity of that country and therefore its ability to pay reparations.

Both the nations under reparations and those who are not should agree to a definite assurance of repayment by placing a tax of, say, 5 or 10 per cent on all exports from that debtor country, to be paid for in the currencies of the countries which receive such exports, and these payments would have, of course, to be held up, not to begin for 2 or 3 years.

In addition to these nine suggestions, I have one further: I believe that if this fund is to be administered with efficiency and economy, the committee should provide that there be appointed an administrator of the fund who can coordinate the various agencies of the Government in procurement, in shipping, in inspection, in these different countries.

That is the more necessary as four or five relief funds are going to be in operation coincidentally with this one.

Now the administration of relief is not, as some people seem to think, a job for welfare-trained people, as much as I appreciate their great qualities and their usefulness to the human race; administration of relief is a tremendous job in logistics.

It is the job of procurement of vast amounts of foods, of preparation of shipping, its transportation not only overseas but on land, and its delivery to certain specific points. The questions which arise of distribution after this food has once arrived in a given country are not difficult, if there is a predetermination of the supply that will be offered for the following 30 days.

If, during that 30 days, the distribution has not been carried out to the satisfaction of the administrator, then the supplies can cease and, in my view, if all the agencies of the Government were brought into cooperation, such a special administration would not need 20 men.

I am therefore not adding a burden of any consequential order upon this appropriation.

Now in conclusion—and I would be glad to amplify this rather condensed statement at any point that the members of the committee may ask—I would like to emphasize that it is such methods as these that would give some protection to the American taxpayer. They would contribute toward bringing an end to this universal giving, and yet would deprive no needy country of relief.

It only calls for cooperation on the part of these governments with the United States to secure efficiency and economy in the use of relief, and in the restoration of productivity which is fundamental for the recovery of the world and in the promotion of fundamental freedom and peace.

The need of relief will extend over the next fiscal year. The proposal in this legislation is for relief only up until January 1, 1948, and therefore is for only half of the next fiscal year.

Further, as I have said, there is no mortal man who can determine what the requirements of these various nations are going to be after the next harvest at the present time. Therefore, what I intended to indicate here was: there should be some provision in this legislation that some time after the forthcoming harvest, say the 1st of September, the Chairman and the ranking Democratic member—I am only just making a proforma suggestion—of the Appropriation Committees of the House and Senate should pass upon the use of the balance of this fund that may remain in hand at that time, and secure its distribution over the whole fiscal year instead of only the first half of the fiscal year.

We must bear in mind that there is a tremendous shortage in world food. I am advised that the amount of food available for distribution to the countries, which it has been stated that this fund will apply to, will not cost, or represent the expenditure of, more than about $125,000,000 before the next harvest. That is not a question of need; it is a question of supply.

I would like also to amplify a little further this question of examination on the ground. I may give you a very pertinent example: Last February I was called upon by the President to take a hand in the world situation. I found that the demands which had been formulated by the different nations as to the food that they would require to get through until the harvest of 1946, amounted to a total of breadstuffs and fats alone of something over 31,000,000 tons. As we had apparently available in the world at that time somewhere under 14,000,000 tons, the situation looked absolutely hopeless. Having had some years of experience during the first war with estimates and with the fact that people in great misery expect to be cut down sometimes, I concluded that nothing would serve except to examine these needs on the ground. With skilled staffs of technicians who could sit down with the technicians of those countries, it was possible to determine fairly accurately the amount month by month for each country that was required to prevent starvation.

When we had canvassed the problem over the entire world, we found that instead of thirty-million-odd tons being needed —if we were to hold to the very minimum levels necessary to prevent mass starvation—that we could succeed with some-where between 17,000,000 and 18,000,000 tons.

Therefore I suggested in my statement that there should be an examination on the ground. These situations look very different from that viewpoint than they do from statistical conclusions.

The Government possesses men in its various departments who are skilled in these problems. It is only a short job, a matter of a week or 10 days for each country. Such an inquiry can quickly determine what minimum program will prevent the loss of life for the given period.

Therefore the amounts of food required are uncertain because of inaccurate estimates of the needs before harvest, but they are also confused by the lack of knowledge as to what the forthcoming harvest will be. These proposals are also deficient as they provide only for one-half of the fiscal year, and I take it you will want to cover for the entire fiscal year rather than meet the problem again in a deficiency appropriation.

On Austrian Agriculture and Food Requirements—Economic Reorganization

Report to The President
[March 11, 1947]

INTRODUCTION

I T IS impossible to make clear the economic and relief problems of Austria without a paragraph on her history.

By the Treaty of Versailles in 1919 Austria was reduced from an empire to a small state of between six and seven million population, over-weighted by the large city of Vienna with its 1,500,000 people.

Being left with too little agriculture to feed herself and too little industry to buy food through export of goods, the deficits between her imports and exports from 1919 to 1931 were met largely by foreign charity and "loans" from institutions and governments, including the United States. She finally crashed into bankruptcy in 1931 setting the fire of financial panic which swept Europe and finally the whole world.

After 1932 the country, rid of accumulated debt, made slow but substantial progress and by 1938 seemed to have reached stability and self-support. At that time she was forcibly annexed by Hitler. After annexation, the Germans stripped the country of the bank reserves, confiscated many industrial establishments, and large farm estates.

The Allied Armies invaded the country in April and May

1945 dividing it into four separate zones for military government under the French, American, British, and Russian Armies.

An election held in November 1945 resulted in the establishment of a constitution and parliamentary government, which government is, however, subject ultimately to the direction of a control commission representing the four Allied Powers.

The people being exhausted of food supplies, relief measures were carried initially by the American and British military authorities. This lasted about twelve months until April 1, 1946, when UNRRA undertook the work. UNRRA (whose funds were 98% American and British Commonwealth) is now winding up its service. The remainder of the fiscal year 1946-47 will fall upon some new organization of relief. Such aid will certainly need to be carried on for the fiscal year 1947-48 and probably considerably longer before recovery of Austrian industry enables her to exchange goods for her necessary food imports.

WAR DESTRUCTION

Aside from the vitality of the state drained by the Germans, there was considerable damage from the war. Fortunately, there was less destruction to manufacturing industry than in most combat areas. The railways suffered considerably but have been generally restored. The largest damage was to housing and to public and important cultural buildings.

In the city of Vienna, which suffered most, some 15,000 buildings were completely destroyed out of 65,000 damaged. Expressed in apartment units, over 110,000, or 21% of the city's shelter, were made uninhabitable with consequent dreadful overcrowding, and thousands living in the rubble.

AGRICULTURAL PRODUCTION

Austrian agriculture never did supply more than 70% of her needs, the balance being imported. Due to the lack of fertilizers and agricultural machinery, the harvest of 1946 was about 60% of normal. Thus, between the normal deficiency in production and the low yields, the present volume of needed imports is very large.

FOOD DISTRIBUTION

The 7,000,000 population, from a food-rationing point of view, can be classified as follows:

"Self-suppliers"	1,200,000
"Partial self-suppliers"	700,000
Expectant and nursing mothers	90,000
Children 1-3	330,000
Children 3-6	370,000
Children 6-12	620,000
"Normal consumers"	2,100,000
"Employees"	600,000
Moderately heavy workers	800,000
Heavy workers	400,000

There is some duplication in these numbers due to "partial self-suppliers." There are some 550,000 displaced persons in Austria, 450,000 of whom are included above, and 100,000 of whom are provided for from non-Austrian sources.

The ration is at present 1550 calories for "normal consumers" with priorities in dairy products and special foods for the mothers group, and children up to twelve years. There are varied supplements in meats, fats, and breadstuffs for the different "workers" groups.

Examination of the nutritional situation of these groups showed that their condition was fairly good. There was no consequential famine edema. The weak spots were the lack of universal school feeding of children and more effective aid for indigent "normal consumers." Therefore, more systematic school feeding is necessary and further provision should be made for the indigent.

The nutritional condition is better than when I examined the situation a year ago. Although the official ration generally parallels that of Germany, insofar as calories are concerned, the condition of the people is distinctly better in Austria.

Compared to Germany the ration is better balanced, especially in the children's group, and there is a larger amount of supplemental food outside the ration. This arises from the larger amounts of unrationed food (such as vegetables except potatoes), larger black market supplies, a certain amount of child-feeding by foreign voluntary agencies and the very large number of food packages sent to friends and relatives from abroad. Altogether it is estimated that these supplements to the rationing system would represent an addition of at least 350 calories *per diem* if evenly distributed, bringing the "normal consumer's" ration up to 1900 calories.

The present food levels appear adequate to prevent any disaster but must be regarded as "emergency maintenance" which cannot be continued over years.

PROPOSED ORGANIZATION OF CONTINUED RELIEF

The United Nations has proposed a fund of $610,000,000 for relief to certain countries of which Austria is one. The United States contribution, recommended by our State Department, is $350,000,000, or 57%. The fund is presumed to cover only the period from the imminent end of UNRRA to the end of 1947—about nine months. The United Nations estimates contemplated a higher food level than that which I have felt possible or necessary during the emergency, and they include certain industrial reconstruction aids in addition to food, medicine and such agricultural supplies as seed, fertilizers and insecticides. While the program recommended by the United Nations is admirable and desirable, I have felt it necessary, in view of world supplies and the drains upon the American taxpayer, to make estimates only for food, medicines and agricultural supplies, and upon more limited levels of caloric intake.

The relief program can be divided into two periods: (a) from the end of UNRRA to the end of the fiscal year 1947, and (b) for the fiscal year 1947-48.

REQUIREMENTS FOR THE REMAINDER OF THE FISCAL YEAR 1946-1947

The program necessary for the period after UNRRA winds up—until July 1, 1947—is difficult to estimate until final amounts of UNRRA supplies are known. However, the requirements of food and medicine beyond the UNRRA program are roughly estimated at about $30,000,000 to July 1st. I have made no estimates for fertilizers or seed for the 1947 crop beyond the UNRRA supplies, as no more could arrive in time.

This sum will need to be provided either from Army deficit appropriations or from the newly proposed $350,000,000 fund. Whatever the source, the control of the distribution of American supplies should be placed in the hands of the American Army Command in Europe. The reason is that these supplies should be coordinated with the supplies for Germany, as both should be procured in common and shipped through the port of Bremen and over German railways. Moreover, Army agents can not only supervise distribution, but can also adjust our activities in relief to that of other nations contributing to Austria.

FISCAL YEAR 1947-1948

As relief must continue at least until the end of the fiscal year 1947-48, I have felt it better to face the fact now rather than renewed appropriations later.

The program for the fiscal year 1947-48 will depend somewhat upon the crop of 1947, which cannot as yet be determined. All estimates should be revised at that time. My preliminary estimate of requirements is:

Cereals	430,000 tons
Meats	5,600 "
Fats	35,000 "

Pulses .... 114,000 "
Sugar .... 9,000 "
Seeds .... 60,000 "
Fertilizers .... 150,000 "
Medicines $5,000,000

The total cost of such a program is estimated at about $125,000,000.

FINANCE

Thus the estimated cost of this program from the end of UNRRA until July 1, 1948, or about 15 months, is about $155,000,000. I have recommended to the Congress certain conditions to be attached to any American contribution.

What amounts the other nations may contribute to Austrian relief have not yet been determined. The British have made a grant of 10,000,000 pounds sterling to Austria but I understand only a minor part can be used for dollar purchases. If the whole $610,000,000 fund be subscribed as recommended by the United Nations, then the 57% of the cost to the American taxpayer would be about $86,000,000. If other nations fail to respond, it may be necessary to lower the level of relief.

The estimates for Austria under the $610,000,000 United Nations program are about $148,000,000 for nine months only, but relief will need to go on at least until July 1, 1948. If it were continued six months more at this same rate, it would entail a further sum of about $100,000,000, or a total of about $248,000,000, as contrasted with $155,000,000 I have estimated.

As said, the lower costs that I propose are due to short world supplies and a food level that while austere is I believe sufficient to maintain health and vigor. Further, the $610,000,-000 program includes support for industrial rehabilitation which I discuss later.

NECESSARY STEPS TO END THE LOAD ON THE AMERICAN TAXPAYER

The problem of how soon Austria can become self-supporting by exports with which to buy her own food is of first interest to the American taxpayer. No report on Austria that does not face this situation is worth preparation. So long as such a balanced economy cannot be created (unless we wish to see terrible starvation) a large part of the deficit will fall upon the taxpayers in the United States and other nations. And this at a time when the whole world is struggling with huge problems of recovery.

There can be no real solution until there is a peace treaty which entirely frees Austrian economy to produce and export.

However, two alternative situations must be considered:

First, the interregnum between now and a peace treaty.

Second, the economic basis of a treaty under which Austria may regain self-support.

THE INTERREGNUM

Austrian economy, even in the interregnum before peace requires the import of machinery, coal, certain raw materials, such as textiles, leather and metals, in order to manufacture both for consumption goods and for export. She already has developed some exports. The Austrian government has set up a sort of pool into which foreign exchange from these exports and otherwise is deposited and from which payments are made for industrial imports. The United Nations estimated her exports and other foreign exchange sources for the year 1947 at about $125,000,000. It is my belief that, at this rate, if the agricultural and food necessities can be provided without present drain on these exchange resources, Austria can manage her own industrial import program, as well as can be expected with the limitations of the times, without calling for aid from taxpayers of other nations in this field.

There is no way to estimate how long it will be before a

constructive treaty shall be concluded. However, there are certain cooperative steps between the occupying powers that could be taken during the interregnum which would decrease needed food imports and increase exports so as to contribute to payment for food.

As I have said, pending peace, the Austrian government is subject to a quadrupartite commission of American, British, Russian and French representatives, and the country is separated into four military zones. The original intention was that there should be economic unity of the zones. That has not been fully carried out and full use of Austrian resources is not being brought into play, the result of which increases the burden upon our taxpayers.

The greatest difficulty in cooperation is with the Russian zone. Under the Potsdam Declaration, each of the four nations was to have as *German* reparations any *German* assets in its Austrian zone. Under these provisions each military government requisitioned such property. A very large segment of Austrian economy is under such requisition. Our American requisitions amounted to some two hundred enterprises but these have been assigned to the Austrian Government to operate in trust pending some settlement of the whole question. The other governments have been urged similarly to assign such ownership so as to increase Austrian productivity, self-support and recovery.

Under the Russian interpretation of the Potsdam Declaration, they have not only requisitioned a large amount of fertile land, but a great number of industrial plants. The Austrians claim that a large part of them were not in reality German assets. Disregarding questions of legality upon which I am not passing judgment, if the produce from these lands were released to Austria, together with relaxation of other requisitions, it would decrease the food imports by at least 70,000 tons per annum. Many of the requisitioned industrial plants are used otherwise than to support Austrian economy or exports. Another way to moderate this load on Austrian food supply would be the reduction of Russian armies to the minor levels of the other powers. In any event, the load upon the taxpayers of other nations during the interregnum is greatly increased, both for food imports and the diminished exports with which to pay for it.

AUSTRIAN ECONOMY IN PEACE

The Allies, in the Moscow Declaration of November 1, 1943, declared the annexation of Austria "null and void," "shall be liberated from German domination," "reestablished a free and independent." Thus classed as a "liberated state," it has been presumed that Austria will be free of reparations.

It can be said at once, however, that if the requisitioned assets are to be removed or operated for other than Austrian economy or by other than the Austrians themselves, there can be little hope that Austria can recover self-support for many, many years.

On the other hand, if Austria's land and industrial equipment were entirely freed by a peace treaty and the burden of foreign armies removed, we might reasonably expect her to begin to contribute to the cost of food imports by the latter part of 1948 and to become self-supporting in two or three years thereafter. Otherwise she is likely again to be the poorhouse of Europe for years to come and her people constantly be dependent for life upon foreign aid.

The Austrian people are making a brave fight to reestablish the principles of Western Civilization. Their officials are able and effective. They should enlist our sympathy, our support and all the influence we can summon in her reconstruction.

On Greek Independence Day

Remarks before Greek War Relief Dinner,
New York City
[March 25, 1947]

THIS day, March 25th, is one of the landmarks in the struggle of Greece over twenty-three centuries for independence and personal liberty. It was 126 years ago today that Greece threw off the Turkish yoke. And in that struggle the American people rallied to her moral and material aid. There is no race that has fought so persistently for these ideals and so valiantly held aloft the torch of freedom. Within the soul of this people there is the fire of freedom which will not be quenched.

Six years ago her independence was submerged by the Germans and Italians, and again, after this desperate war, she has emerged free, but exhausted. Nor has the attack upon her independence and her internal freedoms yet ended.

Greece today, two years after her liberation, is still in political and economic chaos.

America has shown its constant solicitude and has given generously both private and governmental aid. We propose to continue to do so. But a large part of that chaos and misery could be lifted by one man in the world if he be willing. That is Marshal Joseph Stalin. It is within his power to stop the aggressive war in the form of guerrilla raids from Yugoslavian, Bulgarian and Albanian territory. It is within his power to see that the Communist bands in Greece stop killing and abide by constitutional means to express their views. That would bring peace to Greece. Then American aid could be devoted to restoring productivity of the Greek people instead of our wasting our generosity on military equipment.

But our meeting here is to encourage the giving of private and voluntary relief. The generous appropriation of our Government serves to provide the bare necessities of life and defense. It remains for private charity to aid in stamping out the ravages of malaria and tuberculosis, to restore the subnormal children, to provide shelter and to care for the multitude of orphans.

We are here appealing to the heart of the American people for aid.

On the German Food Crisis

Press Statement, New York City

[May 15, 1947]

THE German food crisis is very bad. The situation is, however, temporary. It is in large degree due to the failure of the Germans in both the British and American zones to produce their anticipated collections of indigenous food from their own farmers upon which all calculations have been based. There were considerable losses of indigenous food from the severest season in their history, from undue feeding of livestock and from sales in the black market. The inability to maintain the portion of the full ration from German sources was only developed with the passing of the winter.

In view of the acute world needs we had originally established a program of shipments to Germany which, as in other cases, met only the barest import necessities, and therefore there were no margins in Germany to meet such a development. And again because of the world shortages and the needs of many nations, it has taken a little time to find a solution. But by the energetic actions of the War and Agriculture Departments, enlarged supplies, over and above the otherwise anticipated program of shipments have been obtained and are being put en route, and will, I hope, remedy the deficit in a very few weeks. I understand the special feeding of children has been uninterrupted. However, the whole incident points to the need for the Germans themselves to control their own supplies properly, for America and Britain cannot again be called upon to make good such failures.

The World Food Situation

T HIS meeting was agreed upon three months ago. Its
purpose was to rally for another winter American moral
and spiritual forces engaged in voluntary relief to a
distressed world. During these three months the world outlook
has become even more distressing. The need for privately-
organized charitable aid from the American people has become
more urgent.

In order to emphasize the need I shall summarize the world
food outlook in the simplest terms possible.

1. Food obviously lies at the base of all living, all progress
and all peace. Until we have solved that problem all other
economic and political programs and proposals are in vain.

Due to the failure of agricultural recovery in Europe and
Asia, together with devastating droughts in other parts of the
world—including the American corn crop—the next twelve
months will be a grim food year.

2. There is every indication that the total available food
supplies are no more than those from the harvest of 1945, that
is, two years ago. During the year which followed that harvest
there were the gravest dangers of mass starvation. But by organized measures among the deficit nations, by cooperative action among surplus-producing nations, and by self-denial of
American consumers, we managed to pull through that year
without widespread disaster. During that year, however, hun-

dreds of millions of people had little more than the barest subsistence.

3. The harvest of 1946, that is, the harvest year from July 1, 1946 to last July 1 showed a considerable improvement over the year before. There was a larger production in the deficit nations and larger exports were available from surplus countries. It was possible therefore to get through the past twelve months without such measures as were necessary the year before.

4. The outlook for the twelve months following July 1 of this year is not comfortable. In order that this may be clear I must use statistics. They may not stir emotions, but they are vital to conviction.

The mainstay of the whole hungry world during this past harvest year has been about 30 million tons of cereals and about 4½ million tons of meats and fats and some sugar, which have been moved overseas. This 35 million tons of food was the contribution of all the surplus-producing countries in the world to the hungry countries, to which the United States contributed over 18½ million tons.

Crop reports for this present harvest outside of Russia—that is the harvest the world must live on for the 12 months following last July—show there will be about 4 million tons more bread grains, that is wheat and rye, than in the last harvest. The rice will apparently be about the same. There will be some more sugar. That sounds encouraging, but our trouble is a disastrous decrease in the harvest of coarse grains, that is, corn, oats, barley, etc.; that decrease will exceed 32 million tons. There is also some decrease in European potatoes. Russia has had some crop improvement. We hope it is enough to supply the satellite states.

5. This shortage of approximately 28 million tons in the supply of grains—that is, the difference between a 4 million ton increase in bread grains and a 32 million ton decrease in coarse grains—as contrasted with 30 million tons of grains needed, is not as discouraging as it might look. At famine levels all grains are more or less interchangeable as human food and

animal feed. The major weight of the decrease, therefore, will fall upon animals. Of the 30 million tons of grain exported from surplus countries in the year ended July 1, 1947, 7,600,-000 tons were coarse grains used for human food.

The situation which now confronts us has two major effects. First, there will be less coarse grains in the world available for human consumption than last year. Second, the immense deficit in feed grains will result in a much smaller amount of animal products for export.

6. If large areas of the world are to be saved from mass starvation, several courses of action must be taken:

First, we must impose as much as possible of the burden of food shortage upon animals and not upon human beings. Our farmers must resist the natural tendency to feed wheat to animals when coarse grain feed is scarce. That is, in this world emergency, we must give the preference to human beings. But to rely simply on restricting to a minimum the use of wheat for livestock by no means satisfies the tragic deficit in world supplies. If this were all that is to be done the effect would be to decrease the American contribution to world food supplies by anywhere from 5 to 8 million tons below the 18½ million tons which we supplied during the past harvest year. Therefore we must consider still further measures.

Second, it will be imperative for us to reduce unnecessary human consumption and waste of food. Such measures, in order to secure the best results, must be largely voluntary with some regulation against waste in the processing trades.

Third, even with these additional measures, it would be impossible for the United States alone to meet the world deficit. That can be done only if we have full cooperation from the other surplus-producing countries, and drastic control of distribution and elimination of black markets in the deficit countries.

Fourth, the situation is complicated by rising food prices. Already this has created real privation for many Americans. The increase in food prices over the twelve months ending last July can be very largely ascribed to over-exports of food. I do not

say this in a critical sense as the American people were endeavoring to prevent starvation in all parts of the world. Nevertheless, it is just a fact that if we had exported considerably less
food we would not have had any such upward movement in
prices as has taken place. The accelerated price rise of the last
few months has been in part due to the gradual realization of
an impending world-wide shortage. The remedies for price increases lie in handling of exports with an eye to keeping prices
down, in the stoppage of speculation and hoarding and, above
all, in decreasing unnecessary consumption and waste.

7. The situation will not be solved by panic or over-hasty action. All countries in Europe have their harvests which also
will supply them for some period. In the United States, even
in the most pessimistic view, we have a surplus of human food.
By proper world organization we ought to be able to prevent
disaster as we did in the 1945 harvest year.

8. I should like to add a word of warning. The American
people cannot be expected to make the personal sacrifices which
this program entails unless there is complete cooperation
abroad.

Such events as the present political strikes of farmhands in
Italy which paralyze their production of food do not stimulate
American effort.

9. Primarily, this meeting is concerned with charitable programs. While the broader bases of economic action such as I
have mentioned are necessary if we shall solve this world situation, there is no less need in the world for private effort and
charity. This earth is indeed in need of spiritual and moral
stimulation. Charitable action and the voluntary reduction of
consumption to save human life are among the highest of moral
and spiritual inspirations to mankind. We must call upon these
forces of the spirit if we are to succeed in our economic as well
as our charitable programs. Indeed, the great charitable organizations in the United States which will be putting forth their
efforts to save the individual cases of destitution and hardships,
as distinguished from broad intergovernmental programs, have
a great work to perform—not only in the service they give, but

in the moral and spiritual stimulation they can lend to the American people in these efforts.

The fundamental law of our civilization is based upon compassion and charity. And compassion and charity do not ask whether the sufferer has always been good or bad, whether he has brought his misery upon himself, or is the innocent victim of forces beyond his control.

It is sufficient that there is suffering and that we possess the means to alleviate it. The key to our hearts can always be turned by little children, by mothers, by the aged and the destitute. We are, thank God, sentimentalists. We know that the great bounty that has been placed in our keeping must not be hoarded while others starve and are in pain. We dare not, even in this age of gross and abject materialism, forget that our consciences were forged by tender women and strong men who have built for themselves a world to their liking, always setting aside a mite for the charity that they knew God enjoined upon good people.

And we are a good people. We have in the past responded to every call for human aid.

I hope that the day never comes in this country when all our good works are done through taxes, for then the moral strength that comes from compassion and charity is lost to us.

In this spirit of humility and thankfulness I ask you to increase your effort a thousandfold. Let it never be said that the American heart has grown cold, that the American hand of charity has become palsied. Give for the joy of giving and sing hymns of thankfulness that you have it to give.

Index

Absecon, N. J., speech, Nov. 10, 1945,
44-48
Address at Banquet in Honor of His
Excellency, Prime Minister of
Greece, 267-268
Address before Holland Society of
New York, 58-60
Address before Sons of Revolution,
61-66
Agnosticism, 59, 79
Agricultural products, 113, 129-130,
136, 307
Agriculture, 116, 165, 192, 222, 229,
231, 239, 243, 246, 251, 260, 269, 272-
273, 294, 295, 306; Department of,
187, 193, 288, 305; Secretary of, 169,
216; *See also* Controls, war; *See
also* Food Production
Aid, financial, *see* Loans
Air Transport Command, 216, 270
Albania, 214, 303
Alliance, military, 64-65
Allies, 7, 24, 64, 87, 93, 104, 106, 284,
294, 295, 302
America, Meaning of, 74-79; *see* Uni-
ted States
American Army Command, 298
American Catholic Welfare Associa-
tion, 180, 184
American Occupation Forces, 277; *see
also* Armies, occupation
American Red Cross, 79, 180, 184, 186,
190
American Relief for Czechoslovakia,
180
Anderson, Clinton P., 169
Annexation, 87, 92, 270, 294, 302
Anti-trust acts, 51
Appeasement, 21, 39
Appraisal of World Situation and Our
Policies in Relation to It, 20-21
Appropriations Committees, 135
Arabs, in Palestine, 16-17
Arbitration, in labor disputes, 56
Argentina, 23, 130, 175, 196, 197, 198,
200, 212, 217, 222, 223, 229, 239, 246,
252-253, 257, 258, 259, 260, 262
Armament, 68-70, 290
Armies, occupation, 117, 270, 272-273,

277, 282, 285, 301-302; Russian, 64,
301
Asia, 46, 59, 63, 70, 77, 101, 109, 122-
124, 167, 195, 205, 221, 226, 227, 239,
242, 246, 249, 250, 261, 265, 268, 306
Assets, European in U. S., 11, 112,
128, 134
Atlantic Charter, 25, 39; support of,
21
Atomic bomb, Hoover proposals for
national policies on, 14-15, 21
Atomic power, 33-34, 40
Australia, 23, 196, 198, 199, 201, 202,
205, 212, 217, 223, 230, 242, 250, 252,
259, 260
Austria, 87, 214, 269, 270, 286, 287,
289, 294-302
Austrian Agriculture and Food Requirements—Economic Reorganization, 294-302

Baltic Sea, 283
Bangalore, 203
Bargaining, collective, 56
Belgian-American Educational Foun-
dation, 146
Belgian Relief Commission, 146
Belgium, 146-147, 163, 214, 254, 271,
276
Belsen, 208, 224, 241, 248
Berlin, 273
Bierut, President, 181, 182
Big business, 50, 70
Bill of Rights, 50, 63
Black market, 175-179, 188-189, 193,
242, 249, 275, 297, 305, 308
Bombay, 199, 215
Brazil, 175, 197, 212, 217, 254, 257
Bremen, 298
Bretton Woods, 3
Bridges, Senator H. Styles, 109
Britain, 6, 12, 14, 30, 46, 64, 78, 83, 84,
88, 105, 128, 142, 159, 176, 191, 196,
262, 271, 277, 279, 305; contribution
to relief, 83, 84, 96, 103, 190, 197-
198, 199, 279 ff., 295, 299; food sup-
ply, 90, 163, 195, 196-197, 212, 214,
217, 218, 219, 223, 276, 283

British Empire, 12, 46, 219; *see also* Britain
British Labor Party, 16-17
British Parliament, 284
Buchenwald, 23, 208, 224, 226, 241, 248
Budget, U. S., 69
Bulgaria, 25, 216, 303
Bureaucracy, 35, 45, 71
Burma, 203, 205, 212, 217
Bush, Vannevar, 34

Cairo, 193, 205, 221, 228
California, 100, 159
Calories, see *Food consumption, Rations*
Camacho, Avila, 234
Canada, 23, 79, 130, 175, 196, 197, 199, 212, 217, 223, 252, 257, 259, 262, 263; Prime Minister, 259, 265; St. Lawrence waterway, 18-19
Capital goods, 127, 130, 133
Carran, Mrs. Mollie, 76
Cartels, 13
Central America, 258; *see also* Latin America
Ceylon, 200, 215
Chile, 197, 245, 247-251, 256; President of, 245
China, 23, 98, 123-124, 134, 135, 163, 207, 208, 211, 216, 221, 222, 229, 239, 246, 260, 262, 264
Christianity, 40, 254
Churchill, Winston, in praise of Finland, 25; on Russo-Finnish War, 24
Civil War, 30, 79
Clay, General Lucius, 96, 269
Cochin-China, 206, 215
Collectivism, 45-46, 71, 73; *see also* Totalitarianism
Colombia, 236, 256; President of, 236
Colorado River dam, 19
Combined Food Board, 191, 211, 224, 241, 248, 261, 263
Commerce, Department of, conferences on radio, 141-143; Secretary of, 141, 143, 147
Commodities, exchange of, 7, 110
Commodity credit, 12
Common man, cult of, 41-43
Communism, 45, 49, 54, 59, 101, 120, 122, 254-255, 268
Communist Press Practices, 254-255
Communists, 20, 22, 23, 25, 50, 59-60, 71, 77, 254, 303; in Finnish Ministry, 25
Compton, Dr. Karl, 34
Concentration camps, 20-21, 23, 38, 208, 271; *see also* Forced labor camps; *see also* Work camps

Congress of Industrial Organization, 51
Congress of the United States, 60, 61; and World War I loans, 5-6
Congressional Committee on Postwar Economic Policy, 96-97
Conservation, 212, 220, 227, 231, 242, 261, 262, 309; *see also* Rationing, voluntary
Conservatism, 50, 52
Constitution, U.S., 50, 65
Controls, war, 37, 116
Coolidge, Calvin, 18
Cooperation, 116-118, 123-124, 133, 171, 172, 182, 196, 198, 199, 202, 205, 208, 212, 223, 228, 233, 235, 239, 246, 252, 256, 257, 258, 261, 262, 263, 269, 270, 291, 301, 308, 309; in Western Europe, 65, 121
Cost of living, 113, 287
Credits, 135, 136
Crops, *see* Agricultural products; Food production
Cuba, 197
Currency, 62, 121, 123, 128-129, 133, 134; *see also,* Inflation
Czechoslovakia, 87, 147, 178, 179-180, 214, 270, 271

Davis, Chester, 169
Dawes, Charles G., 3
Debt, national, 10
Declaration of Independence, 50, 63, 78
Defense, 21, 64-66, 69, 115-116, 118, 304
Delinquency, juvenile, 150-151
Demilitarization, 99-101, 104, 106-107; *see also* Disarmament
Denmark, 196, 216, 283
Depression, 32, 76, 121, 147
Destruction at Our Expense, 119
Disarmament, 21, 63, 85-88, 107; *see also* Demilitarization
Displaced persons, 135, 274, 276, 286, 296; *see also* Expellees
Dominions, 11
Draft, 39
Draper, General William, 96, 270
Drought, 221, 222, 229, 230, 239, 243, 246, 250, 260, 264, 306
Dumping of goods, 13

Economic Cooperation Administration, Hoover views on, 120-130
Economic Mission to Germany, Report on, 269-285
Economic Recovery from War, 29-35; *see also* Recovery

Economy, free, 45, 51, 59, 109, 111; Japanese, 99-101; threats to, 50-51; managed or planned, 45, 49, 54, 100-101, 116

Ecuador, 237

Educational institutions, role in recovery, 40-43

Effect of Railroad Strike on Relief to Famine Areas, 232

Effects of Railroad Strike on World Famine, 209

Efficiency, national, means for increasing, 31-32, 46, 55-57

Egypt, 205, 216, 218, 221

Eisenhower, General Dwight, 163

Elections, Congressional, 71

Elections, free, in Japan, 107; in Russian-dominated countries, 23; in Yugoslavia, 22

Emergency Conference on European Cereal Supplies, 187-192

Emergency Food Administration, 169, 171

England, 78; see also Britain

Enterprise, free, 59; see also Economy, free; private, 128, 129, 132, 133, 142

Estonia, 147

Euphrates valley, 16

Europe, 62 ff., 70, 71, 76, 77, 79, 84, 86, 90, 93-97, 108, 119, 122, 124, 126, 128, 133, 147, 205, 211, 212, 219, 221, 222, 227, 230, 239, 242, 246, 249, 250, 261, 265, 268, 285, 286, 294, 298, 302, 306, 309; aid to, see U.S. contribution to relief; assets in U.S., 11, 112, 128, 134; Central, 163; conditions after World War II, 68-71, 86-87, 119, 163-199, 226, 260; Eastern, 38, 46, 59, 163, 260; great depression in, 5; Western, 46, 59, 64-65, 70, 109, 120, 121, 123, 126, 130, 137, 163, 272

European Aid Act, 129

Exchange of Students with Foreign Countries, 146-148

Expellees, 270-272, 284; see also Displaced persons

Export-Import Bank, 3, 10, 111, 117, 128, 130, 132, 133

Exports, see Foreign trade

Faith, 59, 78, 168, 171, 242, 250; see also Christianity

Famine, 23, 77, 163-164, 165-166, 167-168, 169-171, 172-173, 174-175, 176-178, 179-180, 182, 183-184, 185-186, 187-192, 193-198, 199-202, 203-205, 206, 207, 208, 209, 210-220, 221-228, 232, 233-234, 235-236, 237, 238-244,
245-251, 254, 257, 259-266, 267, 269 ff., 296 ff., 306-310; see also Starvation; Food relief

Famine, children, 189-191, 194, 199, 210-211, 225, 226-227, 235, 264-265, 274-275, 277-278, 286, 287, 296, 297, 304

Famine Emergency Committee, 165, 169, 170, 177, 221

Far East, 108, 191, 230; see also Asia

Fascism, 49

Federal Reserve system, 117

Federation of Western Europe, 64

Fifth columns, 60, 68-69

Finland, 5, 24-25, 147, 185-186, 214

FitzGerald, Dr. Dennis A., 83, 187, 193, 264, 269

Food Commission, report, 98

Food consumption, 174, 176-177, 184, [189], 194, 201, 203-204, 223, 240-242, 248, 249, 261, 273, 274, 308; see also Ration

Food deficit, 99, 106, 179-180, 199, 204, 205, 211-212, 219, 220, 225, 227, 234, 235, 241, 248-249, 253, 261, 262, 295-296, 305, 307-308

Food Difficulties in India, 203-205

Food Mission, 237; see also Economic Mission

Food Problem in Philippines, 206

Food production, 116, 180, 225, 230, 243, 249, 272-273, 305, 307-309

Food relief, 3, 12, 23, 46, 59, 103-104, 107, 117, 120, 124-127, 134, 147, 163-310; see also Relief and reconstruction

Food relief, organization of, 229-231, 260, 288-291, 298

Food Situation in France, 176-178

Food Situation in Italy, 174-175; Poland, 183-184

Forced-labor camps, 20-21; see also Concentration camps, work camps

Foreign exchange, 123, 300

Foreign loans, postwar, 3-13; see loans, postwar foreign

Foreign Ministers, conference of, 106

Foreign policies, 3-25, 46, 83-97, 98-102, 103-108, 109-118, 121-130

Foreign relations, 62-63, 148; see also Foreign policies

Foreign trade, 8-9, 13, 110-118, 122-130, 132, 136; Japanese, 99

France, 87, 92, 94, 96, 97, 104, 163, 172-173, 176-178, 197, 212, 214, 217, 218, 254, 264, 271, 276

Free trade, 8, 62; in Germany, 85

Freedom, 49, 52, 59, 66, 67-73, 77-79, 116, 154, 158, 267, 268, 291, 303;

dangers to, 50-53; degeneration and
diminution of, 20-21, 39, 45-46, 53,
126; need for, 37, 45, 66; personal,
59, 86; religious, 78, 154
Fuel relief, 12, 59, 120, 125, 133, 279,
280; see also Relief and reconstruction
Fulbright, Senator J. W., 146

Galpin, Perrin C., 187
George Washington Plan, See Washington, Plan, 62-63
German Agriculture and Food Requirements, 269-285
German Food Crisis, 305
Germany, 6, 21, 38, 70, 83-97, 103-108,
119, 123-124, 127-128, 130, 134, 135,
163, 172, 180, 184, 214, 260, 269-285,
286, 287, 289, 294, 297, 298, 303, 305;
as exponent of collectivism, 45; Finland joins war against, 24; Military
Government of, 95-96; see also New
Germany; see also Occupation, German; see also Occupation zones;
war with Russia, 24
Gibson, Hugh, 83, 187, 269
Gold, 110, 112, 115, 123
Government, centralization of, 45;
philosophy of, 50-51; representative,
59, 70, 71
Greece, 93, 134, 135, 147, 214, 267-268,
303-304; Prime Minister, 267-268
Greek Relief Committee, 267-268
Gridiron Dinner, 152-155

Hamburg, 272, 275
Harriman Report, 127
Hatch, Senator Carl A., 18
Hegel, 79
Helsinki, 185; bombing of, 38
Herter, Representative Christian, 122;
Committee, reports, 131
Hester, Colonel Hugh, 270
Hiroshima, bombing of, 38
Hitler, Adolph, 64, 68, 294
Holland, 60, 94, 163, 196, 214, 276;
example to world, 58-59; surplus
commodities, 12
Hoover, Herbert, on Austrian agriculture and food requirements, 294-
302; on Communist press practices,
254-255; on Congressional election,
54; on Economic Cooperation Administration, 120-130; on effect of
railroad strike on relief to famine
areas, 232; on effects of railroad
strike on world famine, 209; on
exchange of students with foreign
countries, 146-148; on Finland, 24-

25; on food administration in Finland, 185-186; on food and relief
requirements for Germany, Japan
and Korea, 103-108; on food conditions in Czechoslovakia, 179-180; on
food difficulties in India, 203-205;
on food mission, 237; on food needs
of China, 207; on food problem in
Philippines, 206; on food situation
in France, 176-178; on food situation in Poland, 183-184; on food
situation in Italy, 174-175; on German Agriculture and Food Requirements, 269-285; on German food
crisis, 305; on Greek Independence
Day, 303-304; on Japanese food supply, 208; on Japanese reparations,
98-102; on Latin-American food
situation, 256-258; on limits of
American aid to foreign countries,
109-118; on Marshall Plan (ECA),
120-130; on Marshall Plan Bill, 131-
137; on meaning of America, 74-79;
on national policies as to atomic
bomb, 14-15, 21; on necessary steps
for promotion of German exports,
83-97; on Palestine question, 16-17;
on philosophy of government, 49-53;
on President Truman's appeal to
save food, 163-164; on proposals for
post war national defense, 64-65;
115-116, 304; on post-war policies,
21, 85-86, 94-97, 101-102, 103-108,
109-118, 119, 276-285, 286, 293, 297-
302; on relief assistance to countries
devastated by war, 286-293; on Russian attitude toward peace, 20, 23,
68; on support of National Boys'
Club Week, 149-151; on twenty-fifth
anniversary of radio, 141-145; on
world famine, 165-166, 167-168, 169-
171, 172-173, 193-198, 235-236, 238-
244, 245-251, 252-253; on world food
situation, 199-202; on world organization, 64-65; on world situation,
20-21, 67-73; on Yugoslavian incident, 22-23; on postwar policies, 10-
13, 69-73
Housing, 271-272, 295
Hull Cordell, 8
Hungary, 87, 147, 216, 270

Ideals, American, 155
Imports, see Foreign trade
Indemnities, 7
Indemnities, Finnish, 24, 25
India, 23, 163, 199-202, 203-205, 208,
215, 218, 221, 222, 229, 239, 246, 249,
260, 262, 264

Indian Ocean area, 200, 205, 211, 215, 219, 230

Indo-China, 218

Industrial Revolution, 50

Industry, 116, 294, 295; socialization of, 121; *see also* "Level of Industry"

Infant mortality, 163, 184, 189, 194, 195, 226, 264-265

Inflation, 46, 55, 69, 96, 113, 121-123, 125-126, 158, 180

Inter-American Treaty, 64-65

International Children's Emergency Fund, 135

International Bank, 10

International Emergency Food Council, 264, 265, 288

International Radio Conference, 144

International Red Cross, 227

Iowa, 74

Iraq, 16-17, 205, 216, 218, 221

"Iron curtain," 20, 23, 25, 60, 64

Isolationists, 63

Italy, 9, 25, 174-175, 176-178, 214, 254, 276, 303, 309

JCS Order 1067, 88

Japan, 38, 98-102, 103-108, 117, 123-124, 130, 134, 135, 208, 216, 221, 286

Japanese Food Supply, 208

Japanese Reparations, 98-102

Java, 205

Jews, 16

Joint Export-Import Agency, 279, 283

Justice, degeneration of, 38

Korea, 103, 123-124, 130, 134, 135, 208, 216, 221, 286

Kremlin, 68

Labor, 35, 51, 56-57, 125, 129, 271, 272, 273

LaGuardia, Fiorello, 231, 237

Laissez-faire, 45, 51

Latin America, 23, 122-123, 147, 170, 191, 195, 197, 211, 215, 219, 228, 230, 239, 246, 254, 256-258, 262, 283; *see also* Western Hemisphere

Latin-American Food Situation, 256-258

Latvia, 147

Lawrence, Ernest O., 34

Leadership, 41-43, 73, 159

League of Nations, and Russo-Finnish war, 24

Lend-lease, 7, 84, 112; proposals for repayment, 10-11

Lenin, 37, 50

Level of industry, 105, 106, 117; German, 88 ff., 104, 124; Japanese, 98 ff., 124

Liberalism, 50, 52, 71

Liberty, *see* Freedom

Limits of American Aid to Foreign Countries, 109-118

Lincoln, Abraham, 42, 49, 52, 53

Lithuania, 147

Loans, postwar government foreign, 3-13, 84-85, 107-108, 109-114, 129-130, 133

Loans, private, 13, 111, 130, 133, 135, 136

Lochner, Louis, 84, 269

Lodz, 184

Loss in war, intellectual, 28, 39

Lutherans, 186

MacArthur, General Douglas, 100, 107

Madras, 215

Malaya, 200, 215

Manchuria, 20, 23, 208, 260

Manila, 206

Manpower, 135, 260, 271, 290

Markets, free, *see* Free trade

Marshall, General George, 104

Marshall Plan, 62, 64, 120-130

Marshall Plan Bill, 131-137

Martin, Joesph W., 131

Maryland, 78

Marx, Karl, 71, 79

Mason, Frank, 84, 269

McNarney, General Joseph, 269

Meaning of America, 74-79

Mediocrity, dangers of cult, 42-43, 45

Mediterranean, 222, 229, 239, 246, 260

Mexico, 197, 234

Middle East, 211, 219

Militarism, 93, 95, 100, 107, 285

Military governments, 284, 295, 301

Military zones, *see* Occupation zones

Millikan, Robert A., 34

Mohammedan, 17

Mongol invasion, 16

Monopolies, 35, 101, 142

Moral and Spiritual Recovery from War, 36-43

Morale in war, 37

Moratorium, intergovernmental debts, World War I, 5; proposed for World War II, 10-11

Moscow, 25, 104, 255

Moscow Declaration, 302

Mussolini, 71

Mysore, 204, 215

Nagasaki, bombing of, 38

Nanking, bombing of, 38

Napoleonic wars, postwar situation, 30

National Advisory Council on Monetary and Financial Problems, 132-134
National Defense, see Defense
National Socialism, 45; see also Nazis
Nazis, 24, 70, 85, 224, 241, 248, 268, 271, 285; see also National Socialism
Near East, 215
Netherlands, see Holland
New Deal, 45
New England, 78, 149
New Germany, 85 ff.; food supply, 89-90; heavy industry, 87-89, 91; level of industry, 88-94; light industry, 87, 91-93; New World Food Organization Needed, 229-231
New Zealand, 211, 215, 230
Nightingale, Florence, 42
North Africa, 214, 230, 264
North America, 201-202, 205, 206, 227, 242, 250, 264
North Carolina, 78
North Sea, 283
Northern Hemisphere, 199, 202, 229, 233, 235, 238, 243, 245, 250, 252, 256, 260
Norway, 163, 214, 283

Obligation of Republican Party, 49-53
Occupation, German, 172, 179, 183
Occupied zones, Austrian, 295, 301
Occupied zone, German, 84-87, 90, 95-97, 103-106, 117, 119, 124, 269 ff., 305
Ohio, 78
Oil, see Petroleum products
Operation rathole, 124
Oppenheimer, J. Robert, 34

Pacific Ocean area, 211, 216, 219
Palestine, Hoover proposals for, 16-17
Paris, 24, 25, 172, 176-178
"Pastoral State," 88, 92
Pate, Maurice, 187, 195
Patterson, Robert, 98
Peace, 20, 38, 63, 68, 86, 95, 98-99, 101-102, 103, 106-108, 110, 116-118, 121, 124, 137, 163, 166, 168, 172, 182, 192, 198, 200, 224, 225, 227, 228, 231, 244, 251, 259, 263, 285, 288, 291, 300-302, 304, 306
Peace, preservation of, 64-65
Peace, Russo-Finnish, 24-25
Peace, World War I, 20
Peron, President Juan, 252, 253, 257
Persia, 268; see also Iraq
Persian Gulf, 128, 133
Peru, 238, 243, 256; President of, 238, 240, 242, 243

Petroleum products, 133; see also Fuel relief
Philippines, 11, 208, 216, 221
"Planned economy," 101; see also Economy, managed or planned
Plant removal, 124, 134
Poland, 87, 147, 178, 181-182, 183-184, 214, 270, 272, 279
Pope Pius XII, 197, 228, 256
Population, German, 270-271; United States, 50-51
Portugal, 214
Postwar Foreign Loans, 3-13
Potsdam, 87; agreement, 96, 104; Declaration, 88, 282, 301
Prague, 179
Prices, 122, 125, 126, 135, 287, 308-309
Prisoners of war, 271
Productivity, 46, 59, 62, 69, 70, 85-88, 93, 101-102, 104, 107-108, 110, 113-118, 121, 123, 125-126, 129-130, 133, 136, 271, 288, 290, 291, 301, 304
Productivity, national, means for increasing, 31-32, 46, 55-57
Progress, 166, 168, 194, 201, 294, 306
Propaganda, 7, 13, 37
Public health, 194, 201, 287, 289
Punjab, 218
Purges, 60
Puritans, 78

Quaker, 75, 78, 79, 156, 186
Quebec, 88
Quotas, 13

Radio, 141-145
Rationing, 116, 122, 126, 164, 200, 203, 204, 242, 249, 273, 282, 296, 297; see also rations
Rationing, voluntary, 164, 165, 168, 169-170, 191, 196, 201, 225, 308
Rations, 174, 175, 177, 179, 183-184, 185-186, 189, 191, 194, 200, 203-204, 205, 208, 226, 240, 247, 264, 274-281, 296-297, 305
Reconstruction, see Relief and reconstruction; see also Recovery
Reconstruction Finance Corporation, 128
Reconversion, 11
Recovery, Britain, Napoleonic wars, 30
Recovery, Civil War, 30
Recovery, World War I, 30-32, 147
Recovery, World War II, 21, 29, 32-35, 46, 55-57; 83 ff., 98 ff., 103 ff., 109 ff., 119, 120-130, 131-137, 166, 180, 192, 198, 202, 230-231, 244, 251, 259, 291, 295, 300-302, 306

Recovery, moral and spiritual, 36-43, 198, 202, 228, 244, 251, 266

Refugees, 185, 186; see also Displaced persons

Regulation, government, 51, 141, 143-144

Regulation, public, 51; voluntary, 142, 143

Relief and reconstruction, 3 ff., 69-70, 84-97, 103-108, 109-118, 119, 120-130, 130-137, 147, 171, 190, 195, 208, 224, 230-231, 243, 251, 266, 279 ff., 286-293, 295, 297-302, 303-304, 306-310; see also Food relief; see also Fuel relief

Relief Assistance to Countries Devastated by War, 286-293

Renegotiation, intergovernmental debts, World War I, 5-6

Reparations, 38, 86, 87, 92, 94, 96, 97, 104, 106, 117, 130, 270, 284, 290, 301, 302

Reparations, Japanese, 98-102

Reparations and Economic Support to World, 83-137

Repayment, foreign intergovernmental debts, 7 ff., 113; proposals for World War II, 10-11, 133, 136; relief of, 284, 288, 290

Reprisals, 46

Republican Party, 49-50, 52, 54, 67-73

Repudiation, intergovernmental debts, World War I, 5-7

Requisitions, 301-302

Resources, natural, 114-117, 121

Rhineland, 95

Rio de Janeiro, 64

Ripon, Wisconsin, 73

Robertson, General W. M., 270

Rome, 174

Roosevelt, Franklin D., 6; in praise of Finland, 25; and Russo-Finnish war, 24

Roumania, 25, 87, 147, 216

Ruhr, 88, 95, 104, 128, 272

Russia, 6, 38, 42, 59, 65, 68, 87, 88, 95, 96, 97, 104, 107, 137, 184, 185, 186, 191, 196, 197, 198, 200, 208, 212, 217, 218, 254, 270-273, 301, 307

Russia, and peace, 20, 23, 68, 108, 116

Russia, as exponent of collectivism, 44-45

Russia, Finland joins war against, 24

Russia, surplus commodities, 12

Russia, war with Finland, 24

Saar, 87, 88, 104

San Francisco, 209

St. Francis of Assisi, 42

St. Lawrence Waterway Commission, 18

Saville, General Gordon P., 216

Sebrell, Dr. William H., Jr., 83, 269, 276

Security Council, proposed control of uranium, 15

Senate Finance Committee, 292

Senate, Marshall Plan Bill, 131-132, 134-136

Serfs, 21

Sermon on the Mount, 40

Shanghai, 207

Siam, 196, 200, 204-205, 206, 212, 216, 217, 218, 221

Siberia, 23

Sind, 218

Slavery, 59, 68, 71, 77, 78; see also Serfs

Smith, Adam, 41

Socialism, 49, 54, 77; British, 45

South Africa, 195, 210, 211, 215, 222, 229, 230, 239, 246, 260

South America, see Latin America

Soviet Government, 116, 197, 254; see also Russia

Spain, 214

Stabilization Fund, 10, 111-112, 117

Stalin, Marshal Joseph, 68, 303

Standard of living, 69, 101, 110, 203

Stanford University, War Library, 74

Starvation, 46, 116, 167-168, 170, 172, 175, 177, 179, 187, 189, 190, 194, 200, 203, 204, 207, 208, 211, 212, 222-226, 235, 240-242, 247, 248-250, 259, 261-264, 288, 290, 292-293, 300, 306, 308, 309; see also Famine, Food relief

State Department, 132, 136, 297

State, Secretary of, 216

Statism, 49, 51-53

Stockpiling, 115, 118, 133

Stolper, Dr. Gustav, 83, 269

Straits Settlements, 215

Straub, Walter, 169

Strike, Clifford, 98; Report, 100-101

Strike, right to, 55-57

Strikes, 35, 55-56, 70, 209, 232, 309

Students, exchange, 146-148

Sudeten Germans, 271

Surpluses (commodities), 11-12, 110, 114-115, 118, 129-130, 136, 148, 288

Sweden, 94, 190, 216, 223, 277, 283

Switzerland, 176, 190, 214

Taber, John, 103, 117

Taft, William Howard, 152

Tariffs, 8-9, 13, 62

Taxation, 10, 35, 69, 113, 119, 121, 125, 284, 287, 290, 310

Tigris valley, 16
Tito, Marshall, 22
Tokyo, 208
Totalitarianism, 71, 116; *see also* Collectivism
Trading-with-the Enemy Acts, 283
Transportation, future expansion, 33; St. Lawrence waterway, 19
Transvaal, 215
Trieste, 135
Truman, Harry S., 23, 72, 135, 152-155, 163-164, 169, 171, 191-199, 209, 210, 228, 233, 235, 238, 245, 258, 260, 269, 292
Truth, degradation of, 37
Tsaldaris, Constantine, 267
Tuck, William Hallam, 187
Turkey, 93, 134, 135, 303

Unemployment, 8, 113, 115, 133, 136
United Kingdom, 159, 191, 199, 212, 214, 217, 218, 279; *see also* Britain
United Nations, 25, 59, 63-65, 227, 231, 264, 268, 286, 287, 290, 297, 299, 300; charter, 64-65; cooperation with, 21
United Nations Food Administration, 230-231
United Nations, Food and Agricultural Organization, 229
United Nations, proposed control of uranium, 15
United Nations Refugee Organization, 286
United Nations Relief and Rehabilitation Administration (UNRRA), 3, 10, 22, 163, 179, 186, 191, 195, 207, 212, 227, 231, 233, 237, 246, 250, 263, 267, 289, 295, 297, 298, 299
United Nations Security Council, 230
United Provinces, 215
United States, 8, 64-66, 75-79, 83, 98, 101-102, 105, 107-108, 112, 115, 146-147, 157, 165, 176, 181, 196, 197, 206, 208, 210, 212, 217, 223, 232, 236, 252, 257, 259, 262, 268, 283, 288-291, 294, 300, 303, 305, 309; and Finland, 24; champion of world freedom, 45-46, 53, 68; Congress, 5-6, 60, 61, 121, 126, 129, 131, 133-135, 141, 143, 284, 292, 299; Constitution, 50, 65; contribution to relief, 22, 23, 46, 59, 68-70, 83-85, 96, 99, 101-102, 103, 107-108, 109-118, 119, 120-130, 132-137, 175, 177-178, 190, 197, 198, 199, 205, 207, 227, 242, 250, 262, 267, 278, 280-285, 286 ff., 295, 297-299, 304, 307-308; domestic affairs and economics, 29-79, 109-118, 120-130; European assets in, 11, 112, 128, 134; future

federal expenses, 10, 112-113, 124-130, 134, 136, 276, 278-285, 286-293, 297-299; government, organization of, 62; government in relation to St. Lawrence waterway, 19; Hoover on Congressional election, 54; Hoover proposals for postwar economic role, 21, 109-118, 120-130, 132; Hoover proposals for postwar national defense of, 64-65, 115-116, 304; Hoover proposals for postwar policies, 21, 85-86, 94-97, 101-102, 103-108, 109-118, 119, 276-285, 286, 293, 297-302; increase in population, 50-51; influence on nations, 54; policies as to atomic bomb, 14-15, 21; postwar recovery, Civil War, 30; World War I, 30-32; World War II, 32-35; postwar situation, World War II, 9-10, 21, 29-30, 36-43, 45-48, 58-60, 63, 64, 67-73, 109-118, 121; relief to Yugoslavia, 22-23; surplus commodities, 11-12, 129, 148
United States Army, 176, 207
United States Navy, 207
United States Public Health Service, 276, 288
United States Treasury, 128
Uranium, for industrial purposes, 34
Uruguay, 256-257

Valley Forge, 63
Vandenberg, Senator Arthur H., 120, 131-132
Venezuela, 256
Versailles, Treaty of, 85, 107, 294
Vienna, 294, 295
Voorhees, Tracy S., 84, 270

Wages, 122, 125, 126
War Department, 103, 281, 305
War, need to avoid, 60; Secretary of, 216
War potential, German, 88, 92-93; Japanese, 98-100
Warsaw, 38, 181, 183
Washington, 108, 144, 157, 169, 170, 191, 224, 241, 248
Washington, George, 61-63, 65-66
Weir, Sir Cecil, 270
"Welfare State," 49
Western civilization, 58, 68, 70, 86, 108, 118, 268, 285, 302
Western democracies, 6
Western Hemisphere, 59, 64-65, 123, 128, 130, 135, 136, 165, 167, 177, 191, 205, 212, 217, 223, 234, 235, 242, 250
Whig Party, 49

Willcocks, Sir William, 16
Work camps, 271; *see also* Forced-labor camps; *see also* Concentration camps
World Bank, 111, 112, 117, 130
World Famine, 165-166, 167-168, 169-171, 172-173, 210-220, 221-228, 235-236, 238, 244, 250-266
World Food Crisis, 193-198, 245-251, 252-253
World Food Situation, 199-202, 306-310
World War I, postwar conditions, 20,
163-164; relief and rehabilitation, 171, 181, 187, 190, 197, 226, 238, 243, 245-246, 251, 254, 265, 284, 292
World War II, postwar conditions, 20-21, 58, 63, 67-71, 163-310
World War Debt Commission, 5

Yama Conference, 1945, 44
Yugoslavia, 87, 147, 196, 214, 303; army, 22; Communism in, 22; free elections in, 23; relief shipments to, 23; UNRRA contributions to, 22
Yugoslavian Incident, 22-23